Against the Vigilantes

Charles P. Duane, about 1880.
California State Library.

Against the Vigilantes

THE RECOLLECTIONS OF DUTCH CHARLEY DUANE

Edited, with an Introduction and Notes, by
John Boessenecker

UNIVERSITY OF OKLAHOMA PRESS : NORMAN

ALSO BY JOHN BOESSENECKER

Badge and Buckshot: Lawlessness in Old California (Norman, 1988)
(with Mark Dugan) *The Grey Fox: The True Story of Bill Miner—
Last of the Old-Time Bandits* (Norman, 1992)
Lawman: The Life and Times of Harry Morse, 1835–1912 (Norman,
1998)
*Gold Dust and Gunsmoke: Tales of Gold Rush Outlaws, Gunfighters,
Lawmen and Vigilantes* (New York, 1999)

Library of Congress Cataloging-in-Publication Data

Duane, Charles P.
    Against the vigilantes: the recollections of Dutch Charley Duane /
    edited, with an introduction and notes, by John Boessenecker.
       p.   cm.
    Includes bibliographical references and index.
    ISBN 0-8061-3166-7 (cloth: alk. paper)
    1. Duane, Charles P.   2. Outlaws—California—San Francisco
Biography.   3. Politicians—California—San Francisco Biography.
4. Frontier and pioneer life—California—San Francisco.   5. San
Francisco Committee of Vigilance of 1856.   6. Criminal justice,
Administration of—California—San Francisco—History—19th century.
7. San Francisco (Calif.)—Politics and government—19th century.
8. San Francisco (Calif.) Biography.   9. California—Gold
discoveries.   I. Boessenecker, John, 1953– . II. Title.
F869.S353D833   1999
979.4′6104′092—dc21
  [B]   99-21450
                                            CIP

Text design by Gail Carter.

The paper in this book meets the guidelines for permanence and durability of the
Committee on Production Guidelines for Book Longevity of the Council on Library
Resources, Inc.∞

1 2 3 4 5 6 7 8 9 10

For my compadres William B. Secrest and Kevin J. Mullen

Charles P. Duane has for years been a disturber of the peace of this community by repeated assaults, often with deadly weapons, upon unoffending citizens, and by his interference with our elections.
San Francisco Committee of Vigilance, 1856

———

Duane's reputation for lawlessness and brutal aggression has long been established in California.
Bret Harte, 1866

———

Charley Duane was a man of extraordinary character. No charge of dishonest nature . . . was ever brought against him. But he was somewhat prone to fight, and this was the worst that could be charged upon him.
James O'Meara, 1887

———

Charley was always fond of a fracas.
Hubert Howe Bancroft, 1887

Contents

Illustrations

Acknowledgments

THERE have been no prior books about Charles P. Duane. The only way to reconstruct his life was to search for information about Duane and his exploits—good and bad—in the San Francisco newspapers and other contemporary sources. My hunt for information on Charles Duane would never have been completed if not for the unselfish help of my good friends William B. Secrest and Kevin J. Mullen. Both have for many years researched crime and law enforcement in nineteenth-century San Francisco and have generously shared their research on Charley Duane. Bill Secrest has written dozens of articles and monographs on lawlessness in frontier California, as well as two books, *Lawmen and Desperadoes: A Compendium of Noted Early California Peace Officers, Badmen and Outlaws* (1994) and *Dangerous Trails: Five Desperadoes of the Old West Coast* (1995), plus forthcoming biographies of San Francisco police detective Isaiah W. Lees and California Ranger Harry Love. Kevin Mullen, retired deputy police chief of San Francisco, is the author of *Let Justice Be Done: Crime and Politics in Early San Francisco* (1989), as well as a forthcoming history of the San Francisco police. Both unselfishly shared information, advice, and criticism.

Dr. Robert J. Chandler, historian of Wells Fargo Bank in San Francisco and an authority on politics in frontier California, generously read the manuscript and offered his most helpful comments and criticism. Robert Limacher and Joseph T. Silva kindly provided illustrative material from their respective Committee of Vigilance collections.

William and Winifred Medin were kind enough to share with me their collection of documents related to Charles and John Duane. Those materials have greatly enhanced this book.

I am also grateful for the assistance of the staffs of the Bancroft Library, California State Library, California Historical Society Library, and Society of California Pioneers Library.

And a final word of gratitude goes to my wife, Marta S. Diaz, for her patience, love, and support.

Against the Vigilantes

Introduction
The Violent Life of Charles P. Duane

OUTLAWED twice by the San Francisco Committee of Vigilance, first in 1851 and again in 1856, Charles P. "Dutch Charley" Duane was one of the most colorful and controversial figures of the California Gold Rush. He played many roles in his life: politician, fire chief, election rigger, bare-knuckle boxer, gambler, saloonkeeper, gunfighter, and land squatter. As the chief enforcer for California's urban Democratic political boss, David C. Broderick, Dutch Charley rose to the heights of power and prestige in San Francisco until his ignominious downfall at the hands of the vigilantes in 1856.

San Francisco's 1851 and 1856 Committees of Vigilance were the two largest and most important movements of vigilantism in American history. Many writers have examined their actions and debated their motives; whether or not the San Francisco vigilantes were morally justified has been the subject of dispute for more than 140 years. The twin problems of crime and social unrest confronted by the vigilantes are still with us, for today Americans are rightly concerned with violent crime in their communities and the appropriate response to it. Law enforcement agencies increasingly employ a nineteenth-century police technique—community-based policing—and encourage citizens to help suppress crime in their neighborhoods by reporting suspicious persons and occurrences. At the same time, police discourage the public from actually making arrests and advise citizens to leave law enforcement to the professionals. An oft-expressed fear is that citizens who endeavor to fight crime personally will become vigilantes.

The term *vigilante*—once worn with pride by members of the San Francisco committees who were issued ornate certificates, ribbons, and medallions to commemorate their service—has become a dirty word. Today, citizens who use deadly force to defend themselves against crime and crime victims who retaliate against those who have preyed on them are frequently called vigilantes. Both characterizations are wrong. Vigilantism in America has historically been something altogether different.

What, then, is vigilantism? Why did San Franciscans resort to it more than a century ago? Was it right or wrong? Given modern America's concern with crime and violence and the debate over the public's proper role in suppressing it while protecting basic civil rights, a clear understanding of vigilantism and the part it has played in American history is just as important and relevant today as it was in the Gold Rush. Thus, it is both timely and appropriate to examine America's most important vigilance movement through the eyes of one of its most ardent opponents, Charles P. Duane.

In order to understand more fully the San Francisco movements in particular and American vigilantism in general, one must study the men who were targeted by the San Francisco vigilantes. So far scholars who have examined the Committee of Vigilance of 1856 have tended not to do this,[1] perhaps because these men were obscure and information about them is not readily available. Charley Duane is the only one of those deported by the vigilance committee known to have left an account of his experiences during the 1850s. For the most part, the ruffians who were executed or banished by the vigilantes in 1856 have been glossed over by vigilance writers. Current historians have tended to focus on the broader economic, ethnic, and political themes which underlay the 1856 committee without examining those who were arrested by the vigilantes in order to consider whether they were guilty of public offenses and deserved punishment. This is an oversight which I seek to address.[2]

This volume, which examines the colorful life of Charles P. Duane and republishes his recollections of 1850-1856, is one step toward a more complete understanding of American vigilantism.

CHARLES Patrick Duane was born in Tipperary, Ireland, in December 1827. He had four brothers, Thomas, Edward, John, and James, and two sisters, Mary and Katy. The family emigrated to America about 1836 and settled in Albany County, New York. The Duanes were devout Roman Catholics. Charley's sisters and his younger brothers John and James practiced the faith their entire lives, but Charley seems to have been indifferent to religion. He left home at age fifteen and apprenticed himself to a wagon maker in

New York City. He soon joined a volunteer fire brigade and began to "run with the engines."[3]

Such volunteer fire companies were the focal point of social life for young urban males. Fire was one of the greatest dangers of city life. The proliferation of oil lamps, coal stoves, and cheap wood houses combined to make burgeoning cities of the East Coast veritable tinderboxes. Increasingly, beginning in the 1830s, the volunteers were young working-class males. The result was a fundamental change in the organization of these fire companies. Young men from the same neighborhoods, of shared ethnic, religious, and political backgrounds, built hose and engine houses. There they congregated, drank, gambled, and sparred. These fire companies competed with one another, sometimes racing to be first at a fire. But often they competed in the same way as urban gangs, brawling with each other at fire scenes, damaging their adversaries' equipment, and occasionally setting blazes and ambushing a responding rival company.[4]

With their fancy uniforms and lavishly decorated engines, shown off to full advantage in parades, political rallies, and funeral processions, the fire companies were focal points of neighborhood and ethnic pride. Politics became enmeshed in the fire brigades; no local politician stood a chance of election unless he was a member of a volunteer fire company.[5]

For working-class youths like Duane, life consisted of hard labor with minimal opportunity for leisure and pastimes. With urban industrialization, the ancient master-apprentice system declined and workers lost the sense of pride in their craft along with opportunities for moving up, for achieving master status. They lost a certain control over their lives. As a result, in the urban centers of the East Coast, an entire class of young men rejected the old notions of hard work, loyalty to the employer, frugality, sobriety, and self-restraint. Pursuit of leisure, rather than work, came to be a primary goal in life for many working-class males. Before the growth of organized sports in the late nineteenth century, young men in peacetime had few outlets for their competitive, combative, and physical energies. That void was filled as they congregated in saloons, firehouses, political clubs, and militia companies. And leisure was spent imbibing, wagering, sparring, politicking, and whoring. In this cult of masculinity the ethic of personal honor was all-important.

Honor was a vital component of life for the nineteenth-century male and was embraced by men of all classes and all geographical areas. It was manifest in the *code duello* of the southern planter, in the "Code of the West" on the frontier, in the refusal of pugilists and feudists to run from a fight; and it was codified in the legal doctrine of self-defense, "no duty to retreat." Honor meant courage, character, loyalty, respect for womanhood, and especially, a resolve to never back down from an enemy. Conversely, drinking, gambling, fighting, and whoring were not dishonorable. A man possessed honor only if his peers said he did. If his peers failed to accept him as an equal, his honor was gone, and only an act of violent retribution or heroic valor could retrieve it. This concept of personal honor is central to an understanding of Charley Duane, and would govern many of the actions in his life.[6]

Restless, reluctant to be limited by his Irish heritage, Duane sought power in politics and prestige in pugilism. He scorned the Puritan work ethic, abandoned employment as a wagon maker, and relished a life of drinking, gambling, brawling, and womanizing. Charles P. Duane was, part and parcel, a product of the cult of masculinity.[7]

Courage was bred into Charley Duane and fighting the urban conflagrations so common in that era developed his fearless, even reckless, attitude toward danger. Heavy labor had made the youth tough and strong. Duane became well known as an athlete, particularly as a bare-knuckle boxer. As one newspaperman noted many years later, "While not being a professional pugilist, he was recognized as a man who could make it decidedly interesting for any person with an inclination in that line."[8]

Prizefighting was the most popular spectator sport in antebellum America. From its infancy, pugilism was closely tied to the social underworld. It went hand in hand with gangsterism, drinking, gambling, political violence, and blood sports like cock fighting, rat baiting, and dog fighting. Most bare-knuckle boxers were disreputable and brutal rowdies.

In that era prizefighting was more grudge match than sporting event. Challenges were issued and received in writing, much as in a formal duel. Charley Duane fought his share of bloody "mills," or fist fights. When he bested a German fighter nicknamed "Dutch Charley," Duane's friends appropriated the sobriquet for him. Although boxing champion Tom Hyer jokingly changed it to "German Charles," the appellation "Dutch Charley" would cling to Duane until his death.[9]

In New York City, Charley Duane became a close friend of Tom Hyer, who was nine years his senior. Hyer ranked with James "Yankee" Sullivan, John Morrissey, and John C. Heenan as one of the greatest American sports figures of antebellum America.[10] In 1836, at the age of seventeen, Hyer led a vicious street gang on a rampage during which they broke into three brothels, gang-raped a prostitute, destroyed a grocery store, and beat several men. Released from prison in less than a year, Hyer took part in an 1838 raid on another brothel in which a prostitute was beaten senseless. These assaults may have been efforts to extort protection money. Charley Duane idolized him; an indication of Duane's values can be found in his comment on Hyer: "He was one of nature's noblemen."[11]

Tom Hyer's violent capabilities would prove important to New York's Tammany Hall political bosses. Hyer and fellow pugilist Bill Poole, alias "Bill the Butcher," became the leaders of the gang of thugs and political bullies, or "shoulder-strikers," organized by Captain Isaiah Rynders. They were not Irish Democrats, but rather were members of the nativist Know-Nothing Party. Hyer and Charley Duane later became Whigs, and were politically aligned against immigrant Irish. They shared common politics with the Bowery Boys, perhaps New York's most notorious street gang. Like bare-knuckle champions Yankee Sullivan and John McCleester (alias "Country" McCluskey), they also became prized members of volunteer fire brigades. Isaiah Rynders was the political boss of the Sixth Ward and benefactor and commander of the Five Points gangs. Rynders, a former Mississippi River gambler, had first come to New York in the mid-1830s. An astute politician, he became a power in Tammany Hall and for twenty-five years ran the Sixth Ward, which included the notorious Five Points area between Broadway, Canal Street, the Bowery, and Park Row.

Rynders recognized that bruisers could be invaluable on election day, when voting repeatedly, herding voters to the polls, stuffing ballot-boxes, and bullying opposition partisans at the polls were mandatory in the corrupt world of New York politics. Thus the street gangs of young rowdies became as indispensable as the volunteer fire companies to the Tammany Hall bosses. Indeed, many a neighborhood street gang was allied with the local firehouse. About 1841, Rynders founded the Empire Club at No. 28 Park Row, which became the headquarters for the Five Points gangs. At the Empire Club, which was Rynders's political headquarters, prizefighters such as Tom Hyer, Country McCluskey, and Yankee Sullivan gambled, drank, and staged sparring exhibitions.[12]

Within a few years Charley Duane was one of Rynders's loyal henchmen. One day in the late 1840s, Alexander Hamilton, a saloon owner and fight promoter from Troy, New York, visited the Empire Club and engaged in an argument with Dutch Charley. Hamilton's barkeeper in Troy was John Morrissey, who would later become one of the greatest of the bare-knuckle champions. Hamilton boasted that his barkeep could "take the Dutch courage" out of Duane and challenged him to fight Morrissey. Duane, who had never heard of John Morrissey, refused. When young Morrissey discovered that Duane had spurned the challenge, he journeyed to New York and barged into the Empire Club. Finding that Dutch Charley was not there, he foolishly offered to battle any man present. Several ruffians promptly jumped Morrissey and beat him unconscious. This was the inauspicious beginning of one of the most important fighters of the bare-knuckle age.[13]

In December 1848, news of the discovery of gold in California spread like wildfire through the eastern seaboard. Dutch Charley was interested in easy riches, but he was most concerned with a more immediate and equally exciting event. A rivalry, fueled by ethnic and political differences, had long existed between Tom Hyer, hero to American-born Irish, and Yankee Sullivan, the champion of immigrant Irish. In April 1848, in a brawl in a New York oyster bar, young Hyer had beat champion Sullivan senseless. Partisans of the pair, no doubt Duane among them, then armed themselves and prepared for gang warfare. Several weeks later Sullivan published a challenge to Hyer in the *New York Herald*, and in August articles of agreement were signed, providing "a fair stand up fight" for a $10,000 purse. The two fighters spent the next six months training and giving sparring exhibitions.

The contest took place at Still Pond Heights, Maryland, on February 7, 1849. Charley Duane carried Tom Hyer on his brawny shoulders into the ring. Hyer won in sixteen gory rounds, fought in just seventeen minutes. The Hyer-Sullivan fight was one of the greatest American sporting events of the nineteenth century and created tremendous enthusiasm for the sport of pugilism among the American working class.[14]

Three months later Duane took part in the famous Astor Place Riot, one of the bloodiest urban disturbances of that era. Its origins lay in the bitter, long-standing personal and professional rivalry between America's leading actor, Edwin Forrest, and the great English tragedian, William C. Macready. Forrest was a favorite of nativist groups like the Bowery Boys. Isaiah Rynders and his associate, E. Z. C. Judson, a dime novelist better known by his pseudonym, Ned Buntline, took advantage of the actors' feud by using it to foment unrest. On May 7, 1849, Macready performed the role of Macbeth in the Astor Place Opera House in New York City. At the urging of Rynders and Judson, a large contingent of Bowery Boys attended the play. They unfurled an anti-Macready banner, led wild cheers for Forrest, and pelted Macready with eggs until he fled the stage in the third act.

Although police officers were present, they made no effort to interfere. This emboldened the nativist ruffians. At the same time Macready determined that he would not be cowed. Three nights later, amidst tremendous newspaper publicity, he again took the stage. The theater, which seated 1800, was crammed beyond capacity with supporters and opponents of Macready. City authorities anticipated a "serious riot" and saw to it that 325 police officers were stationed in and around the theater. Some 200 state militiamen were in readiness nearby.

By curtain time at 7:30 P.M., Astor Place from Broadway to the Bowery was packed with a mob of ten to twenty thousand men, women, and boys who had come to see the excitement. During the first act, rowdies tried to disrupt the play as they had done three nights earlier, but they were promptly arrested and removed by the police. By the second act, teenage nativist ruffians outside the theater learned of the arrest of their friends and began attacking the theater with barrages of bricks and paving stones that crashed through the windows, injuring police and patrons. Macready and his fellow actors ignored the tumult and continued their performance.

The stoning increased in intensity and the mob gradually overwhelmed the police and prepared to storm the building. Ned Buntline was prominently in their midst, waving a sword and urging the angry crowd on. Now the mayor sent for the militia. The cavalry slowly pushed through the mob, infantry just behind. The rioters attacked them with showers of stones, and thirty of the militiamen were seriously injured. The companies took up positions at both ends of the Opera House. Several shots were fired at the soldiers and some rioters tried to wrestle away their muskets.

An order to fire was given and the soldiers sent a volley into the wall of a house across the street. Instead of cowing the mob, this infuriated them. Rioters began yelling that the militia was armed only with blank charges. As the violence surged out of control, the city recorder, Frederick Tallmadge, and Sheriff J. J. V. Westervelt called on Charley Duane to calm the mob. Tallmadge, as he later reported,

> rushed out into the mob and invoked them to depart, as the military would fire directly upon them. The Sheriff, and Mr. Charles Duane, commonly called "Dutch Charley" (who, I must say, did his duty nobly) accompanied me to the curbstone. While urging the mob to disperse, I was assailed by a volley of stones, and was injured on my ankle and other parts of my body and was forced to retreat into the rear of the military.[15]

The mob was in a frenzy, beyond listening to reason. Now the order to fire was given again and the militia fired three volleys into the crowd, killing thirty-one rioters and spectators. The mob scattered and fled. At least 150 persons, half of them police, had been wounded by stones. Few riots of the antebellum period equaled the bloodshed at Astor Place. Charley Duane had acted responsibly in his efforts to defuse the violence. Though but twenty-one years old, he was recognized by the city's highest authorities as a man of influence over its nativist youth gangs.[16]

Charley Duane's early life was a microcosm of larger events occurring in the urban centers of the East—the emergence of a bachelor cult of masculinity at a time of increasing social unrest between nativist and immigrant groups, accompanied by the rise of street gangs, political ruffianism, firehouse rowdyism, and bare-knuckle pugilism. In the cities of the East Coast in the 1840s and 1850s, politics, saloons, street gangs, volunteer fire companies, and prizefighting all became inextricably intertwined. This connection is indispensable in understanding Charles P. Duane and the rise of vigilance in Gold Rush San Francisco.

NOW Charley Duane turned his attention to a grand adventure—a trip "to see the elephant," as the Forty-niners called it. Duane left New York City on the steamer *Tennessee* on January 17, 1850, and arrived in San Francisco three months later, on April 14. The *Tennessee* carried 551 people, at that time the largest number of passengers brought to California on a single vessel. Duane found San Francisco a rip-roaring boomtown of twenty-five thousand people, with more than five hundred vessels abandoned in the bay, their crews having jumped ship and headed for the gold mines. With George Baker, later judge of the San Francisco Recorder's Court, he opened a saloon, but it quickly burned in one of the city's many fires. Dutch Charley also became a founding member of the city's volunteer fire department.[17]

Soon after his arrival in San Francisco, Duane aligned himself with David C. Broderick, who was already well on his way to becoming boss of the northern, Free-Soil wing of the Democratic party in California. Duane had probably known him in New York City, where Broderick owned a popular saloon, was foreman of a volunteer fire company, and cut his teeth in the rough and tumble world of Tammany Hall politics. Although apparently he was never a member of the Tammany Society, on occasion he received its support. In 1846 Broderick ran for Congress and was defeated. He had been opposed, among others, by Charley Duane's patron, Isaiah Rynders. Broderick joined the Gold Rush and arrived in San Francisco in mid-1849. His political experience in New York City proved invaluable. Many New Yorkers had settled in San Francisco and they helped elect him to the state senate in January 1850. Broderick quickly became one of the most powerful politicians in California.[18]

In San Francisco, David Broderick made good use of his New York connections and the Tammany Hall style of ballot-box stuffing and violent electioneering. He attracted a cadre of political thugs and prizefighters like William "Woolly" Kearney, Yankee Sullivan, Billy Mulligan, and Chris Lilly, all of whom he had no doubt known in New York. Charley Duane and his closest friend, fellow New York bruiser Ira Cole, became Broderick's most loyal henchmen. Although Dutch Charley was a Whig, he greatly admired Broderick, and labored freely on his behalf. Such associations were not uncommon in the tangled, labyrinthine world of San Francisco politics. The journalist James O'Meara, who was a friend of and apologist for Broderick's shoulder-strikers, later wrote of Duane: "No charge of dishonest nature—theft, fraud, swindling, embezzlement, or anything of the kind, was ever brought against him. . . . I am not aware that he was ever accused of crookedness in elections except in his zeal to secure the election of Delos Lake, Whig, as District Judge, in 1851." But O'Meara's opinion should be taken with a generous grain of salt: he also wrote of Billy Mulligan, who was one of the most dangerous ruffians and gunmen on the Pacific Coast, "Beyond his fighting bouts and his conduct in elections . . . there was nothing to warrant his arrest and banishment."[19]

In 1849 and 1850 a series of disastrous fires destroyed much of San Francisco. In June 1850, San Francisco's volunteer fire department was organized. Charley Duane's early popularity and prominence, which he brought with him from New York, were made evident by his election as assistant foreman of St. Francis Hook and Ladder Company No. 1. Joseph Palmer, the prominent but politically corrupt banker of Palmer, Cook & Co., and close political ally of David Broderick, was foreman of the company. Broderick himself was elected foreman of Empire Fire Engine Company No. 1. No doubt Charley Duane played an active role in fighting the massive fires of June 14 and September 17, 1850, and May 3, 1851, in which hundreds of buildings were destroyed. He particularly distinguished himself by leadership, quick thinking, and fearlessness in the fire at the city hospital owned by Dr. Peter Smith on October 31, 1850, which severely injured several patients and caused $250,000 in damage. And in the inferno of June 21, 1851, which left ten blocks burned, Dutch Charley saved a number of houses from the flames.[20]

Less than three months after his arrival in San Francisco, Dutch Charley found himself in trouble with the authorities. On July 3, 1850, he was brought before the recorder's court and charged with assault and battery for "beating and bruising one of the quiet citizens of this city." Two days later Duane was fined a meager six dollars for the offense. This was the first of many times that he would escape punishment in San Francisco, primarily through the influence of David Broderick.[21]

Dutch Charley's next reported affray took place early in September, when he and several cronies were arrested for assault, battery, and "riotous conduct" at a ball on Jackson Street, in what would become known as the Barbary Coast. They were all released when two friendly police officers testified that Duane and his comrades "were peaceably disposed and orderly" and had not been the aggressors. That same month Duane opened the Louisiana Saloon on Portsmouth Square. He employed a full-time bartender who ran the place for him until it burned down the following spring.[22]

In August, Tom Hyer arrived in San Francisco, and soon after the Sacramento Squatter Riot took place. When armed militia and volunteer fire companies were sent by riverboat to restore order, Dutch Charley and Hyer accompanied them. In late September and October, Duane and a group of comrades spent a few weeks on a horseback trip to the El Dorado County mines. There Duane saw the lynching of gambler Irish Dick Cronin, who had killed a man in the El Dorado gambling house. Woolly Kearney was also there, and he tried to rescue Irish Dick from the mob and offered him his horse. But Cronin was captured and strung up to a famous hanging tree that had helped give the camp its nickname, Hangtown.[23]

Dutch Charley returned to San Francisco and was soon in trouble again. On December 18, 1850, a vicious dog had the misfortune to bite him. The enraged Duane whipped out his pistol and shot the animal on the spot. In so doing, he narrowly missed a passerby. The incident was promptly reported to the judge of the recorder's court, who issued a summons for him to appear on a charge of discharging a firearm within the city limits. A police officer named Gould was detailed to serve the paper on Duane. When he did so, Dutch Charley flew into a rage and tore the summons to shreds. Next he seized the officer by the throat, nearly choking him to death, and stomped him several times in the stomach. Brought before the recorder, Frank Tilford, on a charge of assaulting a policeman, Duane claimed that he did not know Gould was an officer but thought he was the dog's owner presenting him with a bill for the dead animal. Although Duane may not have recognized that Gould was a policeman, for San Francisco police did not wear uniforms until 1857, that was no excuse for delivering a savage beating. Nonetheless, Tilford, a fellow Broderick associate, let him off with a $100 fine.[24]

Two months later Dutch Charley's violent temper brought him serious trouble. Early in the morning of February 18, 1851, with Ira Cole and several cronies, he attended the Adelphi Theater on Clay Street, where its troupe of French actors gave a ball. The manager of the ball was an actor named Amedee Fayolle. According to several accounts, the trouble began when Duane entered the ballroom without purchasing a ticket. When confronted, he knocked down the doorkeeper. Dutch Charley then headed upstairs to the dance floor, and when stopped by the attendant, seized him by the throat and head-butted him in the face. In another version, Fayolle accidentally stepped on Dutch Charley's foot during the dance. Perhaps both versions took place. In any event, Fayolle later entered the barroom, where Duane and his friends were drinking. The Frenchman, accompanied by Eugene Mulard and Felix Marchand, gestured toward Duane. Dutch Charley, seeing the gesture as an affront to his personal honor, stepped up to him and asked, "What do you want here?"

Fayolle did not speak English, and a friend of Duane's named Collyer translated for him. Fayolle replied, with Collyer interpreting, "I want nothing. One of my friends will speak to you tomorrow."

Suddenly two heavy jabs from Dutch Charley's huge fists sent the actor reeling to the floor, his face bleeding heavily. Mulard and Marchand came to his assistance, but Dutch Charley knocked down Marchand with a single blow to the head and shoved Mulard across the room. Duane then turned on the prostrate actor and stomped him savagely in the head and body. Fayolle crawled toward the door, so badly beaten that he could not stand, and reached for the doorknob in an effort to get to his feet. As he did so, Duane jerked out a pistol and fired once. At the same time Dutch Charley cried out, "The son of a bitch has got a pistol!"

The ball had torn into Fayolle's back near the spine and lodged in his abdomen. The badly wounded actor was carried to the French hospital. Dutch Charley was brought before the recorder's court of Frank Tilford on a charge of assault with intent to kill. In a two-day hearing, numerous witnesses took the stand; several testified that Fayolle had been unarmed. Duane claimed self-defense, and his friends supported him. They claimed that Fayolle had a small, double-barreled German pistol in his pocket, and that Duane struck him when the actor reached for the weapon; when Fayolle pulled himself up in the doorway, he pointed the pistol at Dutch Charley and tried to cock the hammer. Judge Tilford, however, found that there was sufficient evidence of Duane's guilt to hold him to answer in District Court. The bullet in Fayolle's back raised serious questions about Duane's claim of self-defense and was something that Tilford could not ignore. He released Dutch Charley on a $15,000 bond.[25]

Amedee Fayolle recovered from his wound and Charley Duane was brought to trial a month later. The jury could not agree on a verdict, with eleven jurors voting for conviction and one for acquittal. Vigilantes later charged that the holdout juror had been bribed. Duane's case was transferred to the Court of Sessions. When the

Charley Duane, seated at far left, and friends in San Francisco in 1853. Dave Scannell, later sheriff, is seated, center. Society of California Pioneers Collection.

new trial date arrived on June 26, Fayolle and the other prosecution witnesses failed to appear and the case was dismissed. Fayolle had returned to France; it was reported that David Broderick and other political friends of Duane had raised a large sum to ensure that the Frenchman left town permanently. Although Dutch Charley escaped punishment, he had earned the bitter enmity of San Francisco's large French community.[26]

Dutch Charley was so confident that he was above the law that he continued his violent behavior even while free on bond. On March 12 he entered the jail in the police station house with Police Officer Bryan C. Donnelly and severely clubbed a prisoner against whom he held a grudge. In court the next day, Judge Tilford, who had previously released Duane on bail, expressed outrage "that a man awaiting his trial on a grave charge" was allowed by the police to freely enter the jail and beat a prisoner. Tilford, however, failed to take any action against Duane. Then, while Dutch Charley was awaiting his retrial, he took part in yet another row. A waterfront lot was claimed both by Duane's patron, Palmer, Cook & Co., and by a rival firm that had erected a building on the lot. On May 27, a party of men led by Dutch Charley and George McDougal, brother of Governor John McDougal, began to tear down the building but the police interfered. There was a fight, and Dutch Charley, McDougal, and two others were arrested. Again, Duane escaped serious punishment. This was but the first of many squatter troubles in his life.[27]

The common thread running through almost all of Charley Duane's violent behavior was his refusal to back down from a fight, and his violent redress of verbal insults and physical threats. Ernest de Massey, a French merchant, provided a vivid portrait of Dutch Charley, whom he termed "one of the outstanding American characters in San Francisco":

> He is a man some twenty-five or thirty years old, large, blond, a man of superb physique. He seems to be of more than ordinary intelligence and is generous even to the point of being prodigal. A born leader, ambitious, and a good mixer, he is usually to be found in one of the gambling houses. A notorious politician as well, he has a thousand votes at his command to be disposed of at elections by the simple plan of having his adherents vote three times in different sections of

the city. Naturally he is flattered and bowed down to by all the political leaders. Although he has no visible means of support he lives regally on credit. . . . With his capriciousness, his viciousness, and his undeniable charm he would be a dangerous man in any walk of life—whether in society, political life, or love-affairs.[28]

On February 19, 1851, the day after Duane shot Fayolle, a series of events began that led to the formation of America's largest vigilance movement. A prominent merchant named Charles Jansen was savagely beaten and robbed. Two "Sydney Ducks," or ex-convicts from the Australian penal colony, William Wildred and Thomas Berdue, were arrested the next day as suspects in the crime. Berdue was mistakenly identified as a notorious Australian robber and murderer named James Stuart. On February 22 the two prisoners were escorted by the police to the house where Jansen was recovering from his wounds. On the return trip to the courthouse a lynch mob tried to seize them. Charley Duane related that he and a group of comrades happened by and helped fight off the mob. The next day, however, a huge crowd of eight thousand gathered in Portsmouth Square and seized the prisoners. At the urging of a young merchant, William T. Coleman, they quickly appointed judges and a jury and held an impromptu trial. However, the jury could not agree on their guilt and they were turned back over to the civil authorities. It later developed that the pair were entirely innocent.

These events were not unprecedented. There was a long tradition of vigilantism in America, commencing with the South Carolina Regulators in 1767–69.[29] Now, San Franciscans increasingly feared crime in their city. A series of disastrous fires was rumored to have been started by incendiaries to provide opportunities for looting. Although it has been demonstrated that in fact there was no crime wave in 1851, the fear of crime and the common belief that the courts failed to punish criminals resulted in widespread support for vigilantism. On June 8, 1851, a group of leading citizens met and formed a secret organization they called the Committee of Vigilance.[30]

Two days later, while the committee was enrolling members, an Australian thief, John Jenkins, burglarized a store and was captured trying to escape with a stolen safe in his rowboat. Instead of taking him to jail, his captors turned their prisoner over to the new vigilance committee. They quickly tried Jenkins and sentenced him to hang. Surrounded by vigilantes, Jenkins was marched to Portsmouth Square. David Broderick climbed onto a wagon and pleaded with the crowd of two thousand to rescue the prisoner. His efforts were to no avail, for Jenkins was quickly strung up to a beam of the old Customs House.

The new vigilance committee soon had some seven hundred members. Among the offenders who came under their scrutiny was Charley Duane. On June 26 a petition was presented to the committee asking that Duane be brought before them for his assault on Fayolle, as "the Law has not been effective in administering the punishment that he justly merits." The committee, however resolved to take no action against Duane.[31]

By this time Dutch Charley had developed great animosity toward the vigilantes. On July 9, at an anti-vigilance meeting in the St. Francis Hook and Ladder Company firehouse, Duane and David Broderick were among the featured speakers. Dutch Charley particularly hated one of the vigilantes, Frank Ball, a Mexican War veteran. A popular young singer and jokester, Ball was also one of the jurors who had voted to convict Dutch Charley. The wrathful Duane several times publicly threatened to "kill the red headed son of a bitch, Frank Ball." Dutch Charley was in Clayton's Saloon one night when Ball rendered a comic song about the hanging of John Jenkins. Duane angrily told the crowd that Jenkins was a friend of his. Said Frank Ball later, "After I had sung a song about the execution on the plaza, he called me a puppy, and said that all those who listened to me were puppies and cowards."[32]

Three weeks later, shortly after midnight on July 21, Dutch Charley, Ira Cole, and several comrades attended a masquerade ball at the Cairo Coffee House on Commercial Street. Cole later testified, "We were all pretty tight. . . . Duane had drank more liquor that day than I had ever known him to drink in a single day."

Frank Ball was also present, wearing blackface, petticoats, and a woman's dress. Duane approached him while he was dancing and asked to talk, but Ball refused. Ball's lack of fear of Duane, coupled with his ludicrous feminine attire, was a direct challenge to Dutch Charley's masculinity and to his sense of personal honor. Dutch Charley called Ball "a black Negro," and exclaimed, "You God damned son of a bitch, I want to see you now!"

At the same time Duane delivered a terrific blow to Ball's chin and the young singer dropped to the floor. Duane followed up with a heavy boot to Ball's stomach. Dangerously injured, Ball bled profusely from the mouth and was unconscious for six hours. That same morning the executive committee of the vigilantes ordered that Duane be arrested, but when they were advised that he was already in jail, they took no action. However, the committee issued the following proclamation: "That whereas our brother Frank Ball has been violently assaulted by one Chas. Duane alias Dutch Charley who is now in custody of the Civil Authorities we hereby pledge ourselves that justice shall be meted out to said Chas. Duane."[33]

Dutch Charley was indicted for assault with intent to kill. The Court of Sessions, under pressure to do something quickly for fear that the Committee of Vigilance would act, brought Duane to trial just four days later. The presiding judge was Alexander Campbell, an outspoken opponent of the vigilantes. The court's two associate justices were Edward "Ned" McGowan and Harvey S. Brown, both corrupt associates of David Broderick. Dutch Charley's lawyer asked for a change of venue on the grounds that he could not get a fair trial because of the vigilante excitement and "the influence of the French, among whom a deep seated prejudice prevailed" against him. The motion was denied and Charley Duane was tried and convicted.[34]

The jury returned its verdict on July 26, finding Duane guilty of assault with intent to kill but recommending leniency. Dutch Charley's lawyers moved for a new trial, and the case was continued until the 31st. That morning the courtroom was crowded with members of the vigilance committee as well as Duane's powerful political friends. Judge Campbell denied the motion for a new trial and sentenced him to one year in state prison, the most lenient sentence the law allowed. This result was met with disapproval by the vigilantes. Ned McGowan, no friend of the vigilance committee, provided a vivid description of the scene in court:

> The mobbites who had crowded the court house, jumped on the benches and commenced hissing and showing other marks of disapprobation. They offered no further violence; if they had, many of them would have bitten the dust that day. David C. Broderick, Governor McDougal . . . and the prisoner himself had on a pair of Colt's revolvers, and many others were armed—two or three with double barrel shotguns under their cloaks, and Colonel Jack Hays, the High Sheriff, was in personal attendance on the court.[35]

But Charley Duane did not need the guns of his political cronies to keep him out of prison. On August 17, three weeks after his conviction, his friend Governor John McDougal, at the urging of David Broderick, granted him a full pardon. McDougal knew that his action would be highly unpopular and he endeavored to keep it a secret. But by August 25 rumor of the pardon had leaked out and the members of the Committee of Vigilance were livid. Dutch Charley's public record of seven brawls, including two attempted murders, was too much. The executive committee ordered Duane to "leave this City of San Francisco and not to return under penalty of death." But the vigilantes took no action until September 4, when they received confirmation that the pardon had in fact been granted. The next day the executive committee issued an order for the immediate arrest of Charley Duane. But the vigilantes could not find him. They soon learned that he had shipped out for Panama on September 6 aboard the steamer *Pacific*.[36]

In the meantime, San Francisco's vigilantes had hanged three more criminals. They captured the real James Stuart and executed him on July 11. On August 24 they hanged Samuel Whittaker and Robert McKenzie, a pair of notorious robbers and confederates of Stuart. Having accomplished its goals, the Committee of Vigilance gradually disbanded in the fall of 1851. This encouraged Charley Duane to return to San Francisco. Within three months of his hasty departure he was back in town and back in trouble.

For Duane, the pursuit of leisure included womanizing. Charming, well-spoken, and always dressed in the height of fashion, he reveled in a second nickname, "Handsome Charley." As Ernest de Massey explained, "Girls and women, even those of the highest type, are captivated by his sympathetic manner, his flattery, his delicate attentions, and his pleasing compliments." Duane's close escape from hanging or other punishment at the hands of the vigilantes had changed him little. While he had been gone, an attorney named Tiffany had "interfered with Duane's domestic arrangements." Dutch Charley challenged his rival to a formal duel, but Tiffany had no stomach for the field of honor. On November 24 Duane was arrested, ordered to post a bond to keep the peace, and released. Once again the political influence of David Broderick kept him in good stead.[37]

Dutch Charley was so brazen that he had little fear of the city police. Soon after, he had a run-in with San Francisco policeman

Phineas Blunt, who noted the incident in his journal on January 7, 1852:

> Tonight had difficulty with Charles Duane alias Dutch Charley. Also with John Barmore, Henry Drake and Sandy Rinton. All of them shoulder strikers, one of them offered to cut open [Police Officer] Cornelius Holland, another offered to cut the liver out of me because I had arrested one of them, rather hard spot to be in.[38]

Duane's proclivity for violence seemed limitless. On April 6, 1852, he was arrested for assault and battery on James F. Cook and for "mischievous and riotous conduct" during an affray in the Golden Gate saloon. Duane paid for all the property damage prior to being called into court, where he professed "entire repentance and reform." He was sentenced to a fine of $50 and ordered to post a $1,000 bond to keep the peace for six months.[39]

THERE was a productive side to Charley Duane's violent life. He used his muscular courage to preserve public safety and order, and to become a leader of the volunteer fire department. On December 6, 1852, he was elected assistant chief engineer, the second highest position in the department. Duane took his duties seriously, even over-zealously. On June 6, 1853, he entered the county jail and stomped and broke the arm of a man who had raised a false fire alarm.[40]

Duane excelled as a fireman. His courage in the face of great danger, as well as the leadership qualities he exhibited during the confusion and excitement of raging infernos, earned him respect. On the night of May 2, 1853, a fire erupted in the Rassette House, an elegant five-story wood hotel on Bush Street, trapping more than four hundred sleeping guests inside. Duane played a prominent role in fighting the fire; the occupants were promptly evacuated and no lives were lost. Even though the building was destroyed, the firemen prevented the fire from spreading and only a few adjacent buildings were burned. Five months later, on October 21, Duane led efforts to save the St. Francis Hotel, on the corner of Dupont (Grant) and Clay Streets. Engines were promptly on the scene, and the firemen used a very dangerous but effective technique, running their hoses through the ground-floor doors and windows and fighting the flames from inside the building. Although the upper two floors were blazing, in thirty minutes the fire was out before it had spread to other buildings. This technique is still considered the most effective method of fighting and containing urban fires.[41]

His courage in using this method to fight a factory fire several weeks later was noted by the editor of the *Alta California*: "Mr. Duane . . . regardless of the flames, heat and danger, placed himself in the second story of the frame building which had caught [fire], and by his energy and bravery did much to save it. The upper portion of the building was destroyed."[42]

The city had a law prohibiting the storage of large amounts of blasting powder, which was used to level the city's hills in constructing streets. Several times Duane enforced the "powder ordinance" by seizing kegs of explosives and arresting their owners. Duane also demonstrated his ability at preventing fires. He regularly kept an open eye for fire hazards, especially unsafe stovepipes. In June 1853, he noticed on the roof of a small shack a stovepipe encased by wood, a common cause of fire. The shed was vacant and he forced an entry. Inside, he found a trapdoor in the floor, and below was a three-ton stamping machine and press, plus dies, tools, and coins in denominations of two to fifty dollars. A surprised Duane realized that he had stumbled upon a large-scale counterfeiting operation. He called in the police, who seized the equipment. The culprits were never apprehended.[43]

On December 5, 1853, Charley Duane was elected chief engineer of the fire department. This was perhaps the proudest moment of his life. At the age of only twenty-six he had been chosen to fill one of the most important posts in the city government. At the same time Duane managed the National Hall, the Whig Party headquarters on Kearny Street. Despite his Whig connections, he was close to the Democratic banking house of Palmer, Cook & Co. and kept rooms in its building from 1852 until he was banished by the vigilantes in 1856. For a time he also ran the Magnolia Saloon at Kearny and Commercial Streets.[44]

Duane fully recognized the great responsibility that had been placed on his shoulders, and his behavior began to improve dramatically. But his enthusiasm for his new duties was not shared by many of his peers. Numerous volunteers resigned in protest, and one company, the Lady Washington No. 2, quit *en masse*. After Duane's election, the historian Theodore H. Hittell noted, "The moral character of the department soon showed signs of deterioration.

Some good citizens remained firemen; but most of them retired from active service, and their places were filled by persons who were no credit either to the department or to the city."⁴⁵

Dutch Charley's enemies alleged that many inactive firemen had enrolled in the volunteer department solely so that they could vote for Duane. A correspondent for the *San Francisco Herald* claimed that an entire company, Pacific No. 8, "was organized, not to do fire duty, but to aid in electing Mr. Duane Chief Engineer," and that the fire department rolls had been packed with "a host of political hacks who join the Department to get rid of jury duty and to obtain influence."⁴⁶

On the other hand, sympathetic Democratic newspaper editors saw great nobility in Duane's courageous record as a fireman. They were more than willing to forgive his violent record. The editor of the *Pacific News* spoke of the new fire chief in glowing literary terms and noted a dramatic change in his character:

> We doubt if a more capable man in the entire community could have been chosen. Duane is bold, sensible and energetic, young, enthusiastic and generous. He is yet more than all this: he is reformed and reforming. Two years ago his hardy character assumed the appearance of recklessness, and he became one of the most noted scape graces and dare-devils in the city. He was ready for every forlorn hope, and we are afraid was regarded as an embodiment of that idea himself. Poets talk about the purifying effects of fire, and the cleansing attributes of water. Real life, in this notable instance, has indicated the truths of these metaphors, and Charley Duane comes forth from the blazing rafters of the Rassette, and the old St. Francis, half drowned and half roasted, a redeemed man and useful citizen.
>
> Long may he live to wear his honors. They have been well earned, and will not soon fade. The Fire Department has been the means of saving much to the city of San Francisco; but we doubt whether it has snatched a more noble "brand from the burning" than its present chief officer.⁴⁷

In the same vein, the editor of Sacramento's *Democratic State Journal* added that Duane was "an efficient engineer . . . always on hand where duty or danger calls, using his best energies to preserve the property of his fellow-citizens from the destroying flames. Whatever Mr. Duane has been, he is now a useful and honorable citizen."[48] Even the *Alta California*, one of Duane's harshest critics, commented, "Mr. Duane, whatever may have been his former faults, has for some time past conducted himself in a manner exhibiting a determination to be a good citizen."[49]

Charley Duane proved popular with a majority of the city's firemen. On December 4, 1854, he was reelected to a second one-year term and served until December 13, 1855. In addition to fighting fires, Dutch Charley considered that his role as chief included the broader duty of preserving the peace. He distinguished himself several times by breaking up brawls and disarming lawbreakers.

On February 19, 1854, after battling a fire, Duane, with Woolly Kearney and a group of firemen, was invited into a coffee saloon for free refreshments by its proprietor. Several of them repaid his generosity by getting drunk and smashing up the place. Police Officer Isaiah W. Lees was there, and Woolly Kearney was not happy to see him. Two days earlier, Kearney and several other shoulder-strikers, including James P. Casey, Martin Gallagher, and Bill Lewis, had engaged in a brawl at a political meeting in the Mercantile Hotel. They had been arrested after a vicious battle with Lees and other policemen. Now, in retaliation, Kearney and several companions attacked Lees and beat him. Charley Duane seized Woolly Kearney and dragged him outside. Lees brought Kearney to the station house, where the prizefighter boasted that he would soon be freed by Judge Alexander Wells, a corrupt Broderick associate. Woolly Kearney was found guilty, not of assaulting a police officer, but of the much lesser offense of public drunkenness.[50]

On April 13, 1854, Duane was on the corner of Montgomery and Sacramento Streets talking with John Parrott, the former U.S. consul at Mazatlan, Mexico, and a wealthy merchant, banker, and capitalist. A thirty-six-year-old widow, Hester Farley, walked up to Parrott and complained, "You did not keep your appointment, and I have been waiting for you two hours at Judge Hasting's office." Parrott brushed her off, saying that he was busy and could not go with her at that time. Mrs. Farley angrily responded, "Damn you, you must go with me, or I'll kill you."

At the same time she drew a cocked pistol and raised it to fire. Duane leaped in front of Parrott, seized the weapon, and after a brief tussle, wrenched it away. The distraught woman was arrested and charged with assault with a deadly weapon. The next day, in a preliminary court hearing, Mrs. Farley testified that she had met John Parrott in 1851 on the steamer from Panama to California and that "he had taken liberties with her on board the steamer" and had "ruined her reputation." The judge believed Duane, Parrott, and the attorney, Serranus C. Hastings, who all testified that the woman was incoherent and insane. In retrospect, their testimony seems too pat and was probably fashioned to protect the prominent but erratic Parrott, who was married with a large family, from public embarrassment.[51]

The Democratic primary election of June 19, 1854, one of San Francisco's most violent, illustrated the election lawlessness that gave rise to popular support for vigilantism. Of course, Duane was involved. Reported the *Alta*, "Never have we witnessed such intense excitement, attended with such disgraceful scenes of rowdyism, at any election that has ever taken place in this city. . . . As the day drew to a close, wild riot came . . . [and] black eyes and bloody noses abounded. . . . Knives were drawn and freely used, revolvers discharged with a perfect recklessness." Billy Mulligan was arrested for fighting at the polls and a passerby was shot and wounded while walking past the polls at the Empire Engine Company firehouse.[52]

The worst violence took place that night, after the polls were closed. Duane was in the barroom of the Union Hotel with various cronies, including Barney Mulligan, brother of Billy Mulligan. At that time the Union was a popular gathering place for the political elite. Suddenly J. A. "Jack" Watson burst into the bar and engaged in a heated argument with several men present. Dutch Charley interceded and attempted to quiet Watson, but soon Duane's temper brought him to angry words. Watson turned to leave and strode toward the front door. As suddenly as he had entered, he whirled around, whipped out a revolver, and opened fire on the crowd. Barney Mulligan dropped with a pistol ball in his left thigh. Dutch Charley yanked his own six-shooter and cried out to Watson to shoot at him, not at the crowd. At the same time Duane and several others fired at Watson, who went down with three wounds, one in his thigh, a ball in one hand, and a finger shot off the other hand. Thirteen shots had been exchanged at close quarters, but Duane was not scratched.[53]

On the night of July 4, Dutch Charley was celebrating Independence Day in the Union Hotel bar with David Broderick and

Ned McGowan. A noted ruffian, Jim Campbell, entered and insulted Broderick. Duane let the insult pass, but soon afterward Billy Mulligan entered, dressed to the nines for a fireman's ball. When Mulligan learned of the insult, he doffed his gloves and fancy coat and beat Campbell severely by punching and head-butting. Dutch Charley thought that Mulligan had gone too far and tried to stop the fight, but Ned McGowan told Duane not to interfere. Recalled McGowan years later, "It was a fair fight between two boxers, and I thought it was better to let them have it out." Campbell's injuries kept him bedridden for weeks but did not change his temperament. On September 14 he was killed in a fight with another ruffian, Peter Veeder.[54]

A year later, on the night of June 18, 1855, Dutch Charley was standing at the door of the Metropolitan Theater on Montgomery Street when a brawl broke out across the street between two men named Sutton and Stowell over a $200 debt. High words passed between them when Sutton struck Stowell with his cane. Stowell drew his knife and pursued Sutton across the street, managing to inflict a wound on Sutton's hand. When Duane heard the loud cry of "Murder!" he rushed after the pair and disarmed and arrested them both.[55]

A few weeks later, on the evening of July 6, 1855, Duane and a group of firemen visited the Metropolitan Theater to see a French comedy. A patron in the audience, Leopold Lowenberg, a Merchant Street broker, made a loud hissing noise as Duane's party passed. Dutch Charley, taking this as an affront to the fire department, immediately struck Lowenberg, who had the chief engineer arrested. Once again Duane's political connections saved him from punishment.[56]

Whether criminal rogue or crime stopper, "Handsome Charley" was favored by pretty actresses and made a point of meeting the theatrical stars who visited San Francisco. A number of them gave performances for the benefit of the fire department's charity fund, including the famed Matilda Heron, who sent the dashing fire chief the following letter on June 1, 1854:

> Charles P. Duane, Chief Engineer, Fire Department.
> Dear Sir: Being about to leave San Francisco for my home, I desire to take advantage of the few days left, to make some expression of gratitude to a city which has lavished on me so many kindnesses. Having no way so well to do it, as through

an institution which is its chief affection, pride, and safeguard, I take the liberty of tendering my services for a benefit to the Fire Department Fund, on any evening you may name previous to the sailing of the steamer on the 16th inst.[57]

Duane's genteel response was not what might be expected from a gun-toting rowdy:

Miss Matilda Heron. Respected Miss: Your kind favor of this date, tendering your valuable services in aid of the "Firemen's Charitable Fund," (which you so properly term our city's "chief affection, pride, and safeguard,") is just received; and in behalf of the Department, I hasten to return their grateful thanks for your kindness, and with pleasure accept your generous offer, which will ever be not only remembered, but warmly appreciated by those whose regret at your departure from among us is only equaled by their earnest desire for your success in that profession of which you are so bright an ornament.[58]

Duane later recalled that the actress raised $2,800 for the fund in a single performance. Noted the *California Chronicle*: "Whatever may be said of her acting, the public is bound to believe that she has performed more generous acts than any woman that ever appeared on the California stage."[59]

On November 7, 1855, Dutch Charley's precipitous temper nearly cost him his life. He was in a gambling hall on the corner of Montgomery and Commercial Streets, where a drunken gambler named Gray insulted him. When someone present told Duane that Gray was a thief, the fire chief quickly placed him under arrest. Unknown to Duane, Gray was not a thief but was carrying a large sum of money, and police officer B. C. Donnelley had been assigned to keep an eye on him. Donnelly, the same officer who had assisted Duane in beating a prisoner, interfered with Duane's arrest of Gray and the fight was on. With his club, Donnelly struck Dutch Charley, who retaliated by hammering him with his cane. At that, the policeman jerked his revolver and fired twice at close range. Once again Duane's Irish luck saved his life, for both shots missed. Dutch Charley had Donnelly arrested for assault with intent to kill.[60]

By this time, late 1855, San Francisco's population had mushroomed to 56,000. The most important and modern city in the

Dutch Charley Duane. A woodcut from a daguerreotype taken in San Francisco in 1856. Author's collection.

western U.S., it was the center for commerce, trade, and finance, and was the gateway to the California mining region. San Francisco entrepreneurs made fortunes in banking, shipping, land, manufacture of mining equipment, mercantile pursuits, private express businesses, and a myriad of other endeavors. Their opulent homes vied for space with hundreds of saloons, gambling halls, bordellos, and fandango houses that catered to the population, which was 80 percent male.

The tents and wood shacks of the Gold Rush had long since been replaced with hundreds of multistory modern brick buildings.

Many San Francisco politicians had made fortunes investing in city real estate. Dutch Charley did not have the foresight to invest in city lots, but by 1852 he recognized that the land outside the city would be valuable in the future. He claimed squatter's title to a large tract of land bordering Divisadero Street and including much of Alamo Hill, which would later become part of the Western Addition, incorporated into the city in 1866.[61]

When Duane stepped down as fire chief in December 1855, the editor of the city's *Fireman's Journal* gave his performance a mixed review:

> While we have had occasion to take exception to the course pursued by Mr. Duane on several matters of policy connected with the Department, and while we have had cause to differ with him on matters outside the Department, we cannot withhold from him that meed of commendation to which he is entitled, for the performance of his duties during the two terms he has acted as Chief Engineer. Actuated as he has been on many occasions by an impulsive nature, not at all times under control, and too often by the interested and incompetent counsels of others, yet we entertain the belief that the entire Department will accord to him the very best intentions in the conduct of his office. . . . Mr. Duane leaves the Department with many friends, and of course with enemies.[62]

IT WAS his enemies, political and personal, who would very shortly cause him the greatest trouble of his life, resulting in his permanent downfall as a political power in Gold Rush San Francisco. This time his enemies came in the form of the San Francisco Committee of Vigilance of 1856. From the time of his exile by the vigilantes in 1851, Duane had participated in at least six more altercations, bringing his tally to thirteen. His violent record was very well known, particularly to the vigilantes.

Sympathy for a revival of the 1851 Committee was first stirred in 1855 when Charles Cora, a well-known gambler, shot and killed U.S. Marshal William Richardson in a quarrel on November 17. A crowd quickly gathered and firebrand Sam Brannan, a leader of the 1851 committee, urged the lynching of Cora, without success. Cora

was jailed and James King of William, editor of the newly established
Daily Evening Bulletin, began an editorial campaign against official
corruption. He warned that Cora would escape punishment and
urged the people to hang the sheriff if Cora broke jail. When Cora's
trial resulted in a hung jury in January 1856, King wrote, "Rejoice
ye gamblers and harlots! Rejoice with exceeding gladness!"[63]

On May 14, 1856, King published an attack on James P. Casey, a
member of the city board of supervisors, and publicized his history
as a former convict in Sing Sing prison in New York. Later that day,
as King was walking home, Casey shot and mortally wounded him.
The following day America's largest vigilance movement began to
form. Leading members of the 1851 committee, including William
T. Coleman, quickly reorganized it and accepted applications for
membership. Soon six to eight thousand men had joined the vigilante
ranks. They were organized into some fifty military companies, out-
fitted in militia uniforms, and armed with militia muskets and
bayonets. For the next three months the vigilance committee would
literally run San Francisco. So powerful were the vigilantes that the
local authorities and federal government proved impotent against
them. A blacklist of the worst ruffians and political hacks in the city
was drawn up. Dutch Charley, Yankee Sullivan, and Billy Mulligan
were among those who headed the list. The vigilantes uncovered
evidence of political corruption and even confiscated a trick ballot
box with a false bottom that had been used by Yankee Sullivan and
Woolly Kearney.

On May 22 James Casey and Charles Cora were hanged from
second-story windows of the vigilantes' headquarters, nicknamed
Fort Gunnybags. Dutch Charley was vocal in his denunciation of
the lynching and helped organize efforts to oppose the vigilance
committee. After Casey shot James King of William, a mob gathered
and tried to seize him from the officers. Duane, Billy Mulligan, and
several other friends of Casey held off the would-be lynchers with
their pistols. According to the *Bulletin*, Duane "had matters arranged
to elect himself City Marshal" and oppose the vigilantes. On May
31 Yankee Sullivan, in a fit of delirium tremens, committed suicide
in his Fort Gunnybags jail cell. Because of the animosity between
Sullivan and Tom Hyer, Duane had never been a close friend of
Yankee Sullivan. Nonetheless, he was outraged by Sullivan's arrest
and charged publicly that the famous pugilist had been murdered by
his vigilante guards. Isaac Bluxome, secretary of the 1851 and 1856

committees, later admitted that Duane's subsequent arrest was in retaliation for his allegations that the Vigilance Committee had murdered Yankee Sullivan.[64]

Although Dutch Charley was warned by friends that he had been targeted by the vigilantes and should leave the city, he refused to do so. In his stubborn refusal to kowtow to the vigilantes, Duane demonstrated his strict allegiance to the ethic of personal honor. To run from his enemies was unthinkable. On June 1 he was overpowered and arrested by a band of vigilantes and lodged in Fort Gunnybags in company with Billy Mulligan, Woolly Kearney, and three other shoulder-strikers, Martin Gallagher, Billy Carr, and Edward Bulger.[65]

Duane's trial began on June 3 and ended the following day. The Committee made the following finding:

> Whereas, the evidence brought us establishes conclusively that Charles P. Duane has for years been a disturber of the peace of this community by repeated assaults, often with deadly weapons, upon unoffending citizens, and by his interference with our elections; resolved, that he be sentenced to leave this state in such a manner as shall hereafter be determined, and warned never to return under penalty of death.[66]

On June 5 Duane, Billy Mulligan, and Woolly Kearney were placed aboard the steamer *Golden Age*, bound for Panama. Dutch Charley was enraged by what he considered unjust treatment. His pride would not allow him to go away quietly. When the *Golden Age* docked in Acapulco, he escaped and stowed away on the steamer *John L. Stephens*, bound for San Francisco. Although he was soon found, he demanded to be returned to the city. But the captain forced him to board the first southbound steamer that was encountered and Charley Duane returned to New York.[67]

Dutch Charley's younger brother, John, had arrived in California in 1854 and thereafter was his constant companion and political ally. The vigilantes also placed him on their blacklist but never arrested him or forced him to leave the state.[68]

The vigilantes had moved quickly to round up the worst political ruffians in the city. The committee banished more than forty men from California. Most of them were placed on outgoing ships; a number fled San Francisco to avoid arrest. Two more murderers, Philander Brace and Joseph Hetherington, were hanged before an enormous crowd on July 29, 1856. The Committee of Vigilance soon disbanded, but not before its members formed a political arm, the People's Party, which wielded great power in San Francisco for the next ten years; the profound influence of the vigilantes themselves would be felt in San Francisco for the rest of the century.[69]

THE CONDITIONS which gave rise to vigilance in San Francisco were not unique. They appeared at various other times during the frontier period, such as in the 1853–57 Roach-Belcher feud in Monterey County, California; in Montana Territory's vigilante uprising of 1863–65 involving outlaw-sheriff Henry Plummer and organized thievery; during New Mexico's Lincoln County War of 1878–79; and during the cowboy troubles of southern Arizona in 1880–82, which brought the Earp brothers to prominence. In each of these cases, certain conditions are found in common: society was new and unstable, the courts were incompetent or corrupt, law enforcement was ineffective and partial, the local economy was of the boom-and-bust type, citizens were primarily interested in making money and neglected civic affairs, and politics were controlled by a few powerful individuals. These conditions combined to create a vacuum of legal and moral order. In some cases, vigilantes stepped in to fill this void. In others, bloody feuds resulted.[70]

The 1856 Committee of Vigilance was fundamentally different from that of 1851 in one important respect. In 1851 the vigilantes had targeted thieves and murderers. Although the 1856 committee went after the same types, it was primarily concerned with political criminals: shoulder-strikers and ballot-box stuffers. Because of the political complexion of the 1856 committee, its huge membership, and its deep influence on later vigilance movements, it is the most controversial and has received the most attention from writers and scholars. Thus, the historiography of the 1856 committee is enormous.[71]

Most nineteenth-century chroniclers, such as Hubert Howe Bancroft and Theodore H. Hittell, assigned to the 1856 vigilance committee motives of purity, and agreed with the vigilantes that they had properly targeted crime and political corruption. Modern historians, however, have assigned different motives. Philip J. Ethington has summarized (and disputed) what has become the conventional wisdom. He cites Roger Lotchin (1974), Richard Maxwell Brown (1975), Peter R. Decker (1978), and Robert Senkewicz (1985), who "have argued that the Committee of 1856 was the result of allegedly deeper, more fundamental divisions in San Francisco society, for which the political trappings and stated goals were mere disguise."[72] Those writers have variously blamed the rise of vigilance in 1856 on anti-Irish sentiment, anti-Catholic sentiment, anti-Broderick sentiment, and class conflict between the city's mercantile elite and its Irish working class. Focusing on the undeniable influence of the city's merchants in the committee, they have argued that economic reasons rather than electoral fraud led the vigilantes to target scapegoats under the guise of law and order.[73]

Yet Ethington, who studied the papers and membership records of the 1856 committee, failed to discover evidence of anti-Catholic or anti-Irish motivations by the vigilantes. He did find convincing evidence of fraud in the elections of 1854 and 1855. Yankee Sullivan, before he died, confessed to the vigilantes that he had stuffed ballot boxes. Ethington found that publication of Sullivan's confession added "literally thousands of men to the ranks of the committee." It was this concern with political crime that was the principal reason for the formation of the 1856 vigilance committee.[74]

There is additional evidence of ballot fraud. Well before his arrest by the vigilantes, Yankee Sullivan had boasted that he had used a trick ballot box to elect James Casey. The vigilantes seized and displayed the false-bottomed box. Perhaps the strongest evidence of election fraud came from Charles Duane himself. In a surprisingly blunt admission, he said, "I do not dispute the fact that there was some ground for the Vigilance Committee here in 1856. Politics had become so corrupt that it was impossible to have anything like a fair election. It was a regular thing to elect men as supervisors whose names had not even been mentioned at the polls on election day, just as Casey had been elected. A few men controlled everything, and the votes of the mass of the people counted for nothing."[75]

When James Casey shot James King of William, a mob of five thousand quickly gathered to lynch him. This was not a carefully planned demonstration orchestrated by the city's merchant elite, but a sudden, impromptu gathering of outraged citizens. That a crowd this large would gather so quickly for a uniform purpose, and that six to eight thousand men would soon join an organization to defy established law and authority, demonstrated that the citizenry saw something seriously wrong in San Francisco's criminal justice and political systems.

The vigilance committee made no attempt to obscure the fact that they were targeting violent political criminals. Of Billy Mulligan, Yankee Sullivan, and Martin Gallagher, the vigilantes charged that the three "have for years been disturbers of the peace of our city, destroyers of the purity of our elections, active members and leaders of the organized gang which have invaded the sanctity of our ballot-boxes, and perfect pests to society."[76]

Richard Maxwell Brown has argued that the vigilantes deliberately set out to smash David Broderick's political machine. But, while many of those blacklisted were Broderick men, many members of Broderick's machine were not molested at all. Others that the vigilantes arrested either were unconnected to Broderick or had changed political allegiances. James P. Casey had defected to the Chivalry wing of the Democratic Party; he was supported by Yankee Sullivan, who as poll manager had stuffed his ballot box to elect Casey supervisor in 1855. Chris Lilly was arrested because of his involvement in the San Mateo County election frauds. Some were not political criminals at all. Thomas B. Cunningham was a counterfeiter, Lewis Mahoney and Alexander Purple were robbers and burglars, and Abraham Craft and Dan Aldrich, gamblers. Charles Cora, Philander Brace, and Joseph Hetherington were all hanged for murder and likewise were not political criminals. The men blacklisted by the vigilantes all had one thing in common: they were civil or political criminals. Biographical sketches of twelve of the most notorious men targeted by the vigilantes appear in the notes to this volume.[77]

Historians may debate whether San Francisco vigilantism was morally justified and whether it posed a threat to civil liberties. However, the reason that Dutch Charley and his comrades were targeted seems clear. Charley Duane was arrested and deported by the vigilantes exactly for the reasons that they stated: because he was a disturber of the peace and because of his interference with free elections. There was no secret, underlying reason for his arrest. Certainly his vocal opposition to the committee fueled its animus, but the vigilantes had more than enough cause to arrest him. Duane was not targeted because he was a Broderick supporter, or Irish, or Catholic, but because he was a violent man who was a danger to the public peace as well as to the city's free elections. He had never once received just punishment for his many transgressions in Gold Rush San Francisco. The vigilantes did to him what the courts should have done.

In Gold Rush San Francisco, Charley Duane had acted and reacted the only way he knew. He electioneered and responded to affronts just as he had done back home in New York City—not only with words, but with violence. Dutch Charley was living proof of the blurred class distinctions in Gold Rush San Francisco, and in some ways he was a victim of the mixing of social classes. He socialized with barroom ruffians and firehouse rowdies and at the same time with merchants, capitalists, bankers, lawyers, journalists, actors, and artisans, including such prominent men as Mathew Hall McAllister, Thomas Hayes, Joseph Palmer, and Governor John McDougal. He was a devoted patron of the theater and as chief engineer of the fire department kept company with the leading actresses who visited San Francisco.

In New York, Duane had associated mainly with those of his own class—firehouse rowdies, street ruffians, pugilists, gangsters, political thugs, and gamblers. But in close-knit, socially fluid San Francisco, Duane rubbed elbows with the middle and upper classes. During the Gold Rush, all classes frequented the same theaters, the same gambling houses, and the same saloons. Many members of the upper and middle classes, who fueled the vigilance committees of San Francisco, were exposed for the first time to ruffians like Dutch Charley Duane, and they did not like what they saw. Merchants from small New England communities had never seen crooked elections managed by New York shoulder-strikers. To all appearances, saloon keepers, gamblers, prizefighters, political bullies, and ballot-box stuffers were running the city.

Such men occupied positions of visible power: Edward McGowan as judge of the Court of Sessions, Charley Duane as chief of the fire department, Billy Mulligan as deputy city treasurer and later deputy sheriff in charge of the county jail, James P. Casey as supervisor, John W. Bagley as state assemblyman, and Yankee Sullivan, Billy Carr, Martin Gallagher, James Cusick, Bill Lewis, and Terence Kelly as inspectors of elections in their respective wards. Positions of authority were also held by Tammany Hall politicians from New York City like Sheriff David Scannell and Deputy Sheriff Chris Dowdigan, as well as the corrupt City Marshal Hampton North, who resigned in the middle of the vigilante uprising and left town and returned east with an illicit fortune. It was little wonder that the average San Franciscan thought that the city and its elections were being run by thugs and political criminals.

Charley Duane, Billy Mulligan, Yankee Sullivan, Chris Lilly, and Woolly Kearney were by far the most notorious ruffians in San Francisco in 1856. All had achieved notoriety before they ever came to California. After their arrival, each repeatedly took part in civil and political crime. Certainly there were hundreds of other criminals in the city: robbers, burglars, and thieves. Exceedingly dangerous Gold Rush outlaws like Thomas J. Hodges, alias Tom Bell, and "Rattlesnake Dick" Barter slipped in and out of San Francisco at various times. For most of these criminals, anonymity was their stock-in-trade; often even the police did not know what they looked like. But ruffians like Duane, Mulligan, Sullivan, Lilly, and Kearney were known to everybody. They did not hide from the police like furtive criminals, but instead maintained high public profiles by running saloons and engaging in politics. It was their notoriety, coupled with public outbursts of violence, flagrant violations of the law, and systematic political corruption that caused the vigilantes to take notice and mete out their own punishment.

There may have been economic, ethnic, and political conditions that contributed to the formation of the 1856 committee. No doubt some vigilantes were motivated by anti-Irish, anti-Catholic, or anti-Broderick bias; others may have resented San Francisco's large Irish working class and the cheap labor it provided. However, the overriding reason was a widely held belief that the city's criminal justice system and electoral process were corrupt. That loss of faith in the legal and democratic process was the principal cause of San Francisco vigilantism in 1856.

NOT LONG after Duane's arrival in New York City, he filed lawsuits against William Tell Coleman, James Dows, and Miers F. Truett, all of whom had also returned east. Duane asked for damages because of their actions as leaders of the vigilantes in exiling him. He alleged that his land had been squatted on by a member of the vigilance committee, that he had lost a $60,000 contract to grade a city street, and that he had lost the opportunity to collect money owed him by the city for services as chief engineer. Billy Mulligan and Rube Maloney filed similar lawsuits but all were eventually dismissed on the grounds that New York courts had no jurisdiction over incidents that took place in California.[78]

In March 1857 Dutch Charley visited Washington, D.C., to see David Broderick, who had been elected U.S. senator from California, take his seat in Congress. Broderick honored his old friend by giving him a chair next to his on the Senate floor. It was an extraordinary moment: a member of Congress paying public tribute to a ruffian who had been deported by the vigilantes. Duane's stay in the capitol was at the National Hotel, and the following day he and most of the guests were poisoned after drinking contaminated water from the building's corroded lead pipes. Duane was seriously ill and bedridden for two and a half years, suffering neurological damage that crippled his legs. He was disabled ever after, and could walk only with a cane. Duane's enemies, however, always maintained that his disability was caused by excessive drink.[79]

When Duane recovered, he learned that others who had been exiled, including Martin Gallagher, Billy Carr, Edward Bulger, and Woolly Kearney, had returned to California unmolested. At the end of February 1860, Charley Duane came back to San Francisco without fanfare or controversy. A few weeks later he attended a fire department meeting and his old comrades gave him the seat of honor. His friends also induced the state legislature to pass a bill granting him wages that he claimed were unpaid from his service as chief engineer.[80]

Despite his physical disability, Duane's pugnacious nature was little changed. On the night of July 20, 1860, he quarreled with one Brady on Montgomery Street. When Dutch Charley made a thrust at Brady with his cane, the latter wrestled it away and knocked Duane down with it. As one newspaper reported, "Duane has an affection [sic] in his legs which reduces his power for harm, otherwise Brady might have been the victim of a brutal attack. As it is, it shows that Duane has the same mind as formerly for assaults, and is only prevented by incapacity from doing harm."[81]

Soon after his return to San Francisco, Duane launched a series of lawsuits in federal maritime court against the ship captains who had helped exile him. He was encouraged by a civil action brought by Martin Gallagher in 1858 against the captain of the bark *Yankee*, who had transported Gallagher to Hawaii at the behest of the vigilantes. U.S. District Court Judge Ogden Hoffman ruled that the captain was guilty of "a marine tort of the most flagrant character" and awarded $3,000 in punitive damages to Gallagher. In 1860 Charley Duane sued Captain Watson of the *Golden Age*, asking $50,000 in damages. He also sued Captain Robert Pearson of the *John L. Stephens* for forcibly ejecting him from the ship and putting

Charles Duane, left, and John Duane, right, with unidentified friend, about 1865. From original carte de visite in author's collection.

him on board the *Sonora* to return him to Acapulco. Judge Hoffman, no friend of the vigilance committee, awarded Duane $4,000. Pearson appealed to the U.S. Supreme Court, which found that Captain Pearson was not responsible for "the outrages which he suffered at the hands of the Vigilance Committee" and reduced Duane's judgment to fifty dollars. In another case, Dutch Charley sued Charles Goodall, the tugboat captain who had transported him to the steamer *Golden Age*. That case resulted in a $2,000 payment to Duane. These lawsuits represented far more than an effort to obtain reparations; they were an attempt to restore his personal honor, which had been challenged and blackened by the vigilantes.[82]

The Whig Party passed out of existence in 1856 and many of its members, Charley Duane included, became members of the new Republican Party. Most Irish Catholics were Democrats, and many were Confederate sympathizers, or Copperheads. Duane, on the other hand, was a strong supporter of the Union. Charley's brothers shared his political orientation; James was the Unionist police chief of New Orleans during the Civil War.[83]

On October 15, 1864, Charley and his younger brother, John, took part in a large Union parade on Montgomery Street. A Copperhead named Heffernan spotted Dutch Charley in the crowd and called him an "Irish son of a bitch." The following night the Duanes encountered Heffernan and several other secessionists in the Cosmopolitan saloon. Charley thrashed several of them soundly with his cane, while John held the others off at the point of his pistol. The brothers were arrested. Dutch Charley's testimony in court the next day, as reported by the *Bulletin*, illustrates perfectly his sense of personal honor. He told the judge that he had been "insulted by a crowd of Copperhead Irishmen, who were 'down on him' because he had taken part in the Union procession. . . . That he and his Irish comrades were hissed and hooted at during the entire route of the procession. . . . He was a cripple and unable to defend himself except with his stick, and this he was obliged to use, and intended to use, on all Copperheads who insulted him." The Duanes were convicted of assault and fined $80 each.[84]

But Charley Duane's principal occupation upon his return to San Francisco was his effort to recover the land he had claimed in the Western Addition. His struggles to regain his old squatter's claims and to acquire additional land would consume his life and would result in many battles both in and out of court. The Western Addition was known as the "outside lands" because it was then located outside the city limits. Due to the uncertainty of land titles, the Western Addition was the scene of much squatter violence in the 1860s and '70s. During Duane's four-year absence, rival squatters had settled on the large tract that he had claimed. In 1858 the city took title to a portion of it and established Alamo Square park, bounded by Fulton, Scott, Steiner, and Hayes Streets. By 1866 the federal government ceded its claim to the Western Addition and granted the lands to the city. Those who claimed lots there by adverse possession, or squatting, could still prove their claims in court by showing continuous residence on and improvements to their land. Dutch Charley would spend the rest of his life fighting for his land, with fists, guns, and lawyers. He frequently opposed rival squatters, as well as the city of San Francisco.

In 1860 William G. Ross settled on a portion of the tract that Duane claimed, located at the northwest corner of what is now Fulton and Divisadero Streets. Ross was born in Virginia in 1818. His family settled in Burlington, Iowa, and he came to California in 1849. Prominent in Democratic politics, he filled a number of official positions, including inspector of customs, warden of the port of San Francisco, and stage gauger under Governor John Downey from 1860 to 1862. Ross was a dangerous man with a reputation for being "on the shoot and cut." He boasted that he had killed two men in Iowa. In 1863 he broke a man's arm in a Montgomery Street brawl. In 1866 Duane and Ross were at loggerheads over the property dispute. They also hated each other's politics; Ross was a secessionist and Duane a Unionist. Ross threatened to "shoot the lights out of the Abolition son of a bitch." He made numerous threats to "cook Charley Duane's goose" and said he was "heeled for him." When a mutual friend urged Duane and Ross to settle their dispute, Ross declared, "There is no chance for a settlement. It is war to the knife and the knife to the hilt."[85]

On May 22, 1866, Charley and John Duane drove out to the site and found Ross and some friends building a house. According to several witnesses, Dutch Charley stepped out of his buggy, pistol in one hand and cane in the other. As he walked forward, Ross grabbed a rifle and pulled the trigger. The weapon misfired. Duane left, swore out a complaint against Ross, and returned with police officers who arrested several of Ross's party. That night Ross's house burned to the ground.

The next morning Duane and Ross met in police court. Duane
charged Ross with assault; Ross charged Duane with arson. The two
were released on bonds to keep the peace. At two o'clock that afternoon, Charley and John Duane left the police court in City Hall and
encountered Ross standing on the sidewalk, talking with two friends.
Dutch Charley carried in his pocket a Deane & Adams five-shooter;
his brother had a Remington six-gun and a derringer. Charley
Duane later testified that Ross reached behind himself as if to draw a
pistol. Dutch Charley whipped out his revolver and shot Ross twice
in the back, at the same time shouting, "Draw and fire, damn you!"

Ross dropped to the sidewalk, crying out, "I am murdered!" He
died two days later. No gun was found on his person. The Duanes
were both promptly arrested, John as an accessory. Dutch Charley's
violent past was raked up and recounted by the newspapers. His old
nemesis, the *San Francisco Bulletin*, commented, "Duane bears the
reputation of being an exceedingly bad man; in fact, one of the
worst in the city." The San Francisco press uniformly denounced
Dutch Charley as a back shooter and cold-blooded murderer. Bret
Harte's comments on "the notorious Charles Duane" were just as
critical: "Although the character of his victim was none of the highest, the popular dislike of Duane, whose reputation for lawlessness
and brutal aggression has long been established in California, may
make this last act the culminating one of his career."[86]

The Duanes remained in jail for five months until their trial in
October. Numerous witnesses testified during the eight-day trial,
many describing the threats Ross had made to kill Dutch Charley.
Duane's lawyers argued that it did not matter whether or not Ross
had been armed; if Duane had a reasonable belief that Ross had a
gun and intended to shoot him, the killing was justified. This
argument struck a responsive chord among the jurors. Men in that
era strongly believed in the right of self-defense and in the perceived
right to defend one's person and honor with deadly force. Charley's
attorneys also played on the strong partisan feelings provoked by the
Civil War. They argued, "Do not condemn Duane because he is a
Union man. Do not acquit him because Ross was a Secessionist."

It took the jury less than two hours to return a verdict of not
guilty. The Duanes were immediately released and the charges
against John Duane were dropped. Dutch Charley had once again
demonstrated his ethic of defense of honor and refusal to back
down from an enemy, and once again had escaped punishment.[87]

Duane fascinated Bret Harte, who did not approve of him. The writer supplied a vivid description of Dutch Charley after he returned to San Francisco, and implied that his sexual prowess had been compromised by his illness:

Naturally a splendid animal, of powerful frame and fine physique, dissipation and disease at last reduced him to a paralytic cripple. He walked the streets with a crutch—the miserable wreck and shadow of his former self. He eked a subsistence from the remains of his ill-gotten property. . . . Whatever his fate, it would seem that life to this man, whose force lay only in his physical pre-eminence and whose enjoyments were solely sensual, could be of little satisfaction in his present helpless and impotent condition."[88]

Whether Duane in fact was sexually impotent is unknown. However, in March 1865 he married Mary E. Keefe. The marriage was a success and, although it would produce no children, lasted twenty-two years, until his death.

Now free to continue fighting to preserve his land claims, Duane also became obsessed with speculating in San Francisco real estate. He acquired many lots cheaply because their title was in question. No doubt Duane hoped that his fearsome reputation would dissuade rival claimants from disputing him. Nonetheless, he was often involved in property fights, both in and out of court.

On November 18, 1868, Dutch Charley and several companions were guarding a tract of land located at the mouth of Mission Creek, what is now China Basin. Portions of this tract were under water, and Duane and his men were in a shanty built on piles in the water. When a boatload of rival squatters approached in order to tear down a fence, the Duane party opened fire on them, wounding a squatter named Baxter. Dutch Charley and three comrades were arrested for assault with intent to commit murder. Duane was released, but in 1871 he was again before the courts, accused of perjury. He had allegedly made a false affidavit for the arrest of a man who had squatted on his Divisadero Street property. A jury found him not guilty.[89]

A year later Duane became embroiled in a land dispute with one of his neighbors, William Dowling, a former friend who had testified on his behalf in the Ross trial. When Dowling made the mistake of directing vulgar language toward Dutch Charley, the latter pulled his pistol and fired. Fortunately for Dowling, the bullet passed through his hat and did no other damage. Each pressed charges against the other. Dowling was fined twenty dollars for using vulgar language. Once again Duane's luck held out; he was convicted of a simple misdemeanor and fined but sixty dollars, a pittance when one considers that his offense was far more serious than Dowling's.[90]

There was more squatter trouble the following year, this time over eighty acres claimed by Duane on Haight Street near what later became Golden Gate Park. Duane erected a small shanty on the land and hired seven gunmen (whom he claimed were carpenters) to hold the land. On the night of December 3, 1873, Dutch Charley entered a saloon at Divisadero and Fell Streets and called for liquor. An opposing squatter, Louis French, alias Frenchy, came in and began to abuse Duane, who promptly offered to fight. Frenchy demurred and claimed he was unarmed. When they stepped outside, Dutch Charley saw that Frenchy had a Navy revolver under his coat. After he accused his enemy of trying to lure him outside to kill him, the two went their separate ways.

Duane retired to spend the night in the shanty with his crew of carpenter-gunmen. Because of a heavy rain, Duane foolishly allowed his guards to sleep. At 2:30 that morning a band of nine ruffians led by Frenchy attacked the shanty and riddled it with bullets. Dutch Charley received a bullet in his foot and two of his men were badly wounded. The rest fled but Duane remained and held the ground until daylight, when he was carried to his house nearby to have his wound treated. Louis French and two others were eventually convicted of assault with a deadly weapon.[91]

Duane's involvement in squatter troubles seemed to be endless. In 1876 the *San Francisco Call* ran a story of a "disgraceful outrage" in which "the Duane crowd" forced their way into the Western Addition house of an old man named William Alexander. He was dragged outside to a sand hill while his house was literally chopped to the ground by axe-swinging ruffians. This was an outgrowth of a pending lawsuit over title to the property. Two days later the *Call* published a notarized statement from Charley and John Duane denying the charges against them, but the newspaper did not retract its story.[92]

Dutch Charley received more negative newspaper coverage later that year when the *San Francisco Chronicle* casually referred to him

John Duane, from a tintype taken about 1870. He and older brother Charley were inseparable. Author's collection.

James Duane, Unionist police chief of New Orleans in 1864. Author's collection.

and his brother as "squatters." A few days later, on October 21, an angry Dutch Charley showed up at the *Chronicle*'s offices and up-braided the newspaper's owner, Charles de Young. The publisher offered to print a statement from Duane, but Charley was not satisfied. That afternoon, as de Young was walking down Clay Street, John Duane stepped out from a doorway and struck him several times in the face. The two fell to the ground and bystanders quickly separated them. John Duane was arrested for battery, pled guilty, and was fined $250.[93]

Charley Duane never lost his appetite for politics. He soon saw an opportunity to reassert himself as a political power in San Francisco. An economic depression during the 1870s, coupled with high unemployment and increasing anti-Chinese sentiment, resulted in rioting in San Francisco in July 1877. In the wake of these troubles, the Workingmen's Party of California, with labor agitator Denis

Kearney as its leader, was organized two months later. Kearney's inflammatory public speeches, delivered in open-air meetings, drew large crowds and helped forge the new party into a powerful state-wide political force.[94]

The Workingmen opposed San Francisco's business elite and its political leadership, many of whom had been prominent in the 1856 vigilance movement. Charley Duane quickly saw a chance to position himself as a leader of the new party and at the same time to exact political revenge on his old vigilante enemies. His efforts, however, were thwarted by Denis Kearney, who disapproved of Duane's violent background. Dutch Charley, although a wagon maker by training, had not been a laborer since his arrival in California twenty-seven years earlier. In fact, during his entire work history in California, as shoulder-striker, fight promoter, gambler, saloonkeeper, and squatter, he had studiously avoided labor of any kind. Duane's opportunistic efforts to assert himself as a leader of the Workingmen were transparent to Denis Kearney and his followers.

At a public meeting on December 9, Kearney moved that Duane be expelled from the Workingmen's Party. The motion was passed and the delegates were ordered not to allow Duane to attend or speak at any further meetings. In response, Duane rented a public hall and advertised a Workingmen's meeting a week later. A large crowd showed up, but when Dutch Charley tried to speak it shouted him down. Twice he was hooted off the stage before members of the crowd dispersed at the request of Police Captain John Short. They marched to the U.S. Mint, where Denis Kearney delivered a speech and urged them not to attend any meetings called by Duane. Three months later, on March 16, 1878, a large meeting of tax-payers was held to protest the sale of the Spring Valley Water Works to the city of San Francisco at a purportedly inflated price. Although Denis Kearney had not been invited, he and his supporters seized control of the meeting. Charley Duane was on the stage and Kearney asked Captain Short to eject him from the meeting. Short did so, which resulted in an enraged Duane filing charges against Short before the police commission. This meeting marked the end of Duane's involvement with the Workingmen's Party.[95]

Dutch Charley's pugnacious personality thrived on conflict. He continued to pursue assorted lawsuits, particularly over his land claims, mostly to no avail. In one case he was charged with perjury. In 1877 he lost a trial over his Alamo Square claim; a jury found that it belonged to the city. He later unsuccessfully petitioned the board of supervisors to pay him for his claim to Alamo Square. Despite his disability and ill health, he had not lost his taste for fisticuffs, and in an 1880 Republican Club meeting, he engaged in a fist- and cane-swinging brawl. It ended with Dutch Charley seizing his opponent in a headlock and chewing on his ear.[96]

DUANE'S health continued to fail, and like many men in the twilight of their lives, he reflected upon the prominent role he had played in the early years of San Francisco. No doubt he continued to brood over his perceived unfair treatment by the vigilantes and by the San Francisco press. He wanted future generations to remember his good deeds, not his bad ones. So when a reporter for the *San Francisco Examiner* called on Dutch Charley early in January 1881 to interview him about the Gold Rush days, Duane saw an opportunity to preserve for posterity his adventurous career and at the same time to position his life story in the best light possible.

He told the reporter, "I do not like this business of being interviewed. I have been called upon on many occasions by newspaper men to give some reminiscences of early days in California and I have heretofore invariably refused. But as it seems to me a matter of public interest to learn some little scraps of San Francisco history, I suppose that I will have to reconsider my determination not to appear in print." During the next few weeks, Dutch Charley dictated his recollections to the *Examiner*'s reporter.[97]

Duane seemed to relish the chance to tell his story. Of his first interview with Duane, the reporter wrote, "If relating some occurrence which displayed the patriotism, chivalry, or valor of an old friend, his eye brightens, his expression is animated, and his description is so minute, that it is not difficult for his hearer to see in his imagination the occurrence just as it happened, and to really wish that he had been there."[98]

The first account by Charley Duane appeared in the *Examiner* on Sunday, January 9, 1881. It proved very popular with the newspaper's readers. The *Examiner*'s editor wrote that it "was the cause of considerable comment among the 'old timers' and it was generally admitted that the information . . . was correct." The editor pointed out that "it is a well known fact that two 49ers seldom agree in their recollections" but that pioneers who had read the account "were unanimous in their approval."[99]

Charley Duane's memoirs appear in the following pages exactly as he dictated them, with the exception of a few minor spelling and grammatical corrections. Duane's misspellings of a number of personal names have also been corrected. Chapter titles have been added and, in several cases, material has been reorganized into chronological or topical order.

Fortunately for us, Duane's memory was sharp, considering that the events he related had taken place from twenty-five to thirty years before. The account he left is extremely rare because it provides a firsthand viewpoint of one of the most outspoken opponents of vigilance in San Francisco. Except for Duane and Ned McGowan, none of the men who were blacklisted by the vigilantes in 1856 recorded their memoirs. Many of them did not live long enough to do so. Yankee Sullivan died in vigilante custody, Chris Lilly was slain in 1857, Martin Gallagher was stabbed to death in 1859, Woolly Kearney died in obscurity after years of alcoholism, and Billy Mulligan was shot dead by the San Francisco police in 1865. Those who did survive those days lacked the education, the wherewithal, or the interest to record their memoirs. They were fighting men, sporting men, drinking men—not men of letters.

On the other hand, pro-vigilance accounts are plentiful. Many members of the Committee of Vigilance of 1856 recorded their experiences. Their actions were a source of great pride and were among the most significant incidents of their lives. Then and later they understood that they were participating in something important, something historic, and something controversial that would be remembered and debated for generations to come. Next to Judge Edward McGowan, Charles Duane was the most prominent figure exiled by the vigilantes. His account is one of the most unique and most important of the vigilance movement. It offers a rare, first-person look at the vigilance committee from the other side.

Charley Duane understandably had little to say in his memoirs about the 1851 Committee of Vigilance. Had he said more, he would have had to explain why he had shot unarmed Amedee Fayolle in the back and why he had savagely beaten Frank Ball in retribution for his vote of guilty while serving on the Fayolle jury. He would also have been forced to explain why he had ingloriously fled to Panama after he was placed on the vigilantes' blacklist. Nor did Duane discuss any of his misadventures after his return to

California in 1860. For then he would have had to explain his unsavory career as a squatter, claim jumper, and back shooter. Despite omissions and obvious bias, Charley Duane, by recording his memoirs and presenting his view of the uprising, provided a significant contribution to our understanding of the Committee of Vigilance. And inadvertently, by living a violent life that was closely reported in the city's newspapers, he left a valuable record which helps explain the reasons for vigilantism in Gold Rush San Francisco.

IN 1886 Charley Duane was badly injured when thrown from a buggy. Coupled with his old paralysis, this new injury proved too much for his once stalwart frame. He was bedridden for months and finally passed away at his home, on the corner of Seventh and Howard Streets, on May 13, 1887. He was fifty-nine. Dutch Charley had a long life, considering that most men of his class, due to violence and heavy drinking, did not live past their mid-forties.

Duane's enemies did not mourn his passing. His old antagonist, the *San Francisco Bulletin*, despite many changes in ownership and editorship since the days of James King of William, refused even to note his death. Not surprisingly, Michael de Young, owner of the *Chronicle*, also took no notice. The *San Francisco Call*, the *Alta California*, the *Examiner*, and the *Post* were kinder. Each ran short biographical sketches of his life in mildly positive tones and touched briefly on some of the violent aspects of his life. Their tribute was lukewarm: the *Alta*'s only compliment was that Duane was "a man whose courage was unquestioned." The *Call* termed him "a faithful friend and very bitter enemy," and merely added that "he was a remarkable man in many ways."[100]

Charles P. Duane was indeed a remarkable man. He was intelligent, articulate, and charming. Both men and women gravitated toward him. Early on, he attached himself to the most important Democratic politician on the Pacific Coast and played a significant role in San Francisco politics. Duane was a natural leader of men. Wholly original and independent in thought and action, he always marched to the sound of a different drummer. He was a Whig, not a Democrat like many of his Irish cronies. In New York he came to the aid of several of his vigilante enemies. During the Civil War he was a fierce Unionist and became an avid Republican, a party affiliation he retained until his death.

His splendid physique, his good looks, his dauntless courage, his loyalty toward friends, his success with women, and his strong sense of personal honor all embodied in one man the heroic qualities so admired by the nineteenth-century American male. That was the bright side of Duane's character. The dark side was something else again. Dutch Charley could be bad-tempered, overbearing, bullying, and vicious, especially when drunk. His violence was often directed at inoffensive men who were no match for him in size or strength. He was opportunistic, recklessly ambitious, and politically corrupt. Anger, alcohol, lust for cheap land, and greed for easy riches repeatedly led him into conflict and violence. Dutch Charley Duane represented all that was good and bad in the California Gold Rush.

Charley Duane's historical significance lies in his connection with the vigilantes of 1851 and 1856. For in his story is found a basic truth about vigilantism. All vigilance movements, even those that have political or racist overtones, are a response to crime and fear of crime. And in order to ascertain the reasons behind the formation of a vigilance movement, one must first study the crime that spawned it.

Charles P. Duane left to history an important legacy, for in the microcosm of his violent life can be seen the larger reasons for vigilantism in San Francisco and the American frontier.

CHAPTER 1

Gold Rush San Francisco

WHEN I arrived here in 1849[1] I found the south side of Telegraph Hill and the vicinity of the plaza on Kearny Street, between Clay and Washington, now Portsmouth Square, covered with tents, and the little town looked very much like a soldiers' camp in war times. All the residents of San Francisco, who were not looking for ways and means to reach Sacramento and the mines, were engaged in erecting shanties around the plaza. A long, one story adobe tile-roofed building stood on the Washington Street side of Portsmouth Square, and the prosperous banking house of Palmer, Cook & Co. stood at the south end. On the southwest corner of Clay and Kearny was the City Hotel, which ran on Kearny from Clay to where Commercial Street now is. On the southeast corner of Clay and Kearny, where the drug store is, stood a large adobe building which was fitted up as a general merchandise store. The northeast corner of the streets last mentioned was occupied by the Cockett building, a large structure which was used as a saloon and gambling rooms.

George Baker, who came to this country on the same steamer that I did, and was afterwards police judge, rented a store in the Cockett building with me and we started a first class saloon. We paid $1,100 in advance for one month's rent, and the saloon had been opened just four days when the May fire swept over the town and destroyed nearly every house in the place. This fire occurred on the 4th of May 1850.[2] To show you how lively the times were in those days, I will just state that the least amount of money which we took in over the bar during any one of those four days was $530.

While the fire was still burning, the sporting men set to work building up the town again. Laborers were immediately employed to clear away the debris and others were dispatched to the wharf for lumber, and soon returned with their shoulders heavily laden. We did not then enjoy the luxury of express wagons and trucks. The lumber came here on vessels around the Horn. All the valuables, such as books, furniture, etc., which the residents possessed at the time of the fire were piled up on the plaza, and the night after the fire fully 3,000 people slept on the square in the open air. But the fire did not delay things for any length of time. Everything was life and bustle and carpenters were in demand. The gambling fraternity was the most active in rebuilding the town and inside of ten days after the fire San Francisco was better, as far as the buildings were concerned, than it was previous to the conflagration. The gamblers borrowed the money to rebuild the town from the banking house of Palmer, Cook & Co. That firm was always ready to help any man who showed a disposition to help himself, and I have been informed by Mr. Cook that the house never lost a dollar which they loaned to the "sports" in those times. The bank of Palmer, Cook & Co. was as good as a well-filled treasury to this city in early days. No worthy enterprise was ever suspended while they were in business for lack of money. They were very charitable and liberal to a fault.[3]

In those days California could not boast of many gray-haired men. In fact, I think that Nathaniel Holland was the only man here, as late as 1856, who combed the "silver threads among the black." He was the only one that I saw with gray hair. And women were nearly as scarce as gray-haired men. If a man called a female by the name of "woman" then, as I do now, he ran the risk of being felled to the ground by a pistol in the hands of some chivalrous pioneer. "Lady" was the only term that could be applied with safety to the gentler sex in those days. It did not matter what character she would bear in any well regulated social community; in San Francisco a woman was an object of veneration and respect and could only be spoken of as one entitled to such homage.

When I arrived here there were only twenty-eight American, English, and French ladies in the state,[4] and as one of them passed a group of rough, uneducated men in the street, every hat was raised respectfully, and honest admiration shone in the eyes of the horny-handed sons of toil as their gaze followed her retreating form. This will account to you for the promptness with which an old pioneer invariably rises in a crowded streetcar to give his seat to a lady, and right here I want to say that it would be well for the rising generation if they could feel the same respect for a woman as the old pioneers who knew what it was to be obliged to live without her guiding influence.

David C. Broderick[5] and Fred Kohler,[6] the first chief engineer of the volunteer fire department, arrived here in '49, around the Horn. At the time of their arrival coin was very scarce. There was plenty of gold dust, but as that had to be weighed every time it was received in payment for anything, it was very inconvenient. To the minds of Broderick and Kohler, the latter being an assayer, this lack of coin opened a field for a new enterprise, and they entered into a copartnership to make coin out of gold dust. After melting the dust and pounding it into bars, they cut the bars into various sizes, ranging in value from $5 to $50, and stamped the pieces of gold with the firm name of Broderick & Kohler. They carried on their business in a little shanty which they built opposite the plaza on Clay Street, above Kearny. This was the first "mint" of San Francisco. The coin turned out in this establishment was always found to be worth just as much as was represented, and in many instances, when the bars were weighed, it was discovered they contained more gold than the acknowledged value of the coin.[7]

Shortly after Broderick & Kohler began coining, another "mint" was started for the purpose of coining five dollar pieces. The coin turned out of this establishment was in the shape of our present five dollar pieces and bore the stamp of Moffat & Co.[8] This money was largely circulated all over the state for a short time, but it was soon discovered that the new coins were from 25 to 50 cents short of the proper value, and this fact created a prejudice which stopped the issue of the money.

Between four and five million dollars of the money coined by these two mints, as well as Mexican ounces, silver dollars, etc., were nightly spread upon the gambling tables in the houses around the plaza. The houses were packed with tables and benches, and nearly the whole population of San Francisco could be found any night distributed among the various shanties, courting the fickle goddess. I have seen forty-two tables running in a house which stood on Kearny Street where the old city hall now is. The game of monte occupied the majority of the tables, but faro and other games were also dealt. The tables were rented for two and three ounces per day, and an ounce was estimated to be worth sixteen dollars of our money. In some of the gambling houses there were choice tables which brought very high rents. There were thirteen houses of this description in the immediate vicinity of the plaza and each house had a band of music. The least sum of money paid to any band was

$300 per day, and some of the leading musicians were paid six ounces, or $96 per day.[9]

Thomas Maguire,[10] now of the Baldwin, erected a fine, large three story building in April 1850, on the lot upon which the old city hall stands, and intended to open it on the 5th of May as a gambling house and theater, but he never had a chance to do so, for the fire of May 4th burned the building to the ground. It was a wooden structure and as fine a house as the majority of those in the city today.

The old hall of records, now used as a justice's court, was built by Andy and Jim McCabe[11] and Messrs. Gray and Chamberlain, four well known "sports." They at first built a little shanty on the corner, and after that was burned down, they had the present substantial house put up, and afterwards sold it to the city.

When I came here the town was bounded by Dupont Street on the west, Pacific on the north, Montgomery (which was then the waterfront) on the east, and Sacramento Street on the south. The waters of the bay ran halfway to Kearny on Jackson Street. Where Commercial Street is now, in the center of the block between Kearny and Montgomery, stood the Merchants Exchange Hotel, where a person could get a pretty good breakfast for about three dollars. The St. Francis Hotel, which was on the southwest corner of Clay and Dupont Streets, was the bon-ton hotel of the town. You could be accommodated with a small room, furnished with a cot, and board, for the sum of $100 per week.

On the east side of Dupont Street, about fifty feet north of Clay, stood a splendid large building which was occupied as a restaurant by Zeke Wilson and a man named Robey. This was the finest dining room here. In 1853 or '54 Mr. Wilson put up the first five-story building on the Pacific Coast, on the corner of Sansome and Halleck Streets. He opened it as a hotel under the name of Wilson's Exchange. It is now called the American Exchange. The Graham House, a large three-story hotel, stood on the northwest corner of Pacific and Kearny Streets. The city purchased it in 1850 for a city hall and it was used as such until it was burned down in the June fire, 1851. That fire destroyed the whole town, from Pacific and Stockton to Pine and Sansome Streets, and it was with difficulty that the ships in the harbor were saved.

The late David Mahoney and his brothers owned the first slaughterhouses in the city. They were two in number and were

situated on the other side of Russian Hill, about where Vallejo
Street now crosses. There were three cemeteries for the town. One
was at the foot of Telegraph Hill, a portion of the present Union
Square. Yerba Buena Cemetery was where the new city hall now
stands, and the old Mission was located on Dolores Street where it
still is. In going out to the Mission you would be obliged to follow
a trail through Hayes Valley and pass by the house of Thomas
Hayes,[12] which stood on the corner of Van Ness Avenue and Hayes
Street. The valley was called after Tom Hayes, who fenced in 160
acres of it with a brush fence in 1850. He was then deputy sheriff
under Jack Hays of Texas, who was elected at the first regular
election held in April 1850.[13] He ran against a "sport" named
Bryant,[14] proprietor of the Bryant House, a hotel and gambling-
room situated on Clay Street, about 150 feet above Kearny. After
the fire of May 4, 1850, this was the only house left standing in the
city. John Cotter, the father of the present fire commissioner, and
myself had previous to May 4th leased the building for $6,000 per
month, and the day after the fire we sold the lease to some gamblers
for $10,000 bonus.

Gambling was not against the laws in those days. The first state
legislature which met in San Jose in the Spring of '50 passed an act
licensing games. David C. Broderick, who was in the senate at the
time, vigorously opposed the passage of the bill. The next legislature
passed a law making capital punishment the penalty for stealing. But
this law only remained on the statute book for one year.[15] At the
next meeting Broderick had the act repealed. In those days Broderick
was bitterly opposed by a certain element on account of having been
a fireman and saloon keeper in New York City, but he always
triumphed over his enemies. He was very much interested in fire
department matters and was the founder and foreman of Empire
Company No. 1, which was the first company organized on this
coast.[16] He was a member of it at the time of his death, and out of
respect to his memory the boys changed the name of the company
from Empire to Broderick No. 1. Broderick was a great benefactor
to this city and was respected even by his enemies. He was one of
the few men of early times who did not gamble. In those days nearly
everybody gambled but Broderick never bet on a card. When the
day's business was over there was no resort for the merchant or
mechanic but the gambling shanties. As the darkness of night cast its
shadow over the busy little town, twenty bands of musicians poured

forth their melody upon the night air and temptingly invited the inhabitants of the city to buck against the gilded tiger. The gambling houses were always crowded, as many as 3,000 people being in one place at a time.

The first post office building we had here was situated on Pike Street, now known as Waverly Place.[17] When a steamer arrived you would see a string of people three blocks in length waiting for letters. Businessmen who could not spare the time to get in line and await their turn at the window would give fifty dollars for a good place in the ranks, and some men made considerable money by waiting around and selling their places. There was only one delivery window and it generally took one whole day and night to give out the letters. When the "Noisy Carrier" announced the arrival of a vessel, every man would hastily leave his business and look anxiously toward Telegraph Hill for the signal informing them what kind of a vessel was coming into the harbor. That was how the hill came to be christened "Telegraph." The signal on the hill was a perpendicular pole stuck in the ground, about one hundred feet high, with three or four arms projecting from different sides. One arm represented a brig, another a ship or steamer, so that the people could tell exactly what kind of a vessel was coming. As soon as the signal was given the majority of the people here would rush down to the wharf where the small boats landed the passengers from the steamer.

The men who owned these boats reaped a plentiful harvest on the arrival of a vessel. They charged all they could get and they were often given large sums of money by individuals who were in a great hurry. The freight was brought to the shore on lighters, which came up under Joseph Bideman's house on Montgomery Street, about one hundred feet south of Jackson. The house was built on the water and the cargo was hoisted up through the floor. Men came here from Sacramento and other points a week before a steamer was expected and waited patiently for news from home. The steamers *Senator* and *New World*, commanded by Captains John Van Pelt and Poole, respectively, ran between here and Sacramento. The fare then was thirty-five dollars each way. Captains Van Pelt and Poole were able seamen and splendid, noble-hearted gentlemen.

At that time there were only two blocks in the town sidewalked. Those were on Clay Street, between Kearny and Montgomery, and Kearny Street, between Clay and Washington. These walks were made out of the staves of barrels, and very often a stave would break and the unfortunate pedestrian who happened to be walking on it would go through and have to be pulled out. The first two carriages that were sent here were consigned to Mr. Travers, who died a short time ago, and a man named John Crow. These two gentlemen formed a co-partnership and had a corner in the hack business. It would cost an ounce, or sixteen dollars in coin, to ride a block or two. If a carriage was hired for a day, the charge was one hundred and fifty dollars. For six or eight months these were the only carriages in the town and they did a lively business. There were several livery stables here where saddle horses could be procured but there were no buggies or vehicles of any kind to be had.

A man named Wilson, who came to this country on the same ship with me, built a plank road to the Mission, where Mission Street now is, and he just coined money on the enterprise, collecting toll.

A meeting of the citizens of San Francisco was held at the St. Francis Hotel in June 1850 for the purpose of organizing a volunteer fire department. Gregory Yale, who was then looked upon as the ablest jurist here, was called to the chair. Fred Kohler, who had pre-viously been appointed temporarily by Mayor Geary, was appointed chief engineer at the meeting, and at a regular town election shortly after, he was elected first chief engineer. The department was then composed of the following companies: Empire No. 1, David C. Broderick, foreman; Protection No. 2, Ben Ray, foreman; Howard Hook and Ladder, Folsom (founder of the town of Folsom), fore-man; St. Francis Hook and Ladder No. 1, Joseph Palmer of Palmer, Cook & Co., foreman; and Howard No. 3. I was assistant foreman of St. Francis Hook and Ladder No. 1.

Shortly after the organization of the department the boiler of a steamer about to start for Sacramento exploded, throwing the passengers, among whom was David C. Broderick, on the wharf and into the bay. Some were killed and many were wounded. The alarm was sounded and we turned out and carried the wounded passengers, numbering about thirty, to Peter Smith's Hospital, which was situ-ated on Clay Street, near where Mason now is.

Within ten days of the explosion, and before the patients had recovered, the hospital caught fire.[18] St. Francis Hook and Ladder, which lay on the west side of Dupont Street between Clay and Sacramento, was the first company on the ground. The foreman of the company, Mr. Palmer, being absent, I, as first assistant, took command and set the men to work carrying out the patients. We

The St. Francis Hook and Ladder Company firehouse, 1856. This was the headquarters of Duane's fire brigade during the Gold Rush. William B. Secrest collection.

had got all that we knew of out of the building and were about to
quit when we were informed that there were others in the garret of
the hospital, which was two and one-half stories. Archie Wason,
now Colonel of the Third Regiment, who was then an officer of
Protection No. 2, and I returned and rushed through the flames
and finally succeeded in making our way to the garret. We had to lie
down flat on the floor to avoid the smoke and in that position we
asked as loud as possible if there was anybody in the building. After
repeating the question several times and receiving no response, we
concluded that the patients were all out and we turned to leave,
when we found our egress cut off by the flames. We broke a hole in
the roof and then became involved in a heated discussion as to who
should go first. We both wanted to be the last man to leave the
building, and I finally persuaded Wason to go.

As soon as it was decided that Archie Wason should leave the
burning building first, I assisted him through the hole which we had
knocked in the roof, and after shouting through my trumpet to the
St. Francis Hook and Ladder Company for a ladder to be placed
against the wall of the house, I followed him. We slid to the edge of
the roof where the ladder was hoisted and then went down through
the flames which burst out from the windows on both sides and
singed our hair as we passed. I have the belt which I wore on that
occasion and it shows by its appearance what a close shave we had.
While we were attending to the fire in the hospital the flames were
communicated to the adjoining buildings and while battling with
this new work under the direction of the chief engineer, Fred
Kohler, Mayor Geary[19] appeared upon the scene and issued orders
for the management of the fire which were directly in conflict with
those of the chief.

Kohler informed the mayor that during a conflagration the chief
engineer of the fire department was the presiding officer of the town,
and he ordered him to keep his mouth shut or leave the ground
immediately. Mayor Geary stood upon his dignity and refused to
recognize Kohler's authority, whereupon the latter ordered me to
arrest the mayor and lock him up in the city prison. I placed Geary
under arrest and led him by gentle force down Clay Street. He was
very indignant and commanded me to release him, as he was the
chief magistrate of the city. I told him that I respected his position
and himself, but I was obliged, under the rules of the department,
to obey the orders of my chief. He finally entreated me not to take

him to the city prison and promised that if I would let him go he would not again be guilty of interference at a fire. On the strength of this promise I took him back to Chief Kohler and laid the case before him, at the same time pleading for Geary's release.

"Well," said Kohler, turning to Geary after I had stated the facts, "Clear out of here, and do not interfere any more."

Geary was glad enough to leave when he got the chance, and after that the chief engineer of the fire department was the chief officer of the city during a fire until 1853, when Mayor Garrison[20] interfered with my orders while I was chief. One of the companies in the department had disobeyed my orders at a fire, and to punish the members I took away their engine, which belonged to the city, and put it in the corporation yard. The company complained to Mayor Garrison, and he ordered me to return the engine. This I refused to do, and immediately called a meeting of the board of delegates to settle the question of authority between the mayor and myself. The board had the matter under consideration for three days and three nights and finally sustained me and reprimanded the mayor by a vote of thirty-one ayes to one no. This case was of the same nature as the famous "Gulich" case in New York City and was decided in a like manner.[21]

Frank Whitney[22] was elected second chief engineer to succeed Fred Kohler, but he had not been long in office when he became seriously ill and was obliged to go to the Sandwich Islands, and George Hossefross[23] was elected to fill the vacancy. I succeeded Hossefross and held the office for two successive terms. I was nominated a third time but declined to run. During Hossefross's administration, and while I was first assistant engineer, we started a subscription for a fund to be known as the Fire Department Charitable Fund. The first business house that I called upon was the banking firm of Palmer, Cook & Co. Mr. Palmer took the subscription book and wrote opposite the firm name the figure $1,000, "for a starter," as he modestly expressed it, and Mr. Cook promptly paid me $1,000. The fund increased in three or four years to the large sum of $90,000. The object in starting it was to raise sufficient money to take care of disabled firemen and to support their widows and orphans. It is now under the management and control of the Exempt Fire Company.

Nearly all the star actresses that came here in early days played at least one night for the benefit of the Charitable Fund. Kate Hayes,[24]

San Francisco firemen with hose cart on Meigg's Wharf. From an ambrotype taken in the early 1850s. Bancroft Library.

the celebrated singer, realized $3,000; Madame Biscaccianti[25] had
two benefits, which added considerable to the treasury. Lola Montez[26]
donated the proceeds of one benefit amounting to about $3,000,
and Matilda Heron-Byrne[27] presented $2,800 as the result of one
performance. The largest amount of money realized at any one of
these benefits for the Fund was taken in at a show given by Miss
Sinclair,[28] the wife of Edwin Forrest. The proceeds amounted to
$3,988, which she and her treasurer counted out to me. When she
found that it lacked just twelve dollars of four thousand, she opened
her purse and gave me the twelve dollars. I carried the $4,000 down
to the banking house of Page, Bacon & Co., on the corner of
California and Montgomery Streets, and gave it to Henry Haight,[29]
who was then treasurer of the Fund. I have seen it stated in
reminiscences of pioneers that the amount given by Miss St. Clair
was seven or eight dollars short of four thousand, but I know that it
was not. The Henry Haight mentioned as the treasurer was not the
late Governor Haight.

I mentioned the long line of people who waited their turn on the
arrival of the steamer to get to the post office window. Now such
another string of human beings could be found waiting to get a
look at the first Chinese woman who came to this state. Her name
was Ah Toy and she was a tall, well-built woman.[30] In fact, she was
the finest looking Chinese woman I have ever seen. She could speak
some English, sufficient to make herself understood. When the
Sacramento boat would land in the evening the miners on board
would at once break for Ah Toy's residence. Many of them came
down from the mountains for the sole purpose of seeing her. She
lived in a court or alley which ran off the south side of Clay Street,
between Dupont and Kearny. There were several nice shanties in
this alley and some of them were occupied by respectable men, the
majority of whom were obliged to move away on account of the
nuisance occasioned by the continual visits of the curious miners to
Ah Toy.

I have seen a line of men extending for the length of nearly a
whole block, each man armed with a large pistol in his belt, waiting
his turn to get a chance to gaze on the countenance of the charming
Ah Toy. Those were the days when a strong man could not impose
on a weak one. Every man had to wait for his turn and if he
attempted to break a line he knew that he risked his life in so doing.
When Ah Toy placed herself on exhibition it cost the miners one

ounce of gold dust to satisfy their curiosity, and she had her scales ready to weigh the dust of each visitor so that she could not be cheated.

One day she had two men arrested for passing brass filings and scrapes of brass upon her for gold dust. The case was to be tried before Police Judge George Baker, and when she was placed upon the stand the court was crowded to suffocation. While testifying against the prisoners, Ah Toy picked out a good many men among the spectators who, she said, had been guilty of the same offense charged against the defendants. The judge asked her to show him how much of the brass dust had been passed upon her for gold, and she went over to her house and soon returned with the largest china basin I ever saw, completely filled with brass filings. At this, the spectators gave a loud laugh and the men whom she had picked out in the courtroom hung their heads in conscious guilt. The two men arrested for the deception, in their defense, stated that they had offered the dust for brass and that she had accepted it knowing it to be such. It was two oaths against one, and the judge being obliged to give the prisoners the benefit of the doubt, dismissed the case. After that Ah Toy discarded her Chinese robes and adopted the dress of American females.

Among those who vacated the court where Ah Toy lived was Mr. McAbee, now manager of the Baldwin Hotel. He kept a carpenter shop on the open plaza and did most of the work in the town in his line. Miners and broken sports who had no place to sleep used to crawl at night into the shavings under McAbee's benches on the plaza and he and his men would find them there in the morning when they went to work.

As soon as the steamer *Oregon* arrived here with the news that California had been admitted to the Union, a committee of citizens immediately started to get up a grand ball to celebrate the occasion. The ball was given in a brick building which stood on the northeast corner of Clay and Kearny Streets, the admission price being fixed at twenty dollars a head. The hall was crowded, all the ladies in town being present, and then there was only about one lady to every fifty men. The supper, which was a grand affair, was given at the Union Hotel, a large, four-story brick building that stood on the corner of Merchant and Kearny Streets, where a branch of the county clerk's office now is. It was kept by Mr. Selover,[31] now a broker in Wall Street, New York, and Mr. Hall, late proprietor of a fruit stall in the

California Market. On the day of the ball, Messrs. Selover and Hall had a bridge built from the Union Hotel to the California Exchange, where the dance was held. The bridge, which was being erected by Mr. McAbee, was nicely carpeted and was put up for the accommodation of the ladies, so that they might not be obliged to go out on the street to get to the dining room. This was another notable evidence of the manner in which ladies were appreciated here in those days.

CHAPTER 2

Flush Times

THE first session of the legislature was held at San Jose in 1850. Governor Burnett[1] had been elected at the first state election to the gubernatorial office but shortly after his inauguration he resigned on account of his health, which was very poor. This elevated John McDougal,[2] who had been elected lieutenant governor, to the office of governor. As soon as the legislature met, David C. Broderick, who was in the senate, was elected president of that body, and by virtue of this position he was the acting lieutenant governor. Two or three days before the expiration of his term McDougal resigned to fight a duel, which left Broderick chief executive.

For some time previous to the meeting of the legislature the state treasury had been nearly empty and the government had issued scrip for the payment of current expenses. The scrip drew large interest and was eagerly sought for by the capitalists here. There was a great deal of this paper afloat when California was admitted to the union. When that happy event occurred, Congress decided, in view of the depleted condition of the Treasury, to return to the state a considerable portion of the money which had been collected at this port while California was a territory. When the news of this magnanimous intention on the part of Congress reached here by steamer, the capitalists who had been engaged in the scrip trade set their agents at work to purchase all the paper that they could get. The scrip had been so long in circulation at that time, and the prospects of its redemption in the near future were so doubtful, that it sold at a liberal discount, and when the news of the favorable action of Congress reached here it immediately opened a field for large fortunes to those who were lucky enough to secure the evidence of state indebtedness.

The banking firm of Palmer, Cook & Co. was the leading money power here in those days and they always had a great amount of coin on hand for speculation and enterprise. One of the members of the firm sent for me, and after furnishing me with certified checks to the amount of about $500,000, he directed me to go to the capitol (San Jose) and buy up all the scrip that was for sale at any reasonable figure. My commission for the work was fixed at 25 per cent of the net profits on the transaction.

The weather was very stormy and the roads were in a very bad condition but there was only one way to get to San Jose in those days and I had to brave the storm and take chances on guiding my horse safely over the hills and ditches. I started on my journey at night, accompanied by a gentleman named James Brady, the stepson of Colonel Stevenson.[3] We had to pass out through Hayes' Tract, or Hayes Valley as it is now called, and we stopped at the house of Colonel Thomas Hayes which was situated about where St. Ignatius Church now is. I had never been to San Jose at that time and I was not certain that I could find my way, so I prevailed upon Michael Hayes, a brother of Tom's who was well acquainted with the route, to accompany us. On our way down, when we arrived at a point near the present site of the Industrial School,[4] my horse missed his footing on the top of a high embankment and I had barely time to throw myself from his back before he rolled over and over until he struck the muddy bottom of the gulch below, where he landed on his back. With considerable difficulty I finally got down and liberated him. It was a good distance from the top of the bank where he had fallen off, but he was uninjured. There is a bridge on the spot now, over which railroad cars pass.

We stopped at several ranches on the road and obtained fresh horses, and after a hard ride we arrived in San Jose about daybreak the next morning. I went to the hotel where Broderick stopped and found that gentleman seated in his room reading a paper. I was wet through from the rain and Broderick insisted on putting me to bed in his room and getting dry clothes for me. He would not hear of me attending to the business on which I had gone down there until after I had taken a rest, so I was obliged to content myself with directing another party to buy all the scrip he could find while I was in bed.

Hall McAllister,[5] who was then a young attorney here, had started for San Jose four hours ahead of me on the same errand as myself in the interest of other capitalists, but he did not arrive there until long after my party. Of course he was not as shrewd or experienced then as he is now and before he had been in town long he let the cat out of the bag by telling of the news from Washington and in a short time the scrip was selling for one dollar and ten cents. There was not much profit to be made at that rate but I succeeded in purchasing a sufficient amount to cover my expenses. Early in 1850 I went up to the mines in Placerville, El Dorado County. Nearly every shanty in the town was a gambling saloon and the place presented a very lively appearance. One day a miner attired in a rough buckskin suit came into one of the gambling dens in which I was looking on at the game and put down a bag of dust on a monte layout. He lost his money and the dealer raked in the bag. The miner then bet another bag and lost. He then took out a third sack, and dividing its contents, made two bets, and seeing that he was about to lose, he made a grab at all the money on the table and captured considerable. He had bet in all about two hundred ounces but there was a great deal of money on the table belonging to the bank and other parties. When he made the grab, the dealer of the game and several of the players also grabbed to get their share and in a few seconds there was a scene of wild confusion. Pistols were fired, bright Bowie knives glittered, and things were extremely lively for a short time.

The news of the fight spread through the town and soon there was an angry, excited crowd looking for the man who had caused all the disturbance. In a short time the cry of "Here he is!" rang through the little town and the whole population was soon in pursuit of a tall individual dressed in a buckskin suit who was running through the bushes. He was overtaken and captured and preparations were immediately made to hang him. I had seen the man who created the row in the gambling house while he was playing, and I went to see the prisoner to satisfy myself that the right party had been caught. When I arrived at the spot where the mob had taken their man, I was horrified to see on the back of a mule with a rope around his neck, not the dishonest gambler, but an innocent mule-driver who had only arrived from Missouri a couple of days before, after driving across the plains.

The poor fellow was very much frightened and did not dare to move. They had forced him to mount the mule by covering him with their revolvers, and after putting a rope around his neck, one man led the mule under a tree. The rope was then made fast to a limb of the tree, the mule was led from under him, and the Missouri drover dangled in the air. The fall from the tree was so short it did not break his neck and as the rope began to strangle him he writhed horribly for seven or eight minutes. He then became motionless for a few seconds, after which the convulsions began again. At his second exhibition of agony the man who led the mule from under the innocent victim of mob law said, "Poor fellow, what has he done?"

The real culprit stood among the crowd during the execution and witnessed the murder of another man for his crime. It was afterward learned that the man who had been hung was in the vicinity of the gambling house when the shooting began, and thinking that a wholesale slaughter was about to take place, became scared and ran off in the bushes.[6]

In those days you could raise a cry on any man who was not prominent, and the mob, or vigilance committee, as they styled themselves, would hang him without knowing why they did so. Placerville was particularly noted for this kind of work and it was owing to that peculiar qualification for shedding innocent blood that it was called "Hangtown."

A day or two after the murder which I have just spoken of was committed, I started with ten friends for Coloma. We traveled on horseback. The Indians were very dangerous in that part of the country at that time and we selected one of our number to ride a little in advance of the party and act as a scout. The choice fell on Mose Scott, a well-known politician here in those days. He was mounted on a vicious mule and when he got a short distance from us the animal became unmanageable, and as we afterward learned, ran away with him through the woods. We did not miss him until we arrived at a point where it had been agreed that he should meet us and report. We waited patiently for an hour or so but he did not put in an appearance. The horrible thought that he might have been butchered by Indians filled our minds and we started out to look for him.

We searched for a long time in the woods and finally came to the conclusion that he had been "done for" by the savages. We continued on our journey in sorrow, after finding the trail, and when we arrived at Cold Springs, a point about half way between Coloma and Placerville, we were pleasantly surprised to see Mose Scott stretched out comfortably in front of the public house, sipping a mint julep. He was indignant because it had taken us so long to catch up with him. He explained the reason of his great hurry and we were happy to find that he had suffered nothing more serious than a fast ride on a runaway mule.

On our arrival in Coloma we found a great many gambling houses and a good deal of life and activity. I only saw one white woman in the place and she kept a public house where she entertained the susceptible miner at the rate of fifty cents a drink for chain-lightning whiskey. She was known as "Texas Helen," and was always armed with pistols and Bowie knife. There was no one in the country around that cared to trifle with the Texas maiden and she was highly esteemed by the rough element. She engaged in one fight too many, however, and was shot and killed in her own house.

While in Coloma we called on old Marshall,[7] the man who discovered the first nugget of gold in California in the Sutter mill raceway. He took us to the mill and showed us the very spot where he had discovered the treasure. The raceway was all dug up and a great deal of gold had been taken out. Sutter had built the mill to saw lumber and grind flour. Marshall is still living somewhere in this state. I believe that the legislature gave him a pension four or five sessions ago.

There were no stables in Coloma but our horses were tied to rails in the timber just outside of town where they were fed on wild oats, at great expense to us. We were in the town about four days and we gambled and lost all the money that we had brought with us, and all that we could borrow. On the fourth day there was not one in our party who had a dollar, and we owed considerable for our expenses. While in this condition I met an old Negro who had worked for me in New York City. He had a five-dollar gold piece in his pocket and I concluded to take that and try my luck again. He and his wife had two hundred and fifty dollars in their cabin and he was anxious for me to have that, but as it was some little distance from town I did not care to go for it. I took the five dollars and put it down on a monte table, and when I quit at that game I had six thousand dollars. After paying our expenses we had about thirteen hundred dollars to go home with. On our return to Placerville I came across a man who was digging in a small claim about the size of an adult's grave. I offered him two ounces of gold for the privilege of working in his claim for two hours. He accepted the proposition and at the end of the time specified I had made sixty dollars. This will show you how easy it was to make money in those flush times.

John Kisling,[8] who was an alderman here, I think in 1852, took up a tract of land of one hundred and sixty acres in 1846, which was situated directly southeast of Colonel Thomas Hayes' tract. In 1849 he erected the first brick house in San Francisco in the block where the City Gardens was afterward located, on the edge of Mission Creek. In the regular election of 1855 the Know Nothing party made a very determined fight and was bound to win at all hazards. The Eighth Ward, which then embraced nearly all the territory now included in the Twelfth and Thirteenth Senatorial Districts of this city, had always returned a good Democratic majority and it was therefore an object of much attention to the Know Nothings. The polls were held at the Lodi House, a kind of hotel which was situated on the Mission plank road, about where Twelfth Street now crosses, and Alderman Kisling was one of the inside judges.

On the night of the election the judges and inspectors were, of course, obliged to remain and count the ballots. Between nine and 10 o'clock Mrs. Kisling, wife of the alderman, went to the Lodi House accompanied by her Negro servant, who carried some refreshments for her husband and those engaged in counting the ballots. Upon arriving within a short distance of the house, Mrs. Kisling sent the servant on with the refreshments and seated herself upon the trunk of a tree to await his return. She had not been sitting there very long when a buggy containing two men was driven past and stopped at the back of the house. The occupants then alighted, and taking a large-sized keg, which appeared to be very heavy, out of the buggy, they rolled it under the house, which was built on a wooden foundation, the floor being some distance from the ground. After placing the keg under the house, the parties who had come in the buggy departed.

As soon as her servant returned, Mrs. Kisling, thinking that the barrel which she had seen put under the house contained liquor for the judges and inspectors, directed her servant to go to the house and tell Mr. Kisling that it was there. That gentleman was busily engaged at the time and Colonel Tom Hayes, who was an interested spectator of the count, went out to see about it. He went under the house and upon examination found that the keg contained powder and he came to the conclusion, and it was generally believed, that the Know Nothing managers had placed it there for the purpose of blowing up the house and destroying the ballots in the event of a large Democratic majority in that ward. But there was no necessity for any such work on the part of the Know Nothings, as the city rolled up a solid majority for them. Hayes buried the keg of powder and the Democratic managers, including Broderick, Mayor Garrison,

Kearny Street, San Francisco, in 1856. Telegraph Hill is in the background. William B. Secrest collection.

and others tried to find out who did the work but they never succeeded. In 1850 Mr. Kisling built and owned the first brickyard on
the Pacific Coast, which was situated on the bank of Mission Creek,
about where Harrison and Twelfth Streets now cross.

In 1854 the board of delegates of the fire department offered a
reward of two hundred and fifty dollars for the best plans submitted
for a fireman's certificate. There were thirteen competitors who
presented their ideas and the prize was awarded to an artist named
Nahl[9] who is very prominent here now. The design was excellent
but it was found that it would cost at least five thousand dollars to
get a plate to properly represent it. There was no money in the fire
department funds for such a purpose and the board of alderman
steadily refused to give us that amount of money.

About that time Alderman Van Ness introduced his celebrated
ordinance, which has since made so many people rich in San
Francisco property.[10] He bitterly opposed the petition of the fire
department for the money to get a plate for the certificates, but he
was also very anxious to pass his ordinance. He just wanted one more
vote than he could get to pass his measure, and there happened to
be one representative of the fire department on the board. After he
had tried in vain every other means to gain his end he finally consented to vote for the five thousand dollar appropriation for the fire
department if their representative on the board of aldermen would
vote for his ordinance. In this manner the measure was adopted and
it has occupied a very important place since in the history of San
Francisco.

A man named Thompson,[11] who was one of Tom Hyer's trainers
in his great fight with Sullivan,[12] which took place on the 7th of
February 1849, came to this state about a year after I did. Hyer had
imported him from London, where he was known as Peter Crawley's
"big 'un." When he came here, I took care of him and finally sent
him up to a mine in El Dorado County. I advised him to be very
quiet there and not to put himself up for a fighter because I was
afraid he would be killed. He had only been there a short time when
he sent down word that he had a "job" on hand, which in English
pugilistic circles means a prize fight. His opponent was a man named
Willis. I wanted Thompson to win the fight and I had him well
cared for, sending him the best of wines and liquors, etc. I hired the
race track at Sacramento where the fight took place. At the beginning of the third round Thompson hit Willis and the latter fell to

the ground, and failing to come to time, the fight was won by Thompson.[13] The gate money, amounting to $8,400, I had divided equally between the two men. After the fight Thompson came down here [San Francisco] and opened a ten-pin alley. Shortly after this I was informed that the fight between Thompson and Willis was a prearranged fraud. Of course it made me very angry to think that Thompson had deceived me and I determined to get somebody to whip him.

John Morrissey,[14] since then state senator of New York and Congressman, came here about this time and I made a match between him and Thompson for $1,000 a side. Morrissey had never fought a prize fight but he was strong and muscular and felt confident that, with proper training, he could win the battle. I got Joe Winrow[15] to train him and he used to work on him every day, but did not seem to do him much good. At last I got mad and asked Joe why he did not make more progress with Morrissey. He replied that it was impossible to train him. He would eat what he pleased and when remonstrated with would say, "Oh, I don't want to train to lick the big Englishman." Winrow did the best he could but Morrissey was not in very good condition when he went into the ring. They fought on Mare Island and in the third round the combatants clinched and the friends of Morrissey claimed a foul and the referee decided in favor of him. I mention this fight to show how Morrissey started in as a pugilist.[16]

CHAPTER 3

Hard Citizens

IN 1850 Horace Carpentier[1] had considerable trouble about a large tract of land in Alameda County which he had settled upon. A crowd of squatters jumped the greater portion of it and it was impossible for him to get them to vacate the premises. He finally sent some of his friends to ask me if I would go over to Alameda and protect his land from "jumpers." I felt friendly to Carpentier, and after a little consideration agreed to do so. I mustered a party, consisting of about five personal friends, and we started over. We had to go across the bay in small boats, for which we paid eighty dollars. On our arrival we found the squatters prepared for battle, but we convinced them in a very short time that the best thing they could do would be to leave, and they did it. We held the land until Mr. Carpentier took possession again, and then we returned to San Francisco.

When I arrived in the city, David C. Broderick was very angry and upbraided me severely for going over to Alameda and risking my life to protect Carpentier's claims, not knowing whether he was right or wrong. But I am satisfied now, as I was then, that Carpentier must have been the rightful owner of the property because he has it still and is now living on it. I did not then think of investigating his right to the land. I had known him in New York, and being his friend, took his word for it.

My old companion, Tom Hyer of New York, came here a few months after I did.[2] He was one of the best known men in the country and everybody who knew him liked him. When he walked down Broadway in New York City on a summer afternoon the people would stop to look at him and their gaze would follow his tall, commanding figure until it disappeared from view. He was one of the leaders of the old Whig party and a prominent member of the Unionist Club.

At the time of his arrival in San Francisco Hyer was suffering very much from rheumatism. I took him to Sacramento for a change of

Tom Hyer, champion bare-knuckle fighter. Charley Duane idolized him. Author's collection.

air and we arrived there on the day after the squatter riot.[3] When we left San Francisco we had no knowledge of the riot, as there was no telegraph in those days, and we were hardly prepared for the great excitement which existed in the little town on our arrival. We went to the Columbia Hotel, a large three-story building on Second Street between I and J, close to where the El Dorado building now stands.

There we learned that the riot had been a very serious affair. Many men had been killed and Mayor Bigelow and a number of other prominent citizens had been severely wounded. It was found necessary to cut Bigelow's thumb off. The mayor refused to take drugs of any kind and I held his hand while the operation was being performed. He was a good soul. He died in San Francisco shortly after the riots of cholera and I escorted his remains to Sacramento where he was buried.[4]

After registering our names at the Columbia Hotel, Hyer and I took a stroll around town, and on the levee we found three hundred men drilling under command of some of the law and order citizens. After learning the state of affairs we went to the Empire gambling house, a large place on the corner of J and Second Streets which was kept by Andrew J. Butler, a brother of Ben Butler.[5] You must bear in mind that it was no disgrace to keep a gambling house in those days. Hyer and I began playing faro and monte and in a short time we were flat broke. At this time a party of citizens waited upon me and offered me $5,000 cash if I would induce Hyer to go with me and lead a band of men drilling on the levee against the squatters. Five thousand dollars was a large sum of money for a man who was broke in a strange town, and I immediately sought Hyer and mentioned the proposition to him. His reply was, "You are a fool. Do you think I came so many miles from home to be killed in a squabble of this kind? How do we know which side is right? There is not enough money in Sacramento to induce me to mix in their fight, though I am broke."

I coincided with him and concluded to let the citizens take care of themselves. Benjamin F. Washington,[6] since collector of the Port of San Francisco, and editor of the *Times and Transcript*, Dr. Wake Bryarly,[7] and another man whose name I cannot recollect, felt so incensed at the squatters on account of their outrages upon the mayor and other prominent citizens of Sacramento that they addressed the crowds in the street and called on the law-abiding people to follow them to Sutter's Fort to search for and punish the murderers, as they styled the squatters. A large crowd soon formed, and led by the gentlemen mentioned, started in the direction of Sutter's Fort, but after we had proceeded a short distance the volunteers deserted and I found myself alone with the originators of the avenging party. The four of us kept on our road and upon reaching the fort instituted a thorough search but did not find what we were looking for.

Upon the return of the searching party to Sacramento, Hyer and I started for San Francisco. We landed at the foot of Vallejo Street. Hyer was so sick that he was unable to walk and I laid him down on some rocks while I ran up above the plaza to get the only dray in town to take him home. This was the only vehicle in the place at that time. Hyer returned to New York shortly after and remained there until he died.[8] He was one of nature's noblemen and his ashes now rest peacefully in Greenwood Cemetery, New York. He was the champion of America and was the first one who whipped Yankee Sullivan. The fight was for $10,000 and took place on the 7th day of February 1849. I have the only photograph of him on this coast and it hangs in my office, side by side with the bust of David C. Broderick.

Alexander C. Campbell, Sr.,[9] Ned McGowan,[10] and Harvey Brown were the three County Judges here in 1850 and they sat together as the Court of Sessions. They are all still in the land of the living, hale and hearty. In those days a suit was commenced, tried, and a judgment rendered and executed all on the same day. Speaking of trials reminds me of an incident which nearly resulted in the execution of two innocent men for attempted murder and robbery. On one Sunday evening in the summer of '50 I was returning with a party of friends from a ride, and when passing the corner of Pacific and Kearny Streets, we met a mob of excited men who were actively making preparations to hang two individuals, whom they had surrounded, to the most convenient projection. These men, whose names were Berdue and Wildred, were accused of fracturing the skull of and robbing a man named Jansen who kept a clothing store on Washington Street, just above Montgomery. As soon as I learned the state of affairs I rushed in the mob and with the assistance of my friends succeeded in rescuing the intended victims of lynch law and conveyed them safely to the city prison where they were locked up to await trial.[11]

While Berdue was in jail, I visited him every day, and was generally accompanied by a friend of mine named John Brady. Berdue and Wildred were finally tried on charges of assault to murder and robbery, found guilty, and sentenced to fifteen years' imprisonment in the state prison. Shortly after the sentence, and before the prisoners had been conveyed across the bay, Wildred succeeded in making his escape from the city prison and went to Australia, where he is at present. About the same time an up-country sheriff, who

happened to be in the city, called at the city prison and identified
Berdue as a man named Stuart who was wanted in his county for
murder. He was accordingly given over to the custody of the sheriff
and taken to the place where the crime was committed—I cannot
recall exactly where it was—and was there tried and convicted of
murder in the first degree.[12] The sentence in this case being death,
of course took precedence of the conviction in this city, and
preparations were at once made for a speedy execution.

Berdue during all this time earnestly protested that he was not
the man who was guilty of the crimes for which he was convicted
and that he was mistaken for a man named Stuart who looked like
him, but the circumstantial evidence against him was so strong that
even his friends were forced to believe him guilty. Three days before
the date set for his execution, Mr. Brady, the gentleman who visited
Berdue with me while he was confined here in the city prison, was
walking up California Street, and when he arrived at a point in the
middle of the block between Powell and Stockton Streets, he came
across a man concealed in the bushes whom he took for Berdue.
Being aware of the fact that Berdue had been convicted of murder
in an interior county, Brady was very much astonished, and he said,
"Why, Berdue, how did you get out?"

The man in the bushes replied, "My name is not Berdue."

Brady looked at him for some time and it then dawned upon him
that this individual might be the Stuart for whose crimes Berdue
claimed to be suffering, and he asked the man if his name was not
Stewart. The man said that his name was not Stewart.

"Well," said Brady, "I think your name is Stuart, and I'll bet that
you will not dare to accompany me to the rooms of the Vigilance
Committee."

The man, feeling sure that he would not be identified, expressed
his willingness to go with Brady and they went there together. On
arriving at the fort, Stuart was immediately recognized by parties
who knew him well and he was locked up.[13]

The news was dispatched, as quickly as the limited means at
command would allow, that Stuart had been captured and Berdue
was innocent of all charges against him. Governor McDougal issued
a pardon for Berdue and messengers were sent on different routes for
the town where the execution was to take place, and the document
arrived just in time to stop a judicial murder. Stuart was afterward
tried by the Vigilance Committee at their rooms on Battery Street,

Vigilantes hang James Stuart on the Market Street wharf, July 11, 1851. William B. Secrest collection.

near Pine, and sentenced to death. Colonel Jack Hays, who was sheriff, learning the result of the trial, read the Riot Act on the plaza and called on the citizens to aid him in rescuing Stuart from the Vigilance Committee so as to give him a legal trial in the courts. Ira Cole[14] and I responded to the call but when we got to the committee rooms we found that Stuart had been taken out and hung off the end of Market Street wharf.

When Berdue was first arrested, he had $15,000 but he used it all up in lawyers' fees and other expenses, and on his release he was without a dollar. Some of the citizens subscribed $600 for him and he purchased a horse and cart. He stood on Montgomery Street, north of Jackson, near where Pioneer Hall now is. In '52, when I was elected first assistant engineer and warden of the fire department, I gave him all the cartage. He had the sympathy of the citizens here, but the undeserved disgrace and trouble through which he had passed, broke his heart. He only remained here long enough to make a little money, when he returned to Sydney, his native place.

There were some thieves here from Sydney in those days and a man who hailed from there was set down as a "hard citizen." But this was a great injustice to many gentlemen who came from that country. There was one man named Jenkins here from Sydney who was caught with a small safe in his boat which he had stolen from a store on Long Wharf. The people who caught him dragged him to the plaza and hung him on a joist which projected from the banking house of Palmer, Cook & Co.[15]

I believe it was in 1854 or 1855 that three or four French and English men-of-war arrived in this harbor. This was just after the Russian war with the French and English, and after the capture of the Malakoff tower at Sebastopol.[16] On the arrival of the warships at this port the French and English subjects residing here arranged to give a grand banquet to the officers and crews of the vessels, and it was really a grand one. The tables for the meal were set in a row of tents, spread on a vacant green lot where South Park now stands, and there were seats enough to accommodate about 20,000 people, and I do not think there were any vacant chairs. Every gentleman of any prominence in the state was invited to the feast, and nearly all attended.

At that time I was chief engineer of the fire department and I received an invitation from the Committee of Arrangements for myself and as many members of the department as I chose to bring with me. On receiving the invitation, I called the leading men in the

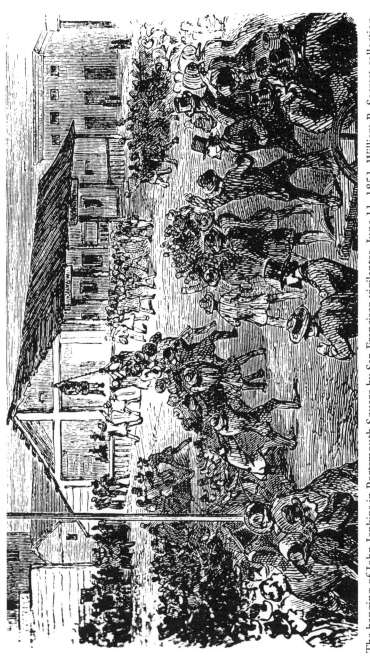

The hanging of John Jenkins in Portsmouth Square by San Francisco vigilantes, June 11, 1851. William B. Secrest collection.

different companies of the fire department together and I laid the matter before them, and invited an expression of opinion as to the number of men I should take to the banquet, and who they should be. After some consultation they concluded that it would be proper to have the fire department represented by the chief engineer, his assistant engineers, and the foreman of each company, and in compliance with their desires, I attended the banquet, accompanied by the parties mentioned.

When I arrived at the scene of the festivity, I was received with much display of courtesy and ceremony, and escorted to a seat between the French and English consuls residing here. Mr. Patrice Dillon was the representative of the French government in this city and Mr. George Aitken officiated in like capacity for the English. They were both very estimable gentlemen and enjoyed the respect and confidence of all who knew them. We passed a very pleasant hour in discussing the menu and matters generally, and at the end of that time an unusual interruption occurred.

In the center of the largest tent, close to where I sat, a large cake, about sixteen feet in circumference, and fourteen feet high, representing the captured tower and the cause of the great rejoicing, was placed on a large platform. The cake, which was of the finest kind of jelly roll, was very artistically fixed around the center pole of the tent in the shape of a tower, and looked very fine. As soon as the French wine, which was passed around with a liberal hand to the sailors, began to have its effect, the sailors of both nations started in to storm the cake tower, which was placed there to be eaten by the guests and not as a target of war. The sailors at first threw their loaves of bread at the tower, and when they had exhausted all their supply of bread, they seized bottles and everything that they could lay their hands on, and fired at the inoffensive cake. After destroying the tower and scattering it all over the tent, a French sailor jumped on the platform where the cake formerly stood with the flag of his nation held aloft. He was immediately followed by an English sailor who, armed with the silken emblem of his nation's honor, was also anxious to display its colors. The French present then gave a rousing cheer for the French flag, which was responded to by the English with a vigorous hurrah for their banner, and in a short time all was excitement and confusion.

In the tent of which I am speaking there was a row of flags, representing all nations with the exception of Russia. The excitement grew so wild in its character that the representatives of all nations present seized their respective flags and jumped on the platform which had held the tower. The platform was not large enough to hold all the patriots, many of whom were very much under the influence of liquor, and the result was that some fell off, others were pushed off, and fired by the wine they had drunk, the English and French sailors and the representatives of the other nations, at least 250 people in all, were soon engaged in a free fight of a desperate character. There were no deadly weapons such as knives or pistols used, but the poles of the respective flags, as well as plates, bottles, clubs, and other convenient arms of an impromptu war were freely handled with dangerous skill.

While all this was going on I sat between the French and English consuls, who addressed the crowd and begged the people to preserve order, but their voices were drowned by the surrounding din and their speeches, of course, had no effect, as they could not be heard. Finally, despairing of being able to do anything themselves, they requested me to ask the members of the fire department present to take charge of the tent under my command and, if possible, quell the riot. I immediately called upon the firemen to assist me and after they had expressed their willingness to aid me, I made arrangements to tie the flags of all the nations represented together, and if possible, hoist them on the large center pole. After I had them on the pole I intended to wave them all together and give one loud cheer for the whole of them. This proposition met with the hearty approval of the firemen and the consuls and I started in to put it into effect.

My men gathered all the flags which they could find but it was almost impossible to get some of them as they were in the hands of the excited patriots covered with blood. We succeeded, however, in getting quite a number, and our next move was to find a pole to tie them to so that they could be reached up to me when I got to the large pole in the center. I rolled up the American flag into a sort of a ball, and making my way through the crowd to the center pole, climbed up about thirty feet with the flag between my teeth. The French and English flags were on a small pole and were handed up to me when I reached the rigging, and then I intended to tie them with the American flag. When I got up thirty feet on the pole, I had to stop suddenly, and looking down, discovered that my feet were firmly clasped to the pole by an English sailor who had climbed up directly after me. He had me in such a position that I could not move and I called out to him to let go.

He replied, "Oh, me bloody Yankee, I've got you."

At this time the row was at its height and the principal part of the fight was going on directly around the base of the pole. I knew that it was almost impossible to make myself heard, still I roared at the top of my voice to the sailor below me, explaining my intention in reference to the flags and asking him to release me, but I could not get a satisfactory answer from him. He still held me in his horny grasp. The manner in which he held me rendered me perfectly helpless and I could neither go up nor down. After trying every inducement to cause the sailor to let go of me, without avail, I at last became angry at his uncalled-for conduct and the prospects of a good long stay on the pole, and so I looked around for some means to rid myself of the healthy incumbrance. I could discover no way in which to release myself until a sudden thought struck me, and stooping down, I caught the sailor by the hair of his head and butted his cranium against the pole. While I was engaged in this unpleasant work, the pole which we were on gave way and we were thrown down upon the heads of the people below.

He had still retained his hold on me when we reached the ground and as soon as we struck terra firma he started to punch me. He was a large, stout, healthy man, and being a sailor, he had the best of me while we were on the mast, but the minute we reached earth his advantage was gone and the tables turned in a very short time. We were soon engaged in a rough-and-tumble fight and in a few minutes the sailors present became aware that one of the comrades was getting the worst of the battle and they jumped in to help him. Things looked very desperate for me for a few seconds, but I was soon backed by the members of the fire department, and then began a general fight between the firemen and the sailors, which resulted in a victory for the firemen.

Previous to the time of the storming of the cake-castle the sailors behaved themselves very well indeed. I never saw such perfect harmony between so large a number of men, and the whole affair was very creditable to the representatives of the two nations who had given the feast. The disturbances which I have mentioned of course broke up the party and the people who did not join in the riot retired in disorder.

There were many people present, both French and English, who did not understand my conduct and they entertained very bitter feelings toward me for the part I had taken in the matter until the

San Francisco in the early 1850s, looking toward the bay. William B. Secrest collection.

respective consuls published cards explaining my conduct and exonerating me from all blame. Still, I am inclined to the opinion that many of these men did not read the letters of the consuls or else were too pigheaded to take any view of the matter but their own, and therefore did not lose the prejudice which existed in their minds on the evening of the banquet. I am satisfied that they showed this prejudice against me when they got the chance in 1856. But if they really had any idea that I was the cause of the disturbance at their jolly feast I do not blame them for feeling bitterly toward me, because I am certain that I would entertain such feeling against them if they disturbed a party of Americans who were holding a jubilee in France or England on the Fourth of July or who were celebrating any other national event.

CHAPTER 4

Dueling in the Gold Rush

THERE are very few people here who are aware of the fact that David C. Broderick ever fought a duel previous to the one in 1859 when he lost his life. In 1852, Broderick received a challenge to fight a duel from Judge Smith,[1] the son of ex-governor Smith of Virginia, who was better known as "Extra Billy" Smith. Judge Smith was also a brother of Austin Smith,[2] who was killed in the late war fighting in the rebel service. At that time a man who refused to accept a challenge was not permitted to move in what was considered in those days good society. He was treated with contempt and looked upon as a coward. Of course, Broderick accepted the challenge and the ground was selected for the duel across the bay, about where the city of Oakland now is. There were but a few shanties there then and they were located on the shore, where the foot of Broadway street is. As soon as the news was spread the place for the fighting had been fixed upon, every Whitehall boat in the harbor was engaged in taking people over the bay. They went back and forth all the night preceding the day of the duel. Ira Cole, two other gentlemen, and I started from this side in a Whitehall boat at one o'clock in the morning of the day of the duel. The fog on the bay was very heavy and after we had gone some distance past Goat Island the tide was very low and we found ourselves on the mud flats. We were obliged to remain there nearly an hour and were surrounded by a great many boats in the same predicament. It was so foggy that we could not distinguish the forms of the occupants of the other boats but we recognized our friends by their voices as they saluted our boat with, "Brig ahoy!" and "Ship ahoy!" and the firing of pistols.

A shot fired by some person hit one of the sailors in our boat in the arm and disabled him. Although we could not see each other, all sorts of bets were made on the result of the duel. After remaining on the flats for an hour, we drew lots in our boat to see who should undress and tow the boat to the shore. I believe Ira Cole cheated me because they all laughed at me when I pulled the short straw by the light of a cigar. As soon as it was decided that I should do the work I immediately took off my clothes and stepped into the cold mud. I took the direction, as I thought, toward shore and I kept hauling until the break of day, when I felt as though I had towed the boat twenty miles. About the time that day dawned I reached the shore and found that I had towed the boat one mile south in a zigzag fashion from where the foot of Broadway now is. After I had dug a hole for the water to come in with the oars of the boat and had taken a bath, we hauled our boat on shore.

We then went over the fields until we sighted two pretty large crowds of people, apparently about one quarter of a mile apart, when we steered our course in that direction and were soon amidst them. One crowd was the friends of Broderick and the others were the friends of Judge Smith, who was on the ground, accompanied by his father, Governor Smith. The duel was to be fought with Navy revolvers at a distance of ten paces, the signal for the shooting being, "One, two, three, fire!" At the word "fire" the parties were to shoot, and if they desired were to advance toward each other, the firing to continue until all the six shots had been used.

John A. McGlynn[3] presented me with a Navy revolver in 1850.[4] It was a very fine one and while I was shooting with it at a target on several occasions the exploded cap caught and prevented the cylinder from revolving. I took it to Brown and Natchez's[5] gun shop, opposite the plaza, and had the cylinder filed so that the cap could not catch. Vi Turner,[6] one of Broderick's seconds, borrowed this pistol from me the day before the duel for Broderick's use. On the field, when the duelists tossed up for the choice of pistols, Judge Smith's second won the choice and he took the pistol which I had loaned to Vi Turner for Broderick. Smith's pistol was the same make but had not been filed as mine had. Previous to the placing of the pistols in the hands of the principals, Broderick pulled out his heavy double-cased gold watch which Howard Engine Company in New York, of which he had been foreman, had presented to him on his departure from New York for California. He handed the watch to Vi Turner and within my hearing Turner said, "Put your watch in your pocket. If you are shot, die like a gentleman."

At this Broderick smiled and replaced the timepiece in his pocket. The pistols were then handed to Broderick and Smith, and the question asked, "Are you ready?"

On both answering in the affirmative, the word "fire" was given and they both commenced firing. I could not tell which of them fired first. After the first shot Broderick's exploded cap caught in the cylinder of his pistol and he did not have strength enough in one hand to cock it in the usual way. He then grabbed it in both hands, and putting the pistol between his knees, proceeded to cock it. While in this position, facing his opponent, he was struck by a bullet from Smith's pistol. The ball hit him in the stomach and staggered him, and his hat fell to the ground. Having succeeded in cocking his pistol, he returned the fire and they both kept shooting until they had fired their six shots. The seconds then rushed up to their respective principals and Turner unbuttoned Broderick's coat. I stood close to him, and on examination we found that the bullet had hit the center of his heavy cased watch and that fragments of the bullet went through both cases and cut his stomach. Judge Smith was not hit at all. After a few moments, Turner asked Broderick if he felt able to renew the duel. His reply was, "Certainly I am."

The people on both sides were ordered back and the seconds of both parties held a consultation with each other and afterwards with their principals. At the consultation of the seconds, Mr. Smith's representatives, on behalf of Judge Smith, said that he acknowledged that Broderick was an honorable gentleman. When Broderick's seconds informed him of this fact he said, "Well, that is sufficient," whereupon the seconds brought their principals half way and Broderick and Smith shook hands. The result was pleasing to all parties concerned.

After the duel it was impossible for all the people to get back to San Francisco on the same day and many walked up to an old house known as the Estudillo Rancho,⁷ a private mansion occupied by Spanish people, which was situated where San Leandro now is. There they obtained horses and rode to San Francisco by way of San Jose.

The Smiths were a fighting family all through. I was informed on good authority that the old gentleman had figured as a participant in several duels in Virginia before he came to the golden shores of California. It appears that his sons were as ready to defend their honor and principles as was the governor. I have seen a great many duels fought here that deserve more prominence than the one which I am about to tell you of, but I mention this simply to show the fighting propensities of the Smith family. In the year 1855, while

David Broderick, U.S. Senator. From a carte de visite by Matthew Brady taken in Washington, D.C., in 1859. Joseph T. Silva collection.

I was chief engineer of the fire department, the late Gregory Yale, one of the ablest lawyers and finest gentlemen in the country, called at my office in the old city hall and stated to me that a young man named Austin Smith, the son of the ex-governor, and a brother of the gentleman who had fought with Broderick, intended to fight a duel with Mr. Henry Truett[8] and that he had already started for the ground. Mr. Yale told me that he was an intimate and personal friend of Governor Smith, who was then in the eastern states, and that previous to his departure, he (Yale) had promised the governor that he would take care of his young son Austin. In compliance with this promise, he considered it his duty to prevent the duel between young Smith and Truett. He had called upon me to see if I would render him any assistance in putting a stop to the fight, at least until such time as Governor Smith should return to California. He asked me as a personal friend to go with him to the scene of the duel and see what could be done in the matter.

I told Mr. Yale that I had made it a rule since the firemen of the city had honored me with the highest position in their gift never to go out of hearing of the fire alarm bell. The city had been burned to the ground and had been almost wholly destroyed nearly every time there was a fire before I was elected chief engineer and I did not propose to let such a catastrophe occur through any neglect of mine. For that reason I told him that I was obliged to refuse him the favor he asked. He said that he honored me for the feeling I had shown and then requested me to accompany him to his office, which was situated on Washington Street, just above Montgomery. On our arrival there he called my attention to his iron safe and proceeded to explain to me the combination by which it was worked. After he had explained the method of operating the safe, he opened it and displayed to my view sixteen thousand dollars in gold which was deposited therein. He then closed the safe, handed me the keys, and told me that in case anything should happen to him through his interference in the duel between Austin Smith and Henry Truett, I would do him a great favor by taking charge of his money and attending to his other effects for the benefit of his family. He also handed me a power of attorney, giving me complete authority in the premises, and stated that he intended to stop the duel if his life had to be sacrificed in the attempt.

Finding that he was so determined in the matter, and being an intimate friend, I became anxious and asked Yale how far from town the duel was to be fought. He replied that he had been informed that it was to take place somewhere in the vicinity of the Sans Souci House. After a little consideration I concluded that I ought to be able to hear the fire bell at that distance, and having made up my mind on this point, informed Yale that I would accompany him to the scene of action. He thanked me warmly and we started. We reached the ground without much difficulty and upon our arrival I found that we were on the block now known as Western Addition Block No. 448, which was then my property and which is now owned and occupied by my brother. We found the principals in the affair of honor, both of whom were intimate friends of mine, upon the ground when we arrived. Chief of Police Hampton North,[9] accompanied by several members of his department, was also present. As soon as I saw him, I thought that I had found a way to end proceedings immediately. I said to North, "You are the chief officer of the police department of San Francisco and I demand of you to uphold the law and stop this duel."

He replied, "I have endeavored to do so, Duane, and the minute I opened my mouth several revolvers were drawn on me and the men in whose hands they were held swore that the first man who laid his hands on either of the principals in the conflict would be killed in his tracks."

He also informed me that it would be useless for any person to attempt to stop the fight, as the principals and their friends were determined to settle the affair by the pistol and nothing short of a miracle could prevent them from carrying out their programme. Truett and Smith were in their places, ten paces apart, at this time, waiting for their respective seconds, for the weapons to be handed to them. Each principal was backed by a crowd of about thirty friends. After receiving the answer from Chief North I immediately walked toward Truett and as I advanced several pistols were leveled at me and I was ordered to "stand back."

I told those who gave the order that I was a sworn officer of the law and intended to do my duty and stop the duel at the risk of my life. I immediately drew my own revolver, and covering the crowd, told them to fire and be [damned]. I then continued my course toward Truett, walking sideways with my face to the crowd. As I got close to my man his friends shouted at him to run and he, acting upon their advice, started off at the top of his speed, with me close to his heels. I pursued him about one block and a half and at the end of that distance I overtook and held him. As soon as I had caught him, his friends gathered around us and demanded his release in a very threatening manner. I refused to let Truett go and the more his friends insisted and threatened the more defiant I became and my grasp upon him grew firmer. The crowd was very noisy and did a good deal of angry talking but not one of them had the nerve to be the first to offer me any violence. Of course, I had the law on my side, and that is what saved me.

I started with my prisoner toward town with the excited crowd following close behind me. I expected every moment to be shot down but I was determined that their friend should go with me if the firing began. I therefore marched Truett in such a position that his friends in firing at me could scarcely fail to endanger his own life, and he, seeing this, after repeated vain efforts to release himself from my grasp, pleaded with his friends to keep quiet and not peril his life. When we got over the hills toward Hayes Valley, Truett begged me to let him go, assuring me on his word of honor that if I granted his plea he would not fight Smith that day. I knew that Truett was an honorable man, and as I had no other interest in the matter except to break up the fight, I consented to release him and the duel was stopped for that day.

The next morning, David C. Broderick sent a messenger to my office with a note requesting me to meet him immediately at the banking house of Palmer, Cook & Co. On my arrival at the bank I found Broderick there and he informed me that the parties whom I had prevented from fighting on the previous day had gone out again, and that this time they had selected the ground outside the county line, somewhere in Santa Clara County. He also stated that Truett's wife had heard of her husband's determination to fight and that she was nearly crazy with terror. He asked me to call upon Mrs. Truett and set her mind at rest by informing her that the duel would again be prevented, if such a thing was possible. He said that she was a very estimable lady and that he felt keenly for her. I asked him why he did not go on the mission of mercy himself. He replied that he could not possibly do it as he and Truett had not been on speaking terms for almost two years. I was aware of this fact because I knew that Truett had left Broderick and had gone over to Gwin's fight when the latter was making the battle for the United States senatorship. Truett was a man of considerable influence and Gwin, being aware of that fact, offered him very great inducements to win him over to his service. He afterwards succeeded in gaining for him a contract for building a portion of the custom house.

Upon leaving Broderick, I immediately went to Truett's house, which was located on the west side of Powell Street, between Jackson and Pacific. I found Mrs. Truett at home, in great distress, crying as if her heart would break. She was surrounded by a number of lady acquaintances residing in the vicinity of her house who were vainly endeavoring by every means at their command to pacify her and relieve her mind. The ladies, who had heard of my interference in the duel on the day before, received me very cordially and hailed me as a guardian angel. I informed Mrs. Truett and her lady friends that I was satisfied that matters would be terminated satisfactorily to both parties without the aid of bloodshed, and that I knew at that time for a positive certainty that the duel would be stopped. This news produced cheerfulness, where but a few moments before all was sorrow and desolation; so you see it is not always best to tell the truth. I said that I would wait for Mr. Truett and I had been in the house about an hour chatting pleasantly with the ladies when I heard some person running up the front stairs. I instantly jumped to the window, thinking it was possibly some messenger with bad news and wishing to be the first to meet him, when to my surprise and joy I found that it was Mr. Truett himself. As soon as he opened the door he was clasped in the arms of his loving wife, who shed tears of gladness over him. She was joined in this pleasant occupation by the majority of the ladies present and there was more salt water flowing than if he had been killed.

Truett and I shook hands and drank a glass of wine, after which he informed me that everything had been settled and there would be no more trouble. The expression of his face as he assured me that the fight was over caused me to doubt his sincerity. I, however, said nothing at the time, but bid the ladies farewell and prepared to depart. Truett then thanked me warmly for the interest I had taken in his family, when I told him that his thanks were not deserved by me, as I had visited his house to comfort his wife at the request of David C. Broderick.

He said, in a tone of great surprise, "Is that so?"

On my replying in the affirmative, he said, "God bless him. He is all man."

Ever after that occurrence I think that Truett was a warm friend of Broderick's. As I was about to leave the house I took hold of Mr.

Truett's arm and asked him to walk a few steps with me. His wife, fearing that he would not return, refused to give him his hat. He accompanied me, however, without a hat, and when we were alone I asked him to explain matters and he informed me that Smith and he had fought the duel and that he had shot Smith in the leg, but he did not think he had wounded him seriously.[10]

In 1851 a duel was fought by Governor McDougal and one of the editors of the *Alta California*, whose name I cannot call to mind at present.[11] McDougal was the governor of this state at the time the challenge was passed and in order to fight the duel he resigned his position as chief executive three days before the expiration of his term. D.C. Broderick was president of the senate at the time and took McDougal's place when the latter resigned.

The ground for the duel was selected on the other side of a creek[12] which divided the counties of San Francisco and Santa Clara, the present county of San Mateo being at that time included in San Francisco County. The weapons chosen were the regular dueling pistols and the distance agreed upon was either ten or twelve paces, I do not recollect which. Billy Owens of Stockton and I drove from here in a buggy and were on hand in time for the fight. There were about twenty-five friends of each principal present. At the words "one, two, three—fire!" both men discharged their weapons simultaneously and McDougal's ball struck his opponent on the right hand, cutting the flesh from three of his fingers and shooting the handle of his pistol off. The same ball entered his body and fractured one of his ribs. The editor did not fall but his second, thinking that his man was seriously wounded, threw up the sponge. He certainly would have been killed if McDougal's ball had not hit the handle of his pistol before entering his body. After the first fire he was willing and did acknowledge that Governor McDougal was an honorable gentleman and reached out his hand, which the governor clasped in his hearty grip.

But the wounded editor said, "Do not shake my hand hard, Governor, for you have wounded me severely."

McDougal, who was one of the noblest of God's creatures in every respect, shook the proffered hand gently, and thus everything was satisfactorily settled. The pistol used by the editor, the handle of which was knocked off by McDougal's bullet, was used many years afterward in a pistol gallery on the plaza. I have shot with it a great many times. I remember that it was in the gallery in 1856 when I was presented with a pair of bracelets by the grateful people of San Francisco in recognition of the services I had rendered while in the fire department. Whether or not the winged editor of the *Alta* is still in the land of the living I cannot say, but the body of my good friend, Governor McDougal, may God bless his soul, reposes quietly in the cemetery, and his spirit I know is with the angel band in Heaven. No truer man than McDougal ever walked the earth and I am satisfied that he is now enjoying his deserved reward.

The *Alta California* had an array of fighting talent on its staff in those days. Another editor named Gilbert,[13] in 1852, challenged and fought General Denver,[14] after whom the city of Denver in Colorado is called. The duel was fought at Oak Grove, about ten miles from the city of Sacramento. The state legislature had passed an act appropriating a certain sum of money to relieve the wants of emigrants crossing the plains to California, and appointing a committee for the proper and impartial distribution of the funds appropriated. Mr. Gilbert, thinking that the money appropriated was not honestly distributed, according to the intention of the act, by the committee appointed, of which General Denver was chairman, gave him a severe dressing in an editorial on the subject which appeared in the *Alta*. The article was answered by Denver in the columns of another journal and in the course of his reply he bitterly attacked and denounced Gilbert. Of course, according to the custom of the country in those days, Gilbert was obliged to challenge Denver, which he did and Denver accepted.

The "code" allowed the challenged party the choice of weapons and Denver selected rifles. The general had a great reputation for the proficiency with which he handled a rifle and when Gilbert was informed of this fact he said, "Well, if Denver is the best shot, he is double my size, and that is to my advantage."

At the first fire both men missed. Denver then told his seconds that he had fired at Gilbert's legs and had no intention of harming him. He said that he did not wish to kill him, and he requested his seconds to induce Gilbert's seconds to advise him (Gilbert) to withdraw his challenge and state that the statements published in the *Alta* reflecting on his (Denver's) character were not true. Denver said that if the challenge was withdrawn and the statement made, he would respond, and the matter could be settled without bloodshed. Gilbert was informed by his seconds of the proposition made by Denver, but he bravely refused to withdraw his challenge or retract anything which he had written. The men were then placed in position for the second shot. Denver remarked that he would not again hazard his own life by shooting at his antagonist's legs, but would aim for his heart. He did so and hit Gilbert, who fell into the arms of his second, Mr. Teschemaker,[15] ex-mayor of this city, mortally wounded. I believe that before the last breath was drawn he was lifted up and he expired in the arms of Harry Livingston,[16] who was then one of the editors of the *Alta*. When Denver learned that Gilbert was dead he wept bitterly and showed real, genuine sorrow. It was generally known that he did all that he honorably could to avoid the duel.

His death cast a gloom over the whole community, as he was looked upon and was a brave, upright man. In those days if the editor of a newspaper scandalized a gentleman he was obliged to go to the front and fight or else lose his position as a journalist and his good standing in the community. Gilbert's body was sent to this city by way of Sacramento, and was received here by the California Guard, the city being draped in mourning. Mr. Gilbert was highly esteemed in this city and to do honor to his memory the supervisors then in office had his picture placed on the wall of their chambers, and it has hung there ever since.

The occurrence of the duel was an event of universal regret and a committee of citizens was appointed to investigate the actions of General Denver as chairman of the Emigrants' Distribution Committee. After a most thorough and searching investigation of all matters pertaining to the subject by Gilbert's friends and the citizen's committee, it was found that Denver had been honorable and just in all his transactions. I was intimately acquainted with both gentlemen and never in all my experience saw a person so seriously affected by anything as General Denver was by this sad occurrence. He was a changed man ever afterward.[17]

In 1851 another editor of the *Alta*, Edward C. Kemble,[18] had a dispute with Mr. George McDougal,[19] a very estimable gentleman. George was a brother of Governor McDougal and possessed a great many of his worthy qualifications as a man. The dispute between him and Kemble occurred in the Union Hotel and the result was that the editor issued a challenge to fight, which was immediately accepted by McDougal. The place elected for the duel was a lot in the rear of a house known as the Red House, which was situated about a mile-and-a-half beyond St. Mary's College, on the old San

Jose Road.[20] This was between six and seven miles from the old City Hall. About forty people, friends of the principals, were on the ground to see the battle of honor. After the men had taken their positions on the field, and while waiting for their weapons, there was a certain party arrived upon the ground, and as soon as he caught sight of him Kemble refused to fight unless the party left the ground. McDougal's seconds and friends appealed to the objectionable party to leave, but he positively refused to do so. When informed of this, Kemble's seconds said that their man would not fight, because if he killed McDougal he would then have to fight the person who had been vainly requested to leave.

The whole party then returned to town, and I believe the matter was subsequently settled without a return to the field. I know that Mr. Kemble was a brave man, and did not refuse to fight from any sense of fear. In those days no coward wished to be looked upon as a man of honor, because he would have too many opportunities of showing his courage. The *Alta* had a staff of fighting editors in the early days, and I think there are fighting editors still in the sanctum, but, thank God, the custom which produced them is now a thing of the past, to be talked of but not indulged in.

I believe it was in the year 1854 that John Cotter,[21] the father of Edward Cotter, ex-president of the Exempt Fire Company, and present Fire Commissioner, fought a duel with John Nugent, editor of the San Francisco *Herald*, which was then the leading paper here.[22] It was during the Broderick-Gwin fight for the United States senatorship, and Cotter was a member of the board of aldermen. Nugent was opposed to Broderick, and was using his paper to benefit William M. Gwin. The members of the Common Council, or aldermen, as they were then called, held Broderick in high esteem as an honorable man, and were disposed to do everything in their power to elevate him to the United States Senate. An editor working on Nugent's paper attacked the council severely upon some of their actions which he thought would be detrimental to Gwin's interests, and Cotter, as a member of the council, and on behalf of that body, challenged John Nugent to fight a duel. The challenge was accepted of course, and it was decided by the respective seconds that the duel should be fought across the bay. Mr. Broderick and I did all that we possibly could to settle this affair without a resort to the "field" but we were unsuccessful in our efforts, as both men were determined to fight and would not entertain any other argument. I felt very

John Nugent, the fiery editor of the *San Francisco Herald*. He was wounded twice in duels and was an outspoken opponent of the 1856 vigilantes. William B. Secrest collection.

sorry about the affair, as Cotter and I had come out on the same steamer together and he was an old gentleman, and in my opinion no match for Nugent. He wore spectacles and knew very little about the business, while Nugent was looked upon as a crack shot. I would not go to see the duel because I did not consider it a fair fight.

The weapons used were regular dueling pistols. Cotter, despite his weak eyesight and inexperience, hit Nugent the first shot, and the latter fell to the ground severely wounded. In fact, the wound was of such a serious nature that grave doubts were entertained of his recovery. His friends thought that he would die before they could get him off of the ground. Mr. Nugent was sick for about eight months from the effect of this wound, but at the end of that time appeared on the streets as usual. The result of this duel placed Mr. Cotter very high in the estimation of the people here, and he could have been nominated to any office in the city government, but he declined all offers with the remark "that he had been abused by his fellow citizens for doing the best he could while alderman, and he would not give them another chance to abuse him by accepting a public position." At that time Mr. Cotter had two sons here, one of whom has since died. Edward, the only surviving member of the family, is still living in this city, and is one of our most worthy citizens. The result of the duel did not have much effect upon Nugent, as far as the policy of his paper was concerned. He was as bold as ever, and was a determined, noble-spirited man to the time of his death, which occurred a few months ago.

Colonel Thomas Hayes, the owner of the Hayes Valley Tract of one hundred and sixty acres which is now known as Hayes Valley, was elected county clerk of San Francisco two or three times. He was a young politician in New York before he came to California, and was opposed to the Broderick wing of the Democracy in that city, and it naturally followed that he and Broderick were not on the best of terms. Tom Hayes and I were brought up together, and were, of course, very intimate. When we came to California and I found that Broderick and Hayes were very distant toward each other, I was very much amazed, because I thought a great deal of them both. I finally succeeded in getting them together for a friendly chat, and had the pleasure of seeing them drop all the ill-feeling which had previously existed between them and become friends.

Broderick elected Tom county clerk, and as the position was a very lucrative one, Hayes was enabled to successfully battle with the numerous squatters who sought to take possession of his property. It was then only one hundred and sixty acres of sand and brush, but now it is valued at about $10,000,000. While he was county clerk, John Nugent attacked him bitterly in the *Herald* for some alleged mismanagement in his office. This was the beginning of a dispute

Thomas Hayes, San Francisco politician and friend of Charley Duane.
Author's collection.

which finally culminated in a duel.[23] Hayes challenged Nugent and
they fought with rifles on a vacant lot just beyond Hayes Valley.
Nugent was hit and fell to the ground. Upon examination the wound
was found to be pretty severe and everybody thought Nugent
would die this time sure, but he recovered, and we used to say that

he was like the cat with nine lives. He suffered for over one year with this wound, and one of his arms, which was affected by the shot, was so severely hurt that he could never after straighten it. When he could just move around comfortably, and while one of his arms was still in a sling, I met him at a public ball and danced in the same set with him. Ned McGowan, a gentleman well known to everybody, who was so shamefully treated by the Vigilance Committee in 1856, was Tom Hayes's second in the duel between him and Nugent, and I believe that he acted as Cotter's second in the first duel.

While I was chief engineer in 1855, James P. Casey[24] and a gentleman named Bagley, who is still residing in this city, went out to fight a duel.[25] I was called upon by the friends of both partici-pants to prevent it. I went out near the Red House, on the old San Jose road, and when I arrived on the ground I found the men in position. I stepped between them and informed them that as an officer of the city I intended to arrest them both. Neither Casey nor Bagley offered any resistance, but the friends of both indulged very freely in threats to shoot me if I attempted to take the men off of the ground. But it was not necessary for me to do so, as I succeeded in stopping the fight without being obliged to bring the participants into town. Shortly after the occurrence I regretted my action in breaking up the duel, as I found that a very bitter feeling existed between all parties concerned, and they were always at loggerheads on account of political differences.

About the time set for this duel, Robert Cushing[26] and Casey met on Kearny Street, between Sacramento and California, directly opposite where Porter & Fenner's livery stable then stood. I was just about to enter the stable when I heard a report, and turning, I saw Cushing and Casey in the middle of the street with their pistols drawn, exchanging shots. Only a few words had passed between them when they stepped into the middle of the street and began firing. They were about twenty feet apart and they had each fired several shots when I sprang between them and said that I would arrest the next man who fired a shot. This caused them to stop shooting, and just then some policemen could be seen coming toward us, so both men pocketed their weapons and went off in different directions.

Shortly after this difficulty there was a Democratic primary election. The polls were held at the corner of Kearny and Pine Streets. Cushing and Casey met soon after the polls were opened and engaged in an angry dispute, which resulted in a desperate fight, pistols and knives being freely used.[27] Ten or twelve shots were fired and things were very lively. I did not see this fight but I learned the particulars from my brother, who was on the ground and saw it all. Cushing was severely wounded in the melee and the policemen, who were attracted to the scene of the row, carried him to the police station in the old city hall. He was unable to stand and they laid him on the floor of the prison, and dispatched a messenger for a surgeon.

I happened in at this time and found Cushing vomiting blood. He recognized me when I spoke to him and he informed me that he was certain that he could not live. A severe cut in his abdomen allowed the intestines to protrude and fall on the floor. I replaced them as well as I could and held them until the arrival of the physician who was summoned. I explained to him what I had done and he informed me that if the intestines were uninjured it might be possible to save Cushing's life. He then sewed up the wound, putting about twenty stitches in all, and placing the injured man upon a door, we carried him to his home on California Street, above Dupont.[28] It was about eight months before he was well enough to leave his bed, but at the end of that time, owing to the careful and tender nursing of his sister, with whom he lived, he was able to walk about. He is still living in this city and is today a prominent member of the Republican Party.

Shortly after the occurrence just mentioned, the grand jury met and took the case under consideration. My brother being an eyewitness of the affair, was subpoenaed to testify in the matter on behalf of the people. Upon learning that my brother John had been summoned, Casey came to me and said that if John testified in the manner in which it was understood he would he must be prepared to suffer the consequences. He advised me to look out for my brother in case he testified as he intended to, as he (Casey) did not propose to allow anybody to testify against him with impunity. I regarded this as a threat, and I knew that Casey, being a desperate man, was capable of executing it, but I told him that my brother had been taught to regard his oath in the proper manner, that he was twenty-one years of age, and in my opinion, capable of taking care of himself. I immediately sought John and informed him of Casey's threat, at the same time providing him with a pistol and Bowie knife to defend himself in case of an attack. He had not been in California long at that time and I instructed him how to act in the matter. That afternoon my brother and I met Casey in company with several desperate characters in Fiske & Loring's saloon, which was situated on Clay Street, between Kearny and Montgomery, where Frank Edwards's carpet store is now. I knew that Casey was waiting to catch John napping, but as he did not make any hostile motion, I of course did not say anything.

This ill-feeling existed between Casey and myself for a long time, although he never attempted to put his threat into execution. Under these circumstances I could not have much love for Casey when he killed James King of William, the founder of the *Bulletin*. In fact, I often regretted that I had prevented the duel between Casey and Bagley. Soon after the row at the polls on the day of the primary election, Casey was sworn in as a supervisor, although he was never elected, and was not even a candidate on the day of election. I am pretty certain that the plan to put him in office was concocted and put into operation after the polls were closed on election day.[29]

CHAPTER 5

A Bullet for James King of William

JAMES King of William[1] was a banker in this city in 1853–1854 and had his office on the southwest corner of Commercial and Montgomery Streets. When he failed there, he became the financial manager for the banking firm of Adams & Co., the place of business of which was located on the northeast corner of Montgomery and Merchant Streets, where the office of the *Evening Bulletin* now is. In those times the fire department always had an annual parade on the anniversary of Washington's birthday. In 1854 the celebration had to be postponed two or three times on account of the inclemency of the weather. I was chief engineer, and of course took considerable pride in the efficiency of the department, and I made it a rule not to retire any night until day began to dawn. I could generally be found in the vicinity of Montgomery and Merchant Streets. The night before the day on which the postponed parade was to take place, I met James King of William as he was coming out of Adams & Co.'s bank. He said to me, "Mr. Duane, I think that you will have a fine day tomorrow for your parade, and you ought to retire early so as to look well in the procession. Here is one hundred dollars from our bank to decorate your engines, and I would advise you to retire early."

It was customary for the bankers and merchants to donate money for the decoration of engines and to pay for music on the day of a parade, so of course I accepted the money. The advice to retire early, coming as it did from one of our leading citizens, was pleasing to me and I followed it. On the next morning the fire department paraded the streets but I noticed that the doors of Adams & Co.'s bank were not opened at 10 o'clock as usual. Later in the day the depositors discovered that the deposits had been removed from the bank the night before. This news spread like wildfire and the town was soon in a great state of excitement, but no one could find out at the time where the money taken from the bank had been placed.

James King of William, editor of the *San Francisco Bulletin*. His murder sparked the 1856 vigilante uprising. Robert Limacher collection.

The depositors, however, learned some time afterward that the money had been removed in the night by James King of William and others to Alsop & Co.'s building, which was situated on California Street, where Hayward's building now stands. I liked King at that time and never, until now, have I made public the circumstance of his presentation of one hundred dollars. Of course, I paid the money into the department fund, but I did not mention the exact manner in which I had received it.[2]

James King of William used the *Bulletin*[3] as a means of redress for his grievances and wrote some very severe articles against persons who were opposed to him politically and otherwise. This system of personal journalism attracted considerable attention and in a short time the *Bulletin* was a very influential paper. Soon after the *Bulletin* made its appearance, James P. Casey started a weekly journal which he called the *Sunday Times*. He was generally looked upon as the editor of the paper but this was a mistake on the part of the public as the editorial chair was occupied by the late John C. Cremony.[4] The latter gentleman, working under the instructions of Casey, bitterly attacked James King of William and many other persons connected with him and his paper.

Thomas King, the brother of James, was at that time endeavoring to obtain a position in the custom house. Casey selected him as a good target and abused him unmercifully every week in the *Times*. While this fight was going on, Mr. Bagley (the gentleman with whom Casey was going to fight the duel which I prevented) and James Hennessey,[5] learning that Casey had earned a very unsavory record for himself in New York before coming to California, employed parties in New York City to hunt up Casey's record and send it out here. In a short time they received an answer which completely satisfied them. This answer contained the full particulars of Casey's arrest and conviction in New York City on a charge of felony and his subsequent incarceration in the penitentiary. Enclosed in the letter were certain copies of the records and proceedings in the matter. Although there were a great many here at that time who had known Casey intimately in New York, there was not one among us who was aware of the fact that he had ever been in state prison.[6] As soon as the documents were received and examined by Bagley and Hennessey, they were given to Mr. Frank Soule,[7] who was then the editor of a paper called the *Chronicle*, the office of which was on Merchant Street, for publication. After reading them, Soule decided that he would not publish Casey's shame until he had consulted with one of his assistant editors whose name was Nisbet,[8] a new arrival from Sydney, and in the meantime he locked the papers in his office safe.

Before Soule had arrived at any decision in reference to the publication of the documents, Nisbet withdrew from the *Chronicle* and went to work for James King of William on the *Bulletin*. While the controversy between the *Bulletin* and the *Sunday Times* was at its most bitter stage, Nisbet called at the *Chronicle* office after some private papers belonging to him which he had forgotten to take with him at the time of his withdrawal from the paper. The papers which he wanted were locked in the same safe that contained the Casey documents and Soule, without any suspicions, gave Nisbet the keys of the safe so that he could get his own property. While ostensibly searching for his letters, Nisbet abstracted the documents proving Casey's incarceration in Sing Sing and gave them to James King of William. Casey was soon informed that the evidence of his disgrace was in the hands of King and would be published in the *Bulletin*.

When the news reached him he immediately went to the editorial rooms of the *Bulletin*, on Merchant and Montgomery Streets, and had an interview with King, during which he begged King not to publish the papers in his possession, at the same time admitting the truth of the information contained in them. He told King that if he would promise not to publish his disgrace he (Casey) would retract all that had been said of him and his brother in the *Sunday Times*, and that he would also make every other retraction that was necessary. While Casey was talking, King sat at his desk with a pistol before him and listened quietly before he was finished. He then turned to Casey and said, "Are you what these documents represent you to be?"

Casey replied that he was.

"Then," said King, "there is the door. Be gone." As he uttered the last word, he placed his hand upon his pistol.

Casey walked toward the door and as he reached it said, "If you publish those papers you or I will fall and suffer the consequences."

That day's issue of the *Bulletin* contained the entire record of Casey's history as a criminal in New York. That afternoon, while on his way home from the editorial rooms, King saw Casey coming toward him on the west side of Montgomery Street, just north of Washington. As soon as Casey caught sight of King he stopped and waited for him to approach. When he came within a few feet of him Casey said, "Draw and defend yourself."

Montgomery Street, 1856, looking north. James King of William walked north in front of the four-story building, the Montgomery Block, then crossed the street, where he was shot by James Casey. William B. Secrest collection.

King was walking with his right hand on his breast inside his coat and when Casey ordered him to "draw," he paid no attention whatsoever but continued on his course directly toward Casey with a sneering expression upon his face. Casey then drew his revolver and fired, hitting King in the breast. The report of the pistol attracted a large crowd of people to the spot and some friends of King carried him into the express office of Buffett and Co., which was situated on the northwest corner of Washington and Montgomery Streets, where Montgomery Avenue now crosses. His coat was opened and a loaded, half-cocked revolver fell upon the floor. After a physician had been summoned and the nature of the wound ascertained, King was carried to a room on the second floor of Montgomery Block where, after lingering for two or three days, he died.[9]

Casey was, of course, immediately arrested and lodged in the city prison. James King of William pursued a very reckless course in his management of the *Bulletin*. He did not appear to care how soon he got killed because he always used to select the most desperate men in the town as the fittest subject for his attacks. After abusing some particular set of fighting men, he would publish a paragraph something after this style: "Oh, you hounds! Why do you not attack me? You dare not. My pistol is getting rusty—the graveyard is on my way as I go home from my office."[10]

All these exact words may not have been written in one paragraph but if the reader will examine the files of the old *Bulletin* it will be found that what I have stated is substantially correct. He attacked many prominent men, and among the number, David C. Broderick. King had many friends who thought a great deal of him and do to this day, but I do not think they knew him as well as I did. A great many members of the Law and Order Party,[11] an association organized in opposition to the Vigilance Committee, showed a very bitter feeling toward Thomas King, the brother of James, when he took charge of the *Bulletin* after his brother's death. He pursued the same course that James had during his lifetime and abused the enemies of his brother in a very vigorous style. I did not blame him for that, however, because I think it is only natural for one brother to take up another's fight.

At the time James King of William was killed I was at a friend's house on Powell Street. After leaving there I was on my way down Washington Street when, just east of Stockton, I met a gentleman named James Hughes, an attorney here, who informed me that

Casey had shot King and that King would surely die. He said that it was more than likely that the affair would result in a general riot. I immediately started down Washington Street on a run and when I reached Montgomery I found about five thousand excited people collected there. Being unable to effect an entrance to Buffett's office where King was lying, I remained on the outskirts of the crowd and endeavored to learn the particulars of the affair. But I could scarcely get an intelligent answer. The people seemed to be perfectly frantic. While I was doing the best I could to keep those in my immediate vicinity quiet, a young gentleman named Lafayette Byrne,[12] a brother of Harry Byrne,[13] then district attorney, called me aside and told me that his brother wished to see me at the city hall. Immediately I walked up Merchant Street, and as I reached the rear of the hall, Chief of Police (or Marshal, as he was called then) Hampton North stopped me and said, "Mr. Duane, I command you to assist me to take the prisoner, James Casey, from the city prison to the county jail."

I was obliged to obey him and expressed my readiness to accompany him. The entrance to the prison then was from Kearny Street, thence through to the courtyard, and then down a flight of stairs. We started for the prison and in the courtyard I found nearly the whole police force stationed, to protect Casey in the event of an attack from the mob. There were some men in the ranks whom I had seen display much excitement with the crowd on Montgomery Street and I came to the conclusion that these men were as dangerous as the mob outside. I communicated my fears to North and advised him to take Casey out by the rear entrance instead of through the courtyard. He agreed to this plan, and placing Casey between us, we marched him out. North was going to put handcuffs on him but I whispered to him not to do so and told him that I should see that he did not get out of our custody until he was safely locked up in the county jail. We then went out in the little alley in the rear of the hall to Washington Street. On our way I told Casey that if he showed any disposition to escape from us he would be killed in his tracks. He then asked me for a pistol to protect himself in case he should be attacked by the mob but we did not think it proper to grant this request. We were willing to risk our lives to defend him from mob law and we considered that sufficient security. When we reached Washington Street North and I drew our revolvers and made our way through the crowd with the prisoner as quietly as possible. But we had not gone far when a yell was heard at Washington and Montgomery Streets, informing the crowd there that Casey was on the street. In a few seconds the whole mob started toward us with wild shouts of, "Hang him! Hang him!" and, "Shoot him down!"

As soon as we saw this, North and I took hold of Casey, one on each side, and started on a fast run up Kearny Street, with the angry mob close in pursuit. I shouted to a hack driver whose carriage was standing on the corner of Washington and Kearny to turn his horses quickly in the direction of Broadway. When this was done we opened the doors of his carriage and pushed Casey in. North also went in with him, while I mounted the driver's box and ordered him to whip up his horses.[14] He did so but before we could get fairly started the carriage was surrounded by the mob, some of whom grabbed the horses by their heads and held them.

I ordered the driver to lay his whip upon the animals with a heavy hand, and drawing my pistol, I leveled it at the crowd around the horses' heads and told them that if they did not let go instantly I would fire. This had the effect of scattering them. By this time the people in the rear of the carriage had taken hold of the back wheels and were about to upset us. I felt the motion, and throwing myself upon the top of the carriage, I reached down with a knife in my hand and told the parties at the wheel that if they did not let go I would cut their hands off. This threat frightened them and they put the carriage on the ground again.

There were about three thousand people congregated about the vehicle but before they hit upon another plan for our destruction the driver struck his horses and we rushed through the crowd to the county jail. At that time there was a large embankment in front of the jail and the entrance could only be reached by the ascension of a flight of wooden stairs. It was in the same location as at present but the street was not graded then. We arrived at the jail and locked Casey up some time before the people who followed on foot got there. The chief of police and I remained outside of the jail on the embankment in front and prevented the people from coming up the stairs. A great many of those below cried out, "Shame on you, Duane, for taking the part of a murderer."

I assured them that I was not upholding Casey in his action in killing King of William, but that I simply wished to see the law carried out. I told them that Casey would not be permitted to

James P. Casey, hanged by the San Francisco vigilantes. William B. Secrest collection.

escape but would be tried by legal process and that justice would surely be done. This did not satisfy them, however. They kept on clamoring for Casey's life and their ranks were constantly increased by new arrivals. They were growing more desperate and determined every moment and North and I expected to see them dash up and capture the jail.

I was at that time a member of the San Francisco Blues, a military organization started by ex-sheriff Gorham, who was our first captain. David Scannell,[15] the present chief engineer of the fire department, was captain of the Blues at the time of King's death and he was also sheriff of this county. When affairs began to assume an alarming aspect, he ordered out the company to aid him as sheriff in keeping the peace. As it was necessary for Scannell to remain at the jail, the company was commanded by Lieutenant B. Farren. There was not over one half of the members of the company present, but a great many citizens promptly responded to the call for volunteers and we soon had a considerable number in ranks. Among these were Hall McAllister, George Hossefross, and many other prominent men.[16] After marching to the armory and securing our weapons, we proceeded with fixed bayonets to the county jail at double-quick time. We were stationed on the embankment directly in front of the jail. Very few of us had on a full uniform but nearly all the members had some part of it.

Sheriff Scannell took command of the company as soon as we were in position, and after we had loaded our guns we were ordered to face the mob and stand in line. Many stones, bricks, and other playthings of that character were thrown at us by the mob, who kept hissing, hooting, and ridiculing us generally. One of the stones hurled from below struck my gun, and glancing off, went through my silk hat and struck my head. It must have severed an artery, for the blood ran down my face and neck in a stream. I saw the party who threw the stone and if I had not been armed I could have dodged it. But I did not think that a soldier stationed in the front ranks had any right to dodge and I was obliged to take the consequences. A great many of my friends in the crowd below shouted that the stone which had cut me was not thrown at me, but it hit me all the same and their good intentions toward me did not have any effect on the result. I have often thought since that it was a great wonder that some of our company were not killed by the stones thrown at us.

I at last became tired of being a target for the crowd below, and I said to Scannell, "You have a great many volunteers here, Captain. Do not allow them to be stoned to death, but give us orders to charge."

He replied, "Stand firm there, sir. Stand firm."

I answered, "I'll be [damned] if I will," and advancing a few steps, I aimed my loaded gun at the party who had thrown the stone at me.

The effect was magical. The five thousand people below all tried to beat each other in getting out of the range of a single weapon and the ground immediately in front of the jail was quickly cleared.[17]

Previous to the arrival of the military company at the jail, Thomas King, the brother of James, was with the mob and he rushed up the stairs to the bank where Marshal North and I were stationed, calling upon those below to follow him and capture the jail. Just as soon as he put his foot on the embankment, I grabbed him and threw him down the bank to the street. He then crossed over to the other side of Broadway Street, entered a house, and shortly after appeared on the veranda and addressed the mob, urging them to storm and capture the jail and hang Casey. His eloquence was interrupted by the arrival of the Blues, upon the appearance of which he immediately subsided. The company remained in front of the jail until dusk, when we were ordered inside, where we remained on guard for several days. By permission of our captain we then formed a company of ten men from the whole company to remain in the jail all the time. We occupied a front room on the upper floor of the jail and no person was allowed to interfere with us. When we had secured the room in the jail we sent a messenger to Natchez's gun store with instructions to purchase all the guns and pistols that were for sale.

In the meantime James King of William had died from the effect of Casey's shot. Between 10 and 11 o'clock on the night of his death, Sheriff Scannell came to the door of the room in which we were stationed and signaled to me to come out in the hall. I obeyed the sign and when I had closed the door of the room behind me Scannell showed me a note from the Executive Committee of a Vigilance Committee which had organized while I was guarding the jail, informing him that the committee would be quiet and that things would run along smoothly if he dismissed me from guard in the jail.

I pleaded with Scannell not to grant the request because I felt sure that if I left the jail would be taken. He said that he was sheriff and that his orders must be obeyed, and he commanded me to leave the jail. I returned to the guardroom for my coat and informed my companions of what had transpired. They immediately sent for Scannell and told him that if he was going to take men away from the guardroom, as he had me, they would not stay there and hazard their lives. He replied that I must go, and my companions then put down their weapons and prepared to accompany me.

I had a full uniform of the San Francisco Blues in the jail and I took this uniform to Casey's cell and shoved it through the wicket in the door, at the same time telling him to put on the clothes and I would endeavor to obtain the sheriff's permission to have him placed on board a man-of-war which was then in the harbor. I made the proposition to Scannell but he refused to entertain it and ordered me to quit the jail. If Scannell had granted my request, it was my intention to have taken Casey over Telegraph Hill to the beach, put him in a small boat, and place him on board the war ship. This would have defeated the Vigilance Committee, because they could not successfully attack the ship. Having failed in this last attempt, I told Casey to prepare for death, and in company with my friends left the jail.

I went to bed immediately and slept soundly until I was awakened between 8 and 9 o'clock on the next morning and informed that the Vigilance Committee, several thousand in number, were marching toward the jail. Hastily dressing myself, I rushed out on Stockton Street and ran toward Broadway, hoping to get to the jail before the arrival of the committee. On reaching Broadway I looked down the street and saw several armed companies with a cannon in their midst stationed in front of the jail. I then continued along Stockton Street to Vallejo. I turned up Vallejo and made for the rear of the jail. Telegraph Hill was literally covered with eager spectators of the scene below.

On my arrival at the rear of the jail I found it guarded by the City Guard, a Vigilance Committee Company under command of Captain Clark. I continued on my way, not heeding the order to "stand back," when a bayonet was thrust at me. I grabbed the weapon and in the struggle the bayonet went through my pantaloons. I then drew my pistol and informed the guard that I would kill the first man who drew on me. I backed slowly, with my eyes on the guards, and in a short time reached the roof of the jail. The skylights were all locked and I rapped on the glass and signaled the sheriff to let me in, but he shook his head and would not open the skylight. After I had been on the roof some time, ladders were placed up at the side of the jail and I, in company with other gentlemen on the roof, among whom was John Hayes, brother of Colonel Thomas Hayes, descended to the courtyard below.

That night the Vigilance Committee appointed seventeen of their number to demand the keys of the jail. They made the demand and Sheriff Scannell delivered up the keys and allowed them to enter the jail. The committee then took Casey and Cora, one after the other, out of the jail, placed them in a carriage surrounded by the armed companies, and escorted them to the rooms of the committee, which were situated on the south side of Sacramento Street, between Front and Davis.[18]

Vigilantes forcibly remove James Casey and Charles Cora from the county jail. Note cannon at right. From the *Illustrated London News*, July 12, 1856. William B. Secrest collection.

CHAPTER 6

"Cora and Casey Are Hanged!"

AFTER Casey and Cora[1] had been locked up, every night for nearly a week a thorough search was carried on in all parts of the city by large bodies of armed men, members of the Vigilance Committee, to discover the hiding place of Edward McGowan. My brother and I followed one party in their parade every night, with weapons, which we intended to give McGowan in case he was captured so that he could defend himself. We would also have rendered him any other assistance in our power, not because it was Ned McGowan, but because we were in favor of law and order and opposed to mob rule. In this manner I made myself very objectionable to the Vigilance Committee. I had many friends among them, some of whom desired me to leave the state during the excitement as I was causing much ill-feeling by my bitter animosity. These men detained the Oregon steamer here two days over time, thinking that they could persuade me to go on board and go to Oregon for a little while. But I would not listen to them and I continued to do everything in my power to prevent the committee from carrying out their intention in reference to Casey and Cora.

While these two men were in the custody of the committee, Belle Cora,[2] a woman who kept a house of disrepute on Waverly Place, and who came to California and was living with Charles Cora, was permitted to visit him, and while in his cell they were married. Charley Cora, although a gambler, was a quiet, unassuming man who never interfered with anybody. Previous to the killing of James King of William by Casey, Cora had been arrested by the authorities on a charge of murder for shooting General Richardson,[3] who was then United States Marshal. During the war between the United States and Mexico, Cora was the proprietor of a gambling house in Mexico and Richardson was connected with the game. After the war was ended Cora and Richardson came to California. Cora followed his old business of sporting and Richardson went to Marysville

118

Charles Cora, hanged with James Casey on May 22, 1856. William B.
Secrest collection.

where he engaged in business. Shortly after President Pierce went
into office he was appointed United States Marshal for California.
Cora and he appeared to be on friendly terms here until they got
into a dispute in a saloon known as the Blue Wing which was situated
on the east side of Montgomery, between Clay and Commercial
Streets, where Riddle's brick building now stands. I do not know
the original cause of the dispute,[4] but after conversing for a little
while they became very angry and talked in a loud tone of voice.
Richardson then said, "Let us not talk here. Come outside."

They went out together and walked slowly as far as the corner of Clay and Montgomery, when they turned down Clay about one hundred feet. This was between 9 and 10 o'clock at night. Some friends of both parties, who were aware of what had taken place in the saloon, followed at a short distance behind, to prevent if possible any serious difficulty. When Cora and Richardson had gone about one hundred feet on Clay Street below Montgomery, Richardson got Cora up against the door of a brick building, which still stands there, and the parties watching the pair heard him use very violent language toward Cora. It was so dark that only the forms of the two men could be distinguished from the corner. While Richardson was still talking in an abusive and threatening manner, the flash of a pistol was seen and a report sounded upon the night air. The friends in waiting rushed up to where Cora and Richardson had been standing and found the latter dead upon the sidewalk. Cora was arrested immediately and taken to the city prison. When questioned as to the cause of the shooting, Cora stated that Richardson had informed him, after they had stopped on Clay, that he had brought him (Cora) there to shoot him and he had attempted to carry out his intention when he was shot.

The death of Richardson created great excitement on account of the elevated position of the deceased. The people, of course, discriminated in his favor because the man who had shot him was a gambler. I was an intimate friend of both these men and I always found them to be quiet, good-natured fellows when they were in their sober senses. But I knew that Richardson was a very violent and dangerous man when under the influence of liquor, and he was intoxicated on the night of his death. It was known that Cora had endeavored to get away when Richardson started the row in the saloon but the latter held on to him.

In a short time after the shooting a great crowd of people had congregated on the corner of Clay and Montgomery Streets and were talking of breaking into the city prison and taking Cora out and hanging him. I did all I could to keep the people quiet, assuring them that justice would be done. They were finally persuaded to abandon their purpose of taking the law into their own hands. I then went down to Richardson's house, which was on Jessie Street, and saw his wife. I informed her, as delicately as I could, of what had happened, and then returned to the city hall, which was surrounded by people.

Cora was indicted for murder and tried in the Fourth District Court, and after a lengthy examination and argument on both sides, the case was given to the jury, which after being out for some time, returned and informed the judge that it was impossible for them to agree upon a verdict. The jury was accordingly discharged, Cora being present in the courtroom at the time. During the trial of the case an angry crowd of people was in constant attendance at the city hall and when the result was announced they became very much excited, and things began to assume an alarming aspect for the prisoner. Before leaving the courtroom, Sheriff Scannell, fearing that he could not take Cora safely to jail without assistance, summoned all his deputies and sent for me and ordered me to help him. With considerable difficulty we got through the crowd with the prisoner and locked him up in the county jail. Cora was defended on his trial by Colonel Baker,[5] one of the ablest lawyers California has ever seen. Before Cora could have another trial the Vigilance Committee was organized and took charge of him and Casey in the manner heretofore stated.

The Thursday after Casey and Cora were taken out of the county jail was the day set for the burial of King. The fire department was called out to parade in the funeral procession. The services were held in a church situated on the west side of Stockton Street, near Sacramento, which is now used by colored people as a place of worship. During the services in the church the companies forming the procession remained in position outside. The fire department was resting on Stockton Street, south of Sacramento. Some person on the corner of Sacramento and Stockton broke from the ranks and ran down Sacramento Street, shouting, "There they go! Cora and Casey are hanged!"

I did not believe what I had heard, because I thought that the Vigilance Committee certainly would not hang men while the funeral services of King were going on. I walked to the corner, however, and looking down Sacramento toward the committee rooms, I saw the bodies of two men hanging from the rafters which projected from the Vigilance Committee building. I ran down Sacramento Street but could not get any nearer to the building than Sansome Street, where a strong guard of the Vigilance Committee was stationed with fixed bayonets to prevent the passage of people. The sight of the two men hanging made me sad, and without saying a word to anybody I went to my rooms and remained there for the rest of the afternoon.

In one of the rarest photographic images of the California Gold Rush, the San Francisco vigilantes hang James Casey and Charles Cora at Fort Gunnybags, May 22, 1856. Their bodies can be seen dangling from the second story, third and fifth windows from the right. From original salt print by pioneer photographer George Fardon in collection of Joseph T. Silva.

I know that there were a great many good men in the original organization of the Vigilance Committee, but the hanging of Cora and Casey intimidated all the thieves and scoundrels in the state and they at once applied to the committee for membership to save their own necks. The committee, desiring to obtain all the strength possible, accepted all who applied for admission.

I do not dispute the fact that there was some ground for the Vigilance Committee here in 1856. Politics had become so corrupt that it was impossible to have anything like a fair election. It was a regular thing to elect men as supervisors whose names had not even been mentioned at the polls on election day, just as Casey had been elected. A few men controlled everything, and the votes of the mass of the people counted for nothing.[6] This system of deliberately depriving the citizens of their birthright was well calculated to arouse their indignation. The courts were sometimes appealed to but the result was not satisfactory, as a general thing. It was the same in the punishment of crimes committed in the course of political differences. But I want you to understand that this state of affairs in the courts was not caused by the negligence or dishonesty of the judges who presided there in those days. It was really the fault of the merchants themselves. They very seldom would serve on a jury and the consequence was that the sheriff picked up every loafer that was available, and with this class of material in the jury box it was not surprising that verdicts of guilty were few and far between.

But if we had an honest deputy sheriff to attend to the selection of juries things might have been different. Chris Dowdigan,[7] the deputy who had charge of that department in the sheriff's office, was a policeman in New York before his departure for California and he was more anxious for the interest of Dowdigan than he was for the welfare of the citizens of San Francisco. He generally waited until the day before "steamer day" when he knew the merchants would be very busy and he would then call around at every business place and summon the proprietor to appear on the next morning at the court for jury duty. Now it was impossible for the merchant to leave his store on steamer day without great loss to himself, and so if he could not dodge the sheriff, he would give him a "slug," or fifty dollars in present coin, and upon payment of the gold the considerate deputy sheriff would invariably let the merchant off. In this way Dowdigan would collect twelve or fifteen hundred dollars. Having failed to summon the merchants, he would then take any person he could find and the result was that the jury was not very select. Dowdegin could be found on the night after his raid on the merchants seated before some faro bank, bucking the tiger with the money that he had realized from his little game. This was really one of the causes of the Vigilance Committee.

At the time that Casey shot James King of William he [Casey] was foreman of Crescent Engine Company No. 10, the house of which stood on the north side of Pacific Street, between Kearny and Montgomery. The building is still standing in the same place. This company was one of the most efficient in the department. After Casey had been hung by the Vigilance Committee, Crescent Company asked the committee for his body, and its request was granted. Casey's remains were then removed to the engine house of the company and he was buried from there on the Sunday following his death. During the administration of George Hossefross, who was chief engineer the term previous to the one in which I was elected, a rule was established that the chief engineer should have charge of the burial of deceased firemen. On the occasion of Casey's burial, I was invited by the company to take charge of the funeral procession in the place of the chief engineer, James Nuttman, who did not make his appearance. I received several notices from members of the Vigilance Committee warning me not to take charge of the funeral ceremonies but I did not pay any attention to them.

The route of the funeral was up Pacific Street to Kearny, thence to Market, to Third, to Mission, thence on the Mission plank toll road across the bridge between Seventh and Eighth Streets to Sixteenth Street, and up Sixteenth Street to the old Mission cemetery on Dolores Street. I was late in arriving at the Crescent engine house and when I got there I found everything at a standstill. Upon inquiring the cause of this, I was informed that a great many men had been intimidated by the Vigilance Committee and were afraid to have anything to do with Casey's funeral. I immediately selected from among the members of the company present the requisite number of men to act as pallbearers and they then took up the coffin and carried it to the hearse, which stood outside the engine house.

The company had strenuously endeavored to obtain a band for the funeral procession but they could not induce any of the musicians here to turn out for love or money, and we therefore had to do without music. The coffin was profusely decorated with flowers and wreaths, which had been presented by the lady friends of the company. After the pallbearers had taken their places on each side of the hearse, I started the procession, which numbered about eight hundred men. The engine houses of those companies which were opposed to the Vigilance Committee floated a flag at half mast as the funeral passed. The sidewalks on the line of march were crowded with spectators. When the coffin had been placed in the grave dug for its reception, the space between the top of the casket and the level of the cemetery was soon filled with floral offerings and some members of the company were obliged to jump into the grave and stamp them down so as to make room for the dirt. The beautiful burial service of the Catholic Church was then read by a priest in attendance and the grave was filled. The people present did not form in line coming back but got to the city as quickly as possible.[8]

CHAPTER 7

Captured by the Vigilantes

A FEW days after Casey's funeral, it was announced on the streets
that Billy Mulligan,[1] Martin Gallagher,[2] Billy Carr,[3] Edward Bulger,[4]
and many others had been arrested by the Vigilance Committee and
taken to their rooms on Sacramento Street. When I was informed of
these arrests I was advised to cease my opposition to the Vigilance
Committee and was told that if I did not do so I also would be
arrested. I defied them to take me. I know now that this defiance on
my part was very foolish, but I was young and would rather sacrifice
my life than humble my pride by associating with them.

After the parties arrested had been incarcerated in the rooms of
the Vigilance Committee it was rumored that Yankee Sullivan had
either committed suicide or had been killed by the Vigilance Committee. This statement soon spread through the town and created
great excitement. I paid no attention to the rumor because I did not
believe that the committee had killed Sullivan and I did not have
much regard for him at any time.[5] But I soon received reliable
information that he was dead and that his body was at the morgue,
which was then situated on the south side of Sacramento Street,
between Kearny and Montgomery, where Gray's undertaking establishment now is. I immediately went there and saw Sullivan's body. I
found that the arteries in his left arm, near the elbow, had been
severed and the arm was nearly cut off.

There was a large crowd in attendance discussing the probable
cause of Sullivan's death. Some said that he had been poisoned by
the Vigilance Committee and others that he had committed suicide.
I wished to ascertain the real cause of his death and for that purpose
summoned Doctors Bowie and Sawyer to make an autopsy of the
body. Doctor Bowie was the leading physician in the state and
Doctor Sawyer was a young man of considerable ability. I knew that
they were both honorable men and that they would make a proper
investigation and report truthfully. They found, after an extended

Bare-knuckle champion James "Yankee" Sullivan. One of the greatest
sports heroes of the antebellum era, he died in vigilante custody in 1856.
Author's collection.

examination, that death had resulted from the wound on the left
arm but they could not tell what instrument had inflicted the fatal
wound. The case knife which Sullivan had used in his cell had been
brought to the morgue with the body and the doctors tried to cut
the flesh with it but found that it was impossible to do so. This
dissipated the theory of suicide in the minds of a great many, but it
has never been ascertained beyond doubt what weapon caused his
death, or by whom it was used. The friends of Sullivan have always
maintained that he was killed by a blow from a sword in the hands

of one Jessel, who had been whipped by Sullivan in New York in a street fight, and who was a guard in the Vigilance Committee's rooms at the time of his death. For a long time I was in doubt as to whether Sullivan had been killed by Jessel or not, but lately, after having talked with members of the Vigilance Committee, I have arrived at the conclusion that Sullivan committed suicide, influenced by the fear that he would be hung.[6]

After the examination by Doctors Bowie and Sawyer, the great crowd on the outside was allowed to enter at the Sacramento Street door and pass through around to Webb Street, viewing the body as they went. Fully 5,000 people passed through in this way. At the request of the friends of Sullivan and those opposed to the Vigilance Committee, who were known as the Law and Order Party, I took charge of the funeral arrangements for the burial of Sullivan.[7] He was to have been buried on the Sunday following his death, but I postponed the ceremony until Monday, for the reason that I intended, after Sullivan had been buried, to march those in attendance down to the Vigilance Committee rooms and capture their fort.

For some time previous to this I had been working quietly and had succeeded in organizing a small company of picked men, and if I had had an opportunity to carry out my intentions on the Monday that Sullivan was to have been buried I am satisfied that I would have been successful. But on the preceding Sunday, the day originally set for the funeral, as I was standing in Fisk & Loring's saloon, on the north side of Clay Street, between Kearny and Montgomery (Palmer, Cook & Co.'s building), I was approached by five or six men led by Joseph Capprise,[8] a man who was assistant engineer in the fire department under me, and whom I considered a warm personal friend of mine, although I knew him to be a member of the Vigilance Committee. He said, addressing me, "Hello, Chief. Come and take a drink."

I replied that I did not drink with any of his kind. I then walked to the door on the Clay Street side of the saloon and stood there for a little while. Capprise followed and wanted to argue with me about his position in joining the Vigilance Committee. He told me, in confidence, that the executive committee wanted me to go down to their rooms and have a talk with them. He said that they had been informed that on the following day (the time set for Sullivan's funeral) I intended to gather a mob and attack them. Capprise said that the committee was determined that I should go to their rooms and talk the matter over, and that they had elected him, as an intimate friend of mine, to ask me to go. He had full liberty to promise that no harm should come to me if I went with him.

I told him that I would not go and bow down to the Vigilance Committee. As I said this, I noticed that he raised his right hand above his head and snapped his fingers. My suspicions were aroused by this action and I asked him what it meant. While he was explaining, the large triangular gong which was rigged on top of the Vigilance Committee rooms sounded and men issued forth on the street all around from the stairs and doorways. As soon as they got out in the street they rushed toward me with drawn pistols. I was not armed at the time, but my rooms were situated upstairs over the saloon where I was and I started through the saloon with the intention of going up to my rooms by the back way to get my arms.

The men who had accompanied Capprise were still in the saloon and attempted to stop me as I ran through, but I scared them off and succeeded in getting out of the saloon and reached the Merchant Street entrance to my rooms, only to find the stairs occupied by a crowd of Vigilance Committee men, all of whom were armed with revolvers. When I found that it was impossible for me to reach my rooms I ran across Merchant Street, intending to go to the police station in the city hall and there obtain arms. On reaching the courtyard of the city hall I found the place filled with members of the Vigilance Committee and policemen, who were acting with them. They surrounded me and, after a struggle in which they all tried to take part, as many as could get a place to hang on grabbed me and dragged me down Merchant Street to Montgomery, along Montgomery to Sacramento, and down Sacramento to the rooms of the Vigilance Committee. There were at least five thousand people in the mob around me. Those who were near enough tore my clothes and abused me as much as they could. Some person tore the front of my shirt out and got a handsome scarf pin valued at one thousand dollars. The pin, I will state, was never returned to me.[9]

On arriving at the Vigilance Committee rooms I was dragged upstairs and placed in a small room opposite the large drill hall which was fitted up as a cell. There was a guard of four men in this room day and night, and the door was never shut. Two men with cocked revolvers sat inside with me and two more armed with muskets and fixed bayonets stood guard on the outside of the door. These guards were relieved every hour or two and their places filled

Fort Gunnybags, headquarters of the vigilantes in 1856. The alarm bell on the roof and the gunnybag fortifications can be clearly seen. William B. Secrest collection.

by fresh men. I remained in that cell four days and during that time nothing in the shape of food, with the exception of two boiled eggs, passed my lips. I refused to eat what they brought me because I was afraid of being poisoned.[10] At the time I ate the eggs there were three handed to me, but as the shell of one was cracked, I would not taste it. I was very much surprised when the time for general drill came on the first day to find among the members of the Vigilance Committee drilling a great many men who were personal friends of mine and who had led me to believe that they belonged to the Law and Order party and were opposed to the Committee of Vigilance. Richard Jessup[11] and Captain Burns,[12] late harbor commissioner, composed the visiting committee and were required to visit the cells every day. They called on me in the room every few hours and treated me kindly but I would not give them even a civil answer. The guards who stood watch over me also treated me well all the time and professed to sympathize with me.

On the third day after my confinement one of the guards on the inside told the other that he would like to speak a few words privately to me and asked him to step out, which he did. The guard who had made the request then stated to me that a certain young lady, mentioning her name, had induced him to join the Vigilance Committee so that he could aid me and that he had succeeded in being appointed a guard over me. He also stated that this young lady had got her father to join the committee and that if I would only remain quiet I would be all right.

I was arrested on the 1st of June 1856 and on the night of the 4th my brother John was permitted to come and see me. When he came into my cell, the guards remained in the room and when I requested them to retire they said that it was against the rules to allow any outsider to converse with a prisoner except in the presence of the guards. I then informed them that my brother had come to me with a message from the lady to whom I was engaged to be married and they certainly did not wish to hear the conversation. After a short consultation they agreed to permit my brother to speak to me in private for a couple of minutes. When the guards had stepped outside John told me that Dr. Ashe,[13] then Naval agent, Judge David S. Terry of the Supreme Court, and others had sent him to tell me to promise the Vigilance Committee to do anything they asked me, so as to get out of the committee rooms, as the captain of the man-of-war which lay in the harbor was going to turn his guns on the building the next morning if the Vigilance Committee did not surrender. I told my brother that I would not do as my friends advised. I then asked the guard to allow my brother to get me something to eat. They, not having the power, went to headquarters, and John was granted permission to bring me a meal, which he did.

The next morning, between the hours of two and three o'clock, two men stepped into my cell, and one of them had a pair of handcuffs which he proceeded to fasten upon my wrists. They then left the room and three other men came in, one of whom was Thomas J. Smiley,[14] then vice-president of the Vigilance Committee. Smiley read a document to me which was in substance as follows: "You must leave the state of California and if you ever return it will be under the penalty of death."

I did not comprehend the words at first and I asked Smiley to read them again, but he replied, "No, I will not."

He was about to leave the room when I told him that unless the document was read again I would not consider it binding, as I did not understand it. One of the men with him asked him to grant my request and he then read it again. About half an hour after this three or four armed men came into the cell and one of them told me to get up and go out with them. They took me out of the building by a rear passage and placed me in a hollow square formed by a military company, which was commanded by Charles Gough,[15] now a deputy license collector. He had been a member of Vigilant Engine Company No. 9 in the fire department and had always professed to be a friend of mine. I was very violent, although being in irons, and used some pretty strong language to those around me. Gough came up to me and said, "Chief, old boy, keep quiet. Your life depends on it, and I am your friend."

He then gave the order, "Forward," and they marched me along Front or Davis Street to Market and down Market Street to the harbor. We found a French company drilling on the wharf when we arrived there. Gough's company left me on the outer edge of the wharf and marched back, leaving the French company to stand guard over me. The latter company kept on drilling, and as I could not understand the French language I thought that I was going to be shot by them. I afterward learned that they asked for the privilege of shooting me but the Vigilance Committee denied their request. Their enmity toward me was caused by my action at the banquet where the Malakoff tower was stormed.[16]

The majority of foreigners here, with the exception of the Irish, joined the Vigilance Committee. There were only about eight or ten Irishmen in the organization.[17] When I had made up my mind that I was to be shot, I put my arms in such a position that my heart would be guarded. My reason for doing this was that I did not wish to die instantly. I wanted to tell them what I thought of them after I had been shot. I stood in this position until my arms were tired and I was obliged to drop them. I then moved slowly to the extreme edge of the wharf so that I could throw myself overboard when the Frenchmen leveled their guns at me. I was a good swimmer and was satisfied that, although being ironed, I could get in under the wharf and cling to one of the piles. It was a very dark night but I could see the glitter of the bayonets by the lights of the ships in the harbor and I was anxiously waiting for them to "present arms." While I was thus waiting, I heard something puffing along by the wharf, and looking around I saw a steamer making fast and the gang plank placed on the wharf.

When the steamer had made fast, Captain Ellis[18] came upon the wharf, accompanied by several members of the military company which he commanded, and walked over to where I stood. He told me that he commanded a company which was then on the steam tug and that he had been ordered to take charge of me. He then gave the order to his men and they took me on board the tug, which was in charge of Captain Goodall,[19] of the firm of Goodall, Perkins & Co., and I was immediately surrounded by a strong guard. While I was wondering what this latest move on the part of the Vigilance Committee meant, I heard the measured tramp of soldiers[20] on the wharf and soon Billy Mulligan, Edward Bulger, Martin Gallagher, Billy Carr, and Woolly Kearney[21] were escorted on board by a squad from Captain Ellis's company.

Just as the day began to dawn, the tug moved away from the wharf and made fast to a large clipper ship lying out in the stream. Our course was then turned toward the Golden Gate. On the way out one of the guards told me that he had overheard a discussion which had taken place in the Vigilance Committee rooms the night before, the subject under discussion being a proposition suggested by a member of the Executive Committee to send away the prisoners then confined upon an old vessel and have her scuttled when we got out to sea. My informant did not know the result of the discussion but he was of the opinion that the ship which the tug was then

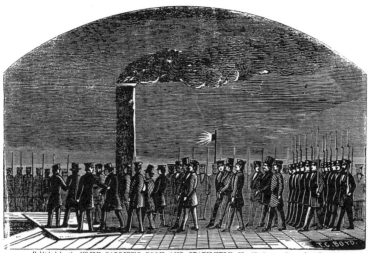

SHIPMENT OF THE PRISONERS.

Charles P. Duane, Martin Gallagher, Billy Mulligan, Wm. Carr, Edward Bulger and Woolly Kearny, sent from the country, by the "Vigilance Committee of San Francisco," at two o'clock, A. M., June 5th, 1856.

In an 1856 lettersheet engraving, Charley Duane is depicted, in top hat at right, being escorted by vigilantes to the steam tug *Hercules*. Dutch Charley and five fellow political ruffians were all deported from California at the same time. Robert Limacher collection.

towing was too fine to be destroyed in the manner proposed. He professed great sympathy for me, but did not know how he could benefit me in the matter. I asked him to show his good feeling by getting the key of the prisoners' irons in his possession and opening my handcuffs when we had reached the Heads, or whenever he thought the time for scuttling was at hand. I would then liberate the hands of my fellow prisoners and we could strike out for our lives. The guard, after some hesitation, agreed to grant my request, and as we got out to sea I informed Mulligan and Gallagher of the arrangement that I had made to obtain possession of the key to our handcuffs. I did not tell any of the other prisoners of my programme because I was afraid that they would expose the matter to benefit themselves.

Shortly after we passed through the Golden Gate, the majority of the soldiers on board the tug became very seasick and their sufferings turned their attention from us entirely. The guard who had promised me the key was very ill, and I went over and asked him to give it to me. He said that he had been unable to get it and he was too sick to make any further attempt. Bulger was the only man among the company who was affected by the rolling waves and if I had only succeeded in obtaining the key which would unlock our irons I would have thrown all of the guns overboard and then, after putting Captains Goodall and Ellis in irons, run the tug ashore on the rocks at the first available place and let each man scramble for himself. I could have accomplished this easily, as the soldiers were too sick to offer any resistance.[22]

At six o'clock in the morning we were about eight miles outside of the heads. The tug then stopped and in a short time the bark *Yankee*, owned by J.B. Post & Brothers, prominent members of the Vigilance Committee, hove in sight and she was hailed by Captain Goodall. Gallagher, Bulger, and Carr were then placed in a small boat and rowed out to the bark and they were taken on board the vessel, which was bound for the Sandwich Islands. Mulligan, Kearney, and I were left on board the tug, which remained where it had hailed the *Yankee* until four o'clock in the afternoon, when the steamship *Golden Age* came out. As soon as she was sighted we were placed in a small boat and were soon aboard the steamer. When the boat from the tug had left the *Golden Age* our handcuffs were taken off and we were ordered to go into the steerage. The vessel was greatly overcrowded and of course there were no bunks for us so we were obliged to sleep wherever we could get a soft place to lie on.

As I walked around the steerage deck during the afternoon, I noticed that the people seemed anxious to avoid me. When I would go to one side of the vessel for the purpose of looking over, the passengers would rush to the other side. As soon as I found that they did really wish to keep away from me, I continued to walk from side to side, just for the fun of seeing them rush back and forth. In this way I had considerable amusement because they would rush so suddenly that the ship would keel over. This, of course, annoyed the captain, and anything which caused annoyance to those assisting in my banishment pleased me.

Governor McDougal, ex-Alderman Corser of the First Ward, and many others of my acquaintance were on board the steamer, bound for Panama. When I had been in the steerage a couple of hours, Governor McDougal came down and insisted upon me returning to his stateroom in the first cabin. I finally consented, and when we had reached there he made me lie down in his berth, which was very inviting as I had not slept much during the preceding four days. I was sleeping soundly a minute after my head touched the pillow. After a very refreshing rest I awoke to find that my friend McDougal had had considerable trouble on my account. As soon as the captain found that I was in his stateroom, he called upon the Governor and informed him that I would have to go in the steerage. Governor McDougal said that his stateroom was his house for the time being and he would defend it with his life, and whoever attempted to interfere with me in his room would have to take the consequences. He stood at the door of his stateroom with a cocked revolver in his hand and protected me while I slept.

Of course when I ascertained the condition of affairs I would not listen to McDougal's invitation to remain where I was because I did not want him to get into any trouble through me. Finding it impossible to keep me with him, he gave me some blankets and a pillow and I returned to the steerage. I had settled myself comfortably on the floor and was again courting nature's restorer when I was aroused by a cabin waiter who informed me that Watson, the purser, had sent him for the blankets and pillow which McDougal had given me. The man was obliged to obey orders but he was kindhearted and he let me keep the pillow and took the pillowcase and blankets. I managed to sleep very well, however, without covering.

Messrs. Hooley[23] and Eph Horn,[24] the minstrels, were among the passengers and they came down to the steerage one evening and took me to their stateroom without the knowledge of anybody on board. When the steamer stopped at Acapulco, all the passengers with the exception of Mulligan, Kearney, and I were allowed to go on shore. I asked Governor McDougal to go and make arrangements with somebody in Acapulco to have a small boat in the rear of the steamer as she started off so that I could jump overboard and be picked up. He went to see about it but soon returned and said that he would not do it because he had been informed by the American consul and others that it was almost certain death for any person to jump overboard in those waters on account of the great number of sharks floating around. I was very much discouraged when I heard this, but I set about to find some other means to gain the shore, as I was determined to land. The minstrels proposed that I should blacken

Duane's friend Billy Mulligan was notorious both in New York City and in San Francisco. The vigilantes deported him from California in 1856. William B. Secrest collection.

my face as a Negro and pass the guard on the gangplank in that disguise, but I was afraid it would not work.

Mr. Corser finally loaned me a blue coat with brass buttons and a large slouch hat, and after putting these on, I armed myself with a Bowie knife and rushed through the crowd down the gangplank. The deckhands were engaged in transferring some chickens from a scow which stood alongside the steamer, and having the slouch hat pulled down over my face, they did not recognize me. I ran along the side of the scow and jumped into a canoe which drifted near and told the man who was in it to pull for shore as fast as he could. He, thinking that I was a thief who had just got some plunder from the steamship, exerted every muscle, and I was on shore before my absence from the vessel was discovered.

I remained in the outskirts of town for two or three hours after the departure of the *Golden Age* and at the end of that time called upon the American consul. I was very agreeably surprised to find in him an old New York friend and he gave me a very warm and hearty reception. After I had told him the story of my grievances, he arranged a couch for me next to his own in the house, which served him for office and dwelling place.

The next morning, while I was still in bed, two Jewish merchants who had previously been engaged in business in San Francisco, entered the room, and in the course of conversation with the consul, gave him the history of the doings of the Vigilance Committee in this city. During the recital one of them said that the Vigilance Committee was running everything to suit themselves and they had sent away the notorious Charley Duane and that he was then on his way to Panama on the *Golden Age*. The consul looked at me and smiled and I remained quiet and took it all in. They boasted that they were members of the Committee, and seemed to take great pleasure in talking against me. After the consul had finished questioning them, I got up out of bed, and winking at him, I advanced toward the brave vigilantes, Bowie knife in hand. I assumed a very threatening manner and in a loud voice said, "So you have sent Charley Duane away, eh? Now, then, you have had your day. This is mine. Prepare for immediate death."

The men, who had recognized me the moment they saw me, fell upon their knees and begged for their lives. Of course, I did not intend to do them any harm and their position was so ridiculous and inconsistent with their talk of a few moments before that the Consul and I could not refrain from laughing. When they had recovered from their scare, they became very friendly with me. They were then on their way to the City of Mexico with some silks and other valuable merchandise. They wanted me to accompany them and I agreed to do so. Two days after, we started on our travels. When we had gone about three miles, my mule stopped suddenly and all my efforts

Members of the Committee of Vigilance in 1856. They are wearing state militia uniforms. Author's collection.

failed to make him move. The merchants wanted to send back for another animal for me but I decided not to go as long as the one I was on refused, and bidding my friends goodbye, I returned to Acapulco. I regarded the mule's refusal to go on the journey as a kind of forewarning of danger but I found out on my return that the brute had been trained by his owners to go so far and no farther. It was lucky for me, however, that I did not keep on the journey, for I afterward learned that the traders had been robbed of their valuable merchandise and then killed by some Mexican highwaymen.

CHAPTER 8

Exiled to Panama and New York

SHORTLY after my return to Acapulco I was stricken down with yellow fever and remained dangerously ill for eleven days. At the end of that time I was able to get around again and I anxiously awaited the arrival of a vessel bound for San Francisco. The first one that put in an appearance was the *John L. Stephens,* under the charge of Captain Pearson,[1] and I went aboard as soon as possible and remained there. She stopped at Acapulco about four hours and then got under way again. I had no money to pay my passage but I met United States Circuit Judge McAllister[2] on board, and when the ship had been about half a day out he went with me to the purser's office to purchase a first class passage ticket to San Francisco for me. The purser went to see Captain Pearson about the matter and he ordered him not to take any fare from me. He had seen the 'Frisco papers at Acapulco and knew all about my trouble with the Vigilance Committee.

Charles Scott, the first country treasurer of this city, was also on board, and he took me to the cabin to have dinner. When Captain Pearson heard about it, he came in and said I should have to go in the steerage. Scott said that I should not go in the steerage and he got up from the cabin table and made me sit in his seat. The servants, by order of Captain Pearson, would not wait on me and Mr. Scott stood behind my chair and helped me to everything. Of course Judge McAllister and Mr. Scott told the other passengers the story of my wrongs and the majority of them did everything they could to make me comfortable.[3]

They kept me in the cabin and matters progressed very favorably until we were within three days' sail of this city when we sighted the steamer *Sonora* bound for Panama. Captain Pearson hailed her and when she stopped he went over from his vessel in a small boat and went on board. In a short time he returned and informed me that he was going to send me back. When they got ready to transfer me to the *Sonora* they were unable to find me, as I had secreted myself under the lifeboat on the upper deck. A thorough search was instituted, and after looking all over the vessel in vain, someone of the crew turned the lifeboat and discovered me. With a cry of, "Here he is," the whole crew rushed toward me but before they reached the boat I had slipped down on the other deck and ran into the toilet room and bolted the door after me. The crowd soon found me and after demanding an entrance and receiving no answer, they proceeded to break in the door.

While they were thus engaged, I got out of a back window and slid down on the lower deck into the cattle pen. Several Mexican steers were confined therein and as I got inside the railing one large beast made a rush at me and enclosed my body between his wide horns, which fastened themselves in the railings on each side of me. I immediately seized the horns and jumped upon the infuriated animal's back and succeeded in getting over the railing on the other side. I then ran up on the promenade deck where the ladies formed a circle with me sitting upon a stool in the middle. This concealed me effectually.

In the meantime the captain and the crew were hunting all over the vessel for me, and many were of the opinion that I had jumped overboard when I went out of the toilet room window. They did not see how I could have jumped anywhere else. Captain Pearson, although not able to find me, would not let the ship proceed on its way, and Judge McAllister, after vainly pleading for me, came to me and said, "Mr. Duane, Captain Pearson is determined not to go any further until he puts you off the vessel, so you had better not resist him. If you hurt anybody aboard, he will hang you to the yard-arm, sure. I have no authority over him on the high seas. I advise you not to go off this ship willingly, but allow yourself to be taken. They have the power to take you."

I took his advice, and putting away my Bowie knife, I gave myself up. As soon as the crew saw that I did not have my weapons they rushed at me with as much vigor and handled me as roughly as the Vigilance Committee had done in San Francisco. Every one seemed to be anxious to take me single handed and the result was that as many as could caught hold of me. As they were taking me down the step ladder, Judge McAllister cried out at the top of his voice, "Captain Pearson, I shall hold you responsible for this gross outrage on the high seas."[4]

Captain Pearson did not reply, but he and his crew dragged me into a boat and rowed over and forced me on board the *Sonora*. Richard Whiting was captain of the *Sonora* and was a good friend of mine. I traveled on his steamer as far as Panama. Before we reached there he gave me a letter to the agent of the steamship company at Aspinwall asking him to give me a passage to New York. We sighted Panama on the morning of the 4th of July 1856, and I was taken on shore in a small boat by Martin Bulger, late superintendent of the Pacific Mail Steamship Company and now president of the Exempt Fire Company.

That night, as I was sitting in the parlor of the hotel, the building was surrounded by a squad of Panama soldiers and five officers came into the room, accompanied by an interpreter. The latter informed me that the object of the visit was to place me under arrest. The military officers had heard the story of my troubles in San Francisco but they looked upon the whole thing as a mere pretense by means of which I would endeavor to establish myself in Panama to scheme against their government. They said they knew that about a month before the time I had left San Francisco, I had organized a body of two hundred men for the purpose of going to Panama and protecting Americans in their troubles on the Isthmus. It was true that I had organized a company for the protection of Americans on the Isthmus of Panama, as several of them had been killed while crossing. This was before the organization of the Vigilance Committee.[5] Of course, I could not afford to admit this to the Panama authorities, but I sent downstairs for a basket of champagne, and while the sparkling beverage was being passed around I told my story, relating all the particulars of my capture and banishment by the Vigilance Committee. I succeed in convincing them that I was telling the truth and when I had finished my recital, they instructed the interpreter to convey their expression of sympathy to me, and after drinking all the champagne on hand they took their departure. Before going, however, they invited me to visit the fort the next day and insisted upon my acceptance of the invitation. Of course I did not dare to refuse, although I thought that their intention was to lock me up after I got in.

About 11 o'clock the next morning I called at the military headquarters and was very kindly received by the officers who had waited on me the evening before. They showed me all around and treated me with the utmost respect and courtesy. After leaving the fort I visited Mr. Ward, the American consul, and asked him to purchase a ticket for me on some steamer which was bound for San Francisco. I had borrowed money from a friend whom I met in Panama but the agents of the steamship companies there refused to sell me a ticket to the city. Mr. Ward interviewed the agents of all the lines and did everything in his power to induce them to take me on one of their steamers but they steadily refused and he had to give it up. When he informed me that it was useless to endeavor to obtain passage from Panama I resolved to try the Nicaragua line, and accordingly went to Aspinwall and took the English steamer *Dee* to Graytown. When I arrived there I found that the Nicaragua company had decided to give up the business and the last steamer on that line, which was the *Tennessee*, had left for San Francisco two days before my arrival in Graytown.

General Walker[6] and his army were encamped about twelve miles from the latter place, and when he heard that I was in town he sent two of his officers to request me to join his expedition. I declined to do so and he then offered me the position of second in command, but I still refused, telling him that my only reason for so doing was because I could not afford to take any chances of being killed until I had sustained my character in San Francisco. I then went to Aspin-wall and presented the letter which Captain Whiting of the *Sonora* had given me to the agent of the steamship company there, whose vessels ran to New York City. The agent treated me very kindly, gave me a through ticket and assigned me to a stateroom on board of a steamer which was to leave for New York that evening. About an hour before the time for the vessel to start the agent came to me and said that I would have to go ashore. I asked him what had caused him to change his mind in reference to me so suddenly, and he replied that his reasons were best known to himself. He would not give me any other explanation of his conduct and I became very angry and informed him that I had a ticket which entitled me to a passage on that steamer, and I intended to remain where I was until I landed in New York City. He left my stateroom with an intimation that I would soon be on shore and in a short time he came on board again, accompanied by twenty or thirty coalheavers. I saw them coming on board and sprang to the door of my stateroom.

The agent pointed at me and said, "There he is, boys. Drag him out and put him ashore."

They advanced toward me and I, drawing my Bowie knife, said, "Boys, listen to me for one moment. I have been persecuted about as much as I intend to be, and I am going to sell my life as dearly as possible. I will certainly kill the first man who enters this room, and as many as I can while my life lasts."

I explained all about my troubles with the Vigilance Committee in San Francisco and when I had concluded the men seemed to sympathize with me, and the leader, turning to the agent, told him to put me off the steamer himself if he wanted to; they would not do it. They all wanted to shake me by the hand but I would not let any of them do so, for fear that they would pull me out of the doorway of the stateroom. As they went on shore again, the agent remained looking at me, undecided as to what course he should pursue. I noticed his hesitation and told him that he had better not try to put me off the steamer as the Isthmus was not large enough for him and me, and one or the other of us would have to suffer. He then left and in a short time the captain of the steamer, an old navy officer, came to my stateroom. He said that he had heard of me before that day, and as those who had spoken to him were esteemed mutual friends, he did not wish to see me get into any trouble. He said that he was captain of the steamer but she was not under his control until she left the wharf, and therefore he could not interfere in the controversy between the agent and myself.

"There is only one way," said the captain, "in which I can settle this matter, and that is by giving you a ticket which will entitle you to a passage on a steamer lying on the other side of the wharf and which leaves for New York via New Orleans at the same time we do tonight."

He advised me to accept this proposition and I told him I would do so on the condition that he would ascertain for me the reason why the agent refused me a passage on his steamer. He said that the people on board objected to traveling with me. I then asked him to give me the names of those who objected and I would then go ashore. He replied, "Certainly I will, Duane. I think it is only fair that you should know that."

He started to get the names of the passengers, and looking out of my stateroom, I saw that the first persons whom he approached were Wheatleigh,[7] the actor, and his wife. Now, I had been very good to Wheatleigh in San Francisco, having arranged a benefit for him and all that sort of thing, and it surprised me very much to find him so ungrateful. When the captain asked him for his name and that of the other passengers who refused to travel with Mr. Duane, he refused to give it, as did all the others, and they hurried off to their staterooms. When the captain found that the virtuously indignant passengers would not give him their names, he returned to my stateroom, and shaking me by the hand, said, "Duane, I believe that you are a great deal better man than those who talk about you, and you shall travel to New York with me. I am able to protect the passengers and you, too."

The agent did not trouble me again and in a short time we started. Ned Batturs,[8] at present deputy assessor, and his brother were on board. During the voyage there was considerable disturbance between the passengers and the captain over the food furnished. I took the side of the captain and we succeeded in bringing the passengers to their senses.

Upon my arrival in New York City, after visiting my friends, I went to the office of a steamship company to purchase a ticket for San Francisco. My friends, Daniel E. Sickles and Tom Hyer, persuaded me to remain in New York until after the presidential election, which was to come off in a short time. They said that they would then send me to San Francisco with a government position, which would prevent any further trouble with the Vigilance Committee, as they would not dare to interfere with a United States officer.

I think it is now my duty to explain a plot to assassinate William T. Coleman,[9] president of the Committee, which was arranged in New York shortly after my arrival there, and while Mr. Coleman was in that city. I made a solemn promise before I was informed of the plot that if I did not agree to assist in it, I would keep the secret. I did not enter into it but I kept my promise in regard to secrecy until I was informed about two years ago by Ned McGowan that the men who had originated the plot had told him all about it. I consider that that fact relieves me of my promise in the matter.

The arrangement was as follows. I was stopping at the Metropolitan Hotel in New York City and one afternoon while I was in the reading room a man by the name of Rube Maloney,[10] one of the parties who had been sent away from here by the Vigilance Committee, came in and invited me to go downstairs with him and drink a glass of wine. We went down to the barroom and upon my entrance I found six or seven men, all of whom had been sent away from California by the Vigilance Committee. They were accompanied by a number of friends. We took a drink and before I had drained my glass I noticed that chairs had been placed over in one corner of the

William T. Coleman, leader of the vigilantes. Author's collection.

room and that my companions had gone over to them and left me quite alone. They consulted together for some time while I stood at the bar, very much surprised, and not knowing what to make of this strange proceeding. I finally heard one of them say, "It is of no use. It will not do."

Rube Maloney replied, "Yes, by [God], he will," at the same time rising from his seat and advancing toward me. He then stated to me that they had a little matter under consideration in which they wanted my assistance. I went over and sat down with them. After being sworn to secrecy, I was informed that a plot had been concocted and everything arranged to kill William T. Coleman. The man to do the work had already been selected and Coleman was to be assassinated on the Bloomingdale Road. The man chosen to do the bloody work was Johnny Franklin, an old partner and friend of Chris Lilly,[11] one of the men who had been sent away from California. A man who was considered very respectable was chosen to swear an alibi for Franklin in case he was arrested for the crime. I do not wish to give his name because he has a daughter and it might injure her. I would not have been let into the secret had it not been that Franklin wanted me to go with him when he was to do the work. When the proposition was stated to me I arose from my chair and said, "If a hair in Coleman's head is harmed I will expose the whole plot."

At this declaration, Billy Mulligan jumped up and said he would stand by me. He was in favor of giving Coleman and every other member of the Vigilance Committee a good, sound thrashing,[12] but he would not agree to his assassination nor take any part in it. This broke up the party. I think that Coleman heard of my conduct because he sent for me several times afterward and I finally called at his office where I was treated very cordially by him, but nothing was said about this matter.

While I was in New York, Miers Truett[13] and other members of the Vigilance Committee arrived there. As soon as I heard that they were in town I went before one of the supreme judges and swore to a warrant for their arrest for their actions while members of the Vigilance Committee. When Truett learned that the warrant was out for him he immediately took passage on board a steamer about to leave for San Francisco and stowed himself away in the baggage room. I knew every move he made, however, and I went on the steamer with the officer who had the warrant.

There was a large crowd on the wharf when we got there and when they discovered that we were looking for a member of the Vigilance Committee of San Francisco they became very much interested and determined to mob him as soon as they caught sight of him. After a long search on the vessel I found him, and then we experienced considerable difficulty in conducting him safely to Eldridge Street jail, where we finally locked him up. When he had been in there about three days, C.K. Garrison, formerly mayor of San Francisco, called on me at the Metropolitan Hotel and informed me that Truett had asked him to go on his bond, but that he would not do so unless I was willing that he should. I told him that I had no objection to his going on Truett's bond, as I did not desire to keep him in jail until after he had been tried.

This was some time before the inauguration of President Buchanan. I went to Washington to see United States Senator Broderick take his seat, and occupied a chair next to him on the floor of the Senate. The day after the inauguration I was poisoned at the National Hotel. Nearly everybody at the hotel was poisoned, by means of drinking water which had passed through corroded lead pipes, and a great many died. I remained in bed for two and one-half years and became paralyzed. That is the cause of my lameness.

Of course I could not return to New York to prosecute Truett and the others who had been arrested at my desire, and they were discharged. While I was in New York, Trenor W. Park,[14] a member of the Vigilance Committee, arrived in town. This was in the summer of 1856. I was in the barroom of the St. Nicholas Hotel when Park came in, accompanied by Rube Maloney. The saloon was very large and a great many of Maloney's friends, including many men who had been sent away by the Vigilance Committee, were there. As Maloney passed me, he winked and pointed at Park. He then invited us all to take a drink, and I stood at the bar next to Park. As he was about to raise the glass of liquor to his lips, a man put a pistol to his side. I immediately knocked the man's arm away, and placing Park behind me, I backed clear across the long saloon until we reached the office of the hotel. I asked him if he was stopping there. He replied in the affirmative, and I then told him to go to his room immediately and to remain there until he was ready to leave town, as he would surely be killed if he appeared on the streets. He took my advice and I have never seen him since.

When I placed myself in front of Park, the man who would have killed him, but for my interference, leveled his pistol at me, and Maloney and others threatened to kill me unless I got out of the way, but they did not dare to do it. Maloney and those men always hated me for my actions in protecting the lives of members of the Vigilance Committee in New York, and they used to tell people that I was a traitor because I would not stand in to murder men. I do not know whether the members of the Vigilance Committee feel proud of their record, but I certainly do of mine.

CHAPTER 9

Judge Terry and the Vigilantes

IN THE month of June 1856, after the Vigilance Committee had taken possession of the county jail and confiscated all the arms that they could lay their hands upon, General Sherman,[1] who was then a banker in this city and major general of the state militia, came to the conclusion that if he had a sufficient quantity of arms and ammunition to supply the Law and Order party men with, he could break up the organization of the Vigilance Committee and maintain the dignity of the law. In accordance with this idea he chartered a vessel and dispatched several members of the Law and Order party, among whom were Rube Maloney, John Phillips, Deputy County Treasurer under Robert Woods, and James McNabb to Benecia with a letter addressed to General Wool of the regular army of the United States, asking for all the guns and ammunition that he could possibly spare. They reached Benecia without interference and presented the letter to General Wool, who after a little consideration, granted the request of General Sherman and gave them an order for the weapons. Having secured all that they could, they started on their homeward trip, and while sailing along in San Pablo Bay the Law and Order party were considerably surprised to see a heavy vessel come up alongside their craft and order them to "heave to."

The schooner which Sherman had chartered was a very light one and was not built to stand a battle, and as the vessel of their party looked rather formidable, the volunteer army considered discretion to be the better part of valor and therefore promptly obeyed the summons to stop. As soon as they had come to a standstill they were informed that the other boat was the property of the Vigilance Committee and working under its orders and they were commanded to surrender the arms on board their schooner and deliver themselves up as prisoners. Resistance was useless against such superior numbers and after a short consultation Sherman's party yielded and was conveyed in a small boat to the vessel of the Vigilance Committee.

The arms and ammunition were then transferred, after which the schooner was scuttled and left to sink.[2]

The Vigilance Committee's vessel, which was under the command of John L. Durkee,[3] the present fire marshal, then started for this city with the prisoners and plunder and landed at Sacramento Street wharf where the Law and Order men were released from custody with a solemn warning that if any one of them said a word about what had happened in San Pablo Bay he would be arrested and punished by the Vigilance Committee.

Shortly after this Durkee and his company were arrested by the United States Marshal on a charge of piracy and were tried before Judge McAllister of the United States Circuit Court. The judge was satisfied of the guilt of the defendants, for it was clearly proven, but as the crime charged had been committed in San Pablo Bay, within the jurisdiction of the state law and not on the high seas, he did not see any way for him to interfere. This fact alone saved Durkee and the others implicated with him from a severe sentence, as piracy is, of course, a very grievous offense against the United States laws. When General Sherman found that it was impossible for him to do anything, owing to his inability to obtain the necessary weapons of war, he resigned his position as chief in command of the state militia and was succeeded by Volney E. Howard.[4]

In the meantime, Rube Maloney, who was very prominent among the opponents of the Vigilance Committee, had told several parties about the piracy in San Pablo Bay and he became very bitter in his denunciation of those who had taken part in that attack. The Executive Committee of the Vigilance Committee heard of this and they issued an order for Maloney's arrest and placed the warrant in the hands of a man named Hopkins[5] to serve. He started out, accompanied by a posse of six members of the Committee, armed with the order, and he found Maloney in Dr. Ashe's office, which was then in the rooms over Palmer, Cook & Co.'s bank, on the corner of Washington and Kearny Streets, under the protection of Dr. Ashe, David S. Terry,[6] and others. Dr. Ashe was the Naval Officer of the Pacific Coast and David S. Terry was then Chief Justice of the Supreme Court and a very intimate friend of the doctor's.

At the time that the arresting party arrived to take Maloney, Judge Terry was in Ashe's office. When the doctor was informed of the object of his visitors, he told Hopkins that no person should be arrested out of his office except by legal authority, and Judge Terry

David S. Terry, chief justice of the California Supreme Court and one of the most prominent opponents of the vigilance committee in 1856. William B. Secrest collection.

backed him in his assertion, declaring the whole affair an outrage, and as Chief Justice of the Supreme Court he warned Hopkins not to arrest Maloney. The Vigilance Committee men were finally compelled to leave the office without their prisoner. Hopkins left with the exclamation, "I will show you whether I arrest him or not," and soon the gong on top of the Committee's room on Sacramento Street was sounded.

Rube Maloney was very much frightened and he asked Judge Terry, Dr. Ashe, Martin Reese, and others who were in the office to accompany him to one of the armories of the state militia, which was located on the corner of Dupont and Pacific Streets. Judge Terry announced his willingness to assist any citizen in his rights against mob law and told Maloney that he, as an officer of the law, would defend him at the risk of his life. He and the others in the office then started with Maloney. They went down Kearny Street to Jackson and turned up Jackson. When they had reached a point about half way up the block, a large body of Vigilance Committee men, with Hopkins at their head, rushed upon their party. Hopkins, with pistol in hand, immediately attacked Judge Terry and caught him by the throat. The judge, after vainly trying to shake his assailant off, drew a Bowie knife and plunged it into Hopkins, who then let go his hold and fell upon the ground. As soon as their leader fell, the vigilante crowd became demoralized and they scattered in all directions, while Terry and his friends continued on their way and conducted Maloney in safety to the armory.

Shortly after this the Vigilance Committee gathered in large numbers, surrounded the building, and with their cannon in front demanded the surrender of the armory and guards. Dr. Ashe, seeing that there was no possible chance to successfully battle with such large numbers, sent word of the condition of affairs to Volney E. Howard, chief in command, and upon receiving an answer, finally surrendered. Every man in the armory, numbering in all about fifty or sixty, was marched down to the Committee rooms, on the corner of Front and Sacramento Streets.

After locking up the prisoners, several companies of the Vigilance Committee went to the other state armory, which was situated on the northeast corner of Clay and Kearny Streets. Volney E. Howard, Rodney West,[7] and John Nugent were in charge of the troops at this station and they were called upon to surrender. West and Nugent did not want to give up to the Vigilance Committee. They said that they would much rather die fighting them, but Howard finally yielded to the Committee's demands, to the great disgust of Nugent and West. The latter has since that time served his country as a general in the war of the rebellion and as United States Senator from Louisiana. The men in the second armory were also locked up in the Vigilance Committee rooms and had their arms confiscated. They were kept in confinement for a short time and then released in small numbers.

After these captures the Vigilance Committee had full control of the town. They deprived Judge Terry of his liberty for nearly a month, until Hopkins was pronounced out of danger. If he had died, it was understood that Terry was to have been hung out of the window, just as Casey and the others had been murdered. I am glad that Hopkins did not die at that time, because he was reserved for a worse fate and suffered it. He was trampled to death while running away from the battlefield in a skirmish in the late war.

While Terry was a prisoner in Fort Gunnybags, his wife was informed that the Vigilance Committee wanted him to resign from the Supreme bench and that he would suffer death unless he did so. She went down to the Committee rooms accompanied by Mrs. Colonel Jack Hays of Texas and told the judge not to resign as Chief Justice under any circumstances, as she would rather see him hanged than bring disgrace upon himself and his children by yielding to the vigilance mob. He assured her that there was no danger of his resigning—that he would suffer death first, and he was as good as his word.

The majority of the members of the Vigilance Committee were anxious to hang Terry and the Executive Committee had all they could do to hold them back. They became so clamorous at last that his life was not considered safe in the Committee's rooms and one morning, between two and three o'clock, Miers Truett, Nick Arrington, Tom Smiley, and others of the Executive Committee who were friendly to Terry quietly took him out of the rooms through a rear passage, and by traveling along the outskirts of the town, succeeded in reaching the home of Colonel Jack Hays, on Powell Street, between Pacific and Broadway, without attracting attention. After he had been there some time a consultation was held by his friends who were members of the Vigilance Committee and it was decided that he should go on board the *John Adams*, a man-of-war then lying in the stream under command of Captain

Front and back views of silver medallion issued to members of the 1856 Committee of Vigilance. The "all-seeing eye" was the emblem of the vigilantes. Robert Limacher collection.

Farragut.[8] It was arranged that Terry should go down to the foot of Vallejo Street alone, so as to not attract attention, and arming himself, he followed instructions, and on arriving there found a boat waiting for him, by which he was conveyed to the war ship, where he remained for a long time.

When the mass of the Vigilance Committee mob found that Judge Terry was out of their grasp they became wild, and it required the most prompt and determined action on the part of the Executive Committee to prevent them from hanging Truett, Nick Arrington, and others of the Committee who had assisted Terry in getting to the man-of-war. If the mob had succeeded in hanging the members of their own Executive Committee, I would have been very sorry, of course, because it would have savored of inconsistency on the part of those good people.

The knife with which Terry stabbed Hopkins was the property of George S. Evans,[9] present Harbor Commissioner, and the manner in which Judge Terry came in possession of it will clearly prove that he did not seek the trouble with Hopkins or the Vigilance Committee, and that he had no idea of what did occur. Judge Taliaferro,[10] at present a notary public and attorney in this city, was one of the judges here at the time I am speaking of. The day before Terry's trouble with the Vigilance Committee, Mr. Taliaferro had gone down to what is now San Mateo County to dispossess a man named

Sanchez who occupied a ranch unlawfully there. Before going he borrowed a Bowie knife from George S. Evans, who told him to be sure and give it to him immediately on his return, as it was a unique and valuable one and much prized by him (Evans). It was a seven-inch blade, with a fine, silver-mounted handle, and was very fancy.[11] Judge Taliaferro, upon his return from San Mateo, went to Dr. Ashe's office, where Evans was generally to be found, for the purpose of returning the knife. Evans was not there, however, and Ashe said, "Oh, leave it on top of my desk there, Judge. George will be along in a little while and I will give it to him."

The judge laid the knife down as directed. Terry had just come down from Sacramento the evening previous, and as I before stated, was in Ashe's office when Maloney came and asked for protection. When Judge Terry started to accompany him to the armory, he was unarmed, and glancing on Ashe's desk he saw the Bowie knife which had been left by Judge Taliaferro, and put it in his pocket to defend himself and Maloney, if necessary. As the result showed, it was very lucky for him that the knife was there.

Judge Terry and I were always good friends here before I was sent away by the Vigilance Committee, but when I heard in New York that he had killed my friend, David C. Broderick, under circumstances that some considered unfair for the latter, I felt very bitter toward him. On the impulse of the moment I admitted the idea to my mind, as did all of Broderick's friends who were not personally cognizant of the facts, that he had taken an unfair advantage of Broderick in the duel,[12] and for a long time after my return to San Francisco I felt very hostile to him, and we did not speak. But it is now nearly a quarter of a century since that unfortunate occurrence happened and I think Terry really feels worse over the result of that duel than the majority of those people who are now trying to make political capital out of the affair to his detriment. A large number of them never knew Broderick and many of them were his bitterest enemies when he was alive. I am sure no person in this state or anywhere else will doubt my close friendship with Broderick, and I feel now, after mature consideration, that Terry was as honest in his position in that affair as was Broderick, and that if Broderick had been advised by the right kind of men, the duel would never have been fought.

Terry has shown by his refusal to fight when challenged since that lamentable occurrence that he does not thirst for the blood of his fellow man,[13] and I feel sure that he has more respect for the memory of Broderick today than many of those who are howling against him on that issue. He displayed his courage in the Vigilance Committee times when few men dared to do it, and he must be respected for it by all lovers of law and liberty.

Notes

INTRODUCTION

1. The voluminous papers of the 1851 committee have provided abundant data on the criminals who were targeted by the vigilantes; later writers have provided additional details. See Hubert Howe Bancroft, *Popular Tribunals* (1887); Mary Floyd Williams, *Papers of the San Francisco Committee of Vigilance of 1851* (1919) and *History of the San Francisco Committee of Vigilance of 1851* (1921); George R. Stewart, *Committee of Vigilance: Revolution in San Francisco, 1851* (1964); and Kevin J. Mullen, *Let Justice Be Done: Crime and Politics in Early San Francisco* (1989). However, Bancroft's information on those targeted by the 1856 committee is sparse, and later writers have done little to shed light on the histories of men like Charles Duane who were banished by the 1856 committee. Apparently, only two articles have been published on men deported by the 1856 vigilantes: William B. Secrest, "There Once was a Badman Named Mulligan," *Real West* 27 (August 1984); and Kevin J. Mullen, "Dutch Charley Duane," *Old West* 33, no. 1 (Fall 1996).

2. There are but two other known accounts left by men who were targeted by the vigilantes. Judge Edward "Ned" McGowan, who was black-listed by the vigilantes and fled to avoid arrest, wrote his *Narrative of Edward McGowan, Including a Full Account of the Author's Adventures and Perils While Persecuted by the San Francisco Vigilance Committee of 1856* (San Francisco, 1857), which was reprinted twice, the most available edition being *McGowan v. California Vigilantes* with a foreword by Joseph A. Sullivan (1946). Additionally, McGowan's memoirs were published in numerous installments in the *Argonaut* (May–June 1878), the *San Francisco Post* (July 1878–April 1879), and the *Alta California,* (October–December 1884). These recollections of life in California during the Gold Rush are fascinating and generally reliable. The same cannot be said of the veracity of his writings about the vigilantes. He is so extraordinarily biased against his purported tormentors that the historical value of those memoirs is greatly diluted.

McGowan's editorship of two Sacramento scandal sheets; his false accusations against members of the committee; and his penchant for dishonesty, intrigue, and corruption further serve to damage his credibility. The only other memoir left by a man who was arrested by the committee was that of Alfred A. Green, a lawyer who in 1878 gave historian Hubert Howe Bancroft a dictation entitled "The Life and Adventures of a '47er of California." Green's memoir provides details of his arrest and brief imprisonment by the vigilantes on charges that he stole the title papers for the Mexican pueblo of San Francisco. However, he was never a political criminal or a member of the group of ruffians and shoulder-strikers who were blacklisted by the vigilantes.

    3. *San Francisco Bulletin*, October 25, 1866; *San Francisco Call*, May 15, 1887.

    4. David R. Johnson, *Policing the Urban Underworld* (1979), 84–86.

    5. Kevin Mullen, *Let Justice Be Done: Crime and Politics in Early San Francisco* (1989), 84–85.

    6. On personal honor and the cult of masculinity, see Elliot J. Gorn, *The Manly Art: Bare-Knuckle Prize Fighting in America.* (1986), 141–44, and Michael T. Isenberg, *John L. Sullivan and His America* (1988), 39–59. On personal honor and its link to the *code duello* and the "Code of the West," see Gary L. Roberts, *Death Comes for the Chief Justice* (1990), pp. 138–41. Studies of honor in the South are Bertram Wyatt Brown, *Southern Honor: Ethics and Behavior in the Old South* (1982), esp. chaps. 2, 6, and 13; and Edward L. Ayers, *Vengeance and Justice: Crime and Punishment in the Nineteenth Century American South* (1984), 9–33, 263–68. On the legal doctrine of no duty to retreat, see Richard Maxwell Brown, *No Duty to Retreat: Violence and Values in American History and Society* (1991), 3–37.

    7. Gorn, *The Manly Art,* is a brilliant analysis not only of bare-knuckle prizefighting, but of masculinity in nineteenth-century America. See, in particular, chap. 4.

    8. *San Francisco Call,* May 15, 1887; *San Francisco Bulletin,* October 25, 1866; Mullen, "Dutch Charley Duane": 35–37.

    9. *San Francisco Call,* May 15, 1887; James O'Meara, *The Vigilance Committee of 1856* (1887), 47.

    10. Born in 1819, Hyer was the son of Jacob Hyer, a butcher by trade and a pugilist by temperament, who in 1816 boxed one of the first ring fights in America. The elder Hyer trained his son Tom in the "manly art" and the youth soon became a champion prize fighter. Peter Gammie, "Pugilists and Politicians in Antebellum New York: The Life and Times of Tom Hyer," *New York History* 75, no. 3 (July 1994): 267; Gorn, *The Manly Art,* 83–97.

11. Gammie, "Pugilists and Politicians in Antebellum New York: The Life and Times of Tom Hyer": 269–70. Duane's quote is from the *San Francisco Examiner*, January 16, 1881.

12. Herbert Asbury, *The Gangs of New York* (1928), 5, 43–44, 73, 77–79; Gammie, "Pugilists and Politicians in Antebellum New York": 270.

13. Gorn, *The Manly Art*, 109.

14. Ibid., 81–97; Gammie, "Pugilists and Politicians in Antebellum New York": 274–83.

15. Richard Moody, *The Astor Place Riot* (1958), 154.

16. On the Astor Place Riot, see Moody, *The Astor Place Riot*, and R. H. Ranney, *Account of the Terrific and Fatal Riot at the Astor Place Opera House* (1849). Another account of the riot was published in the *New York Telegram* in 1882 and reprinted in the *San Francisco Call*, January 2, 1882. On Ned Buntline, see Jay Monaghan, *The Great Rascal* (1951), especially chap. 15.

17. See trial testimony of Charles Duane in *John H. Baird et al. v. Charles P. Duane et al.*, District Court, Fourth Judicial District, San Francisco, February 13, 1864, p. 81; and *Alta California*, November 17, 1856. Duane's name was not on the passenger list published in the *Alta* on April 15, 1850, which indicates that he may have been a crew member, or, perhaps, a stowaway.

18. David A. Williams, *David Broderick: A Political Portrait* (1969), chap. 2; Arthur Quinn, *The Rivals: William Gwin, David Broderick, and the Birth of California* (1994), 40–47.

19. O'Meara, *The Vigilance Committee of 1856*, 47–48.

20. *San Francisco Examiner*, January 16, 1881; *Alta California*, June 22, 24, 1851; Bancroft, *History of California*, 6: 203; Kevin J. Mullen, "Torching Old-Time San Francisco," *The Californians* 8, no. 5 (January–February 1991): 26–33.

21. *Alta California*, July 4, 6, 1850; Mullen, "Dutch Charley Duane": 35–36.

22. *Alta California*, September 4, 1850.

23. Williams, *Papers of the San Francisco Committee of Vigilance of 1851*, 556; Bancroft, *Popular Tribunals*, 1: 155–56.

24. Ibid., December 19, 20, 1850; R. A. Burchell, *The San Francisco Irish* (1980), 123–24.

25. *Alta California*, February 19, 21, 22, 1851; George R. MacMinn, *The Theater of the Golden Age in California* (1941), 131–32; Ernest de Massey, "A Frenchman in the Gold Rush," *California Historical Society*

Quarterly 6, no. 1, (March 1927): 48–49; Mullen, "Dutch Charley Duane": 36–37.

26. *Alta California*, June 27, 1851; Mullen, "Dutch Charley Duane": 37; Williams, *Papers of the San Francisco Committee of Vigilance* (1919), 96; de Massey, "A Frenchman in the Gold Rush": 49; Herbert Asbury, *The Barbary Coast* (1933), 80. De Massey claims that the payment to Fayolle was $50,000, which seems inordinately high.

27. *Alta California*, March 13, May 28, 1851.

28. De Massey, "A Frenchman in the Gold Rush": 48. De Massey was a book dealer in San Francisco from 1852 to 1856. He returned to France in 1857.

29. California's first vigilance movement took place in Los Angeles in 1835 during the Mexican period. During the first year of the Gold Rush, criminals were executed in Santa Barbara, San Jose, and Placerville by tribunals that ranged from traditional vigilance committees to provisional courts that combined extralegal and legal elements. In July 1849 members of an extralegal movement in San Francisco arrested, tried, and banished a gang of New York criminals called the Hounds.

30. Kevin J. Mullen surveyed San Francisco newspapers for the period 1848–52 and found that, contrary to the claims of the vigilantes and their supporters, there had been no drastic increase in property crime before the committee was formed. He found further that the oft-touted claim that there had been 1,200 murders in San Francisco between 1850 and 1853 was a gross exaggeration. Mullen, *Let Justice Be Done*, 129–38, 158–59, 237.

31. Williams, *Papers of the San Francisco Committee of Vigilance*, 96–98.

32. Bancroft, *Popular Tribunals*, 1: 320; *Alta California*, July 26, 1851.

33. Williams, *Papers of the San Francisco Committee of Vigilance*, 333.

34. *Alta California*, July 22, 26, 1851; George R. Stewart, *Committee of Vigilance: Revolution in San Francisco, 1851* (1964), 219–33.

35. Quoted in John Myers Myers, *San Francisco's Reign of Terror* (1966), 55–56. See also *Sacramento Daily Union*, August 2, 1851.

36. Williams, *Papers of the San Francisco Committee of Vigilance*, 551, 588, 590, 597. Evidently all evidence of the pardon was destroyed. There is no copy of it in the Governors' Pardon Papers in the California State Archives, which are otherwise remarkably complete.

37. *Alta California*, November 25, 1851; *Sacramento Daily Union*, November 27, 1851; de Massey, "A Frenchman in the Gold Rush": 48. The attorney, Tiffany, was obscure enough that his name does not appear in the city directories.

38. Phineas Blunt, *Journal* (in Bancroft Library); transcript provided to author by courtesy of Kevin J. Mullen.

39. *Alta California*, April 6, 1852.

40. Mullen, "Dutch Charley Duane": 38.

41. *Alta California*, May 3, 4; October 23, 1853.

42. Ibid., November 9, 1853.

43. Ibid., September 29, October 6, 1853; *San Francisco Whig*, quoted in the (Stockton) *San Joaquin Republican*, July 2, 1853.

44. *John H. Baird et al. v. Charles P. Duane et al.*, 94, 184–85; *Alta California*, May 15, 1887. A disreputable dance hall known as "Dutch Charley's," located on the corner of Pacific Street and Murderer's Alley in what became known as the Barbary Coast, was closed by the police in 1855. It does not appear to have been associated with Charley Duane. *San Francisco Herald*, August 28, 31, September 1, 1855.

45. *San Francisco Herald*, December 8, 10, 1853; *Alta California*, December 8, 1853; Mullen, "Dutch Charley Duane": 38; Theodore H. Hittell, *History of California* (1897), 3: 362.

46. *San Francisco Herald*, December 10, 1853.

47. Quoted in (Sacramento) *Democratic State Journal*, December 9, 1853.

48. Ibid.

49. *Alta California*, December 8, 1853.

50. Ibid., February 20, 1854; *San Francisco Herald*, February 21, 1854; William B. Secrest, *Lawmen and Desperadoes* (1994), 76–77, 197–98.

51. *California Chronicle*, April 13, 1854. Of Parrott, a contemporary wrote that "he was most excentric [*sic*] in his feelings and rather slack in his moral principles." J. C. Jones to Thomas O. Larkin, quoted in George P. Hammond, ed., *The Larkin Papers*, (1953), 4: 28.

52. *Alta California*, June 29, 1854; *San Francisco Herald*, June 21, 1854.

53. *California Chronicle*, June 20, 1854.

54. *San Francisco Post*, July 27, 1878; *California Chronicle*, December 30, 1854.

55. *Alta California*, June 19, 1855.

56. Ibid., July 7, 1855.

57. *California Chronicle*, June 2, 1854.

58. Ibid.

59. Ibid. On Matilda Heron, see n. 27 for chap. 1 of this book.

60. *San Francisco Herald*, November 15, 1855.

61. Mullen, "Dutch Charley Duane": 38; *San Francisco Bulletin,* July 20, 1877.

62. San Francisco *Fireman's Journal,* December 15, 1855.

63. Robert M. Senkewicz, *Vigilantes in Gold Rush San Francisco* (1985), 7.

64. Bancroft claimed that Duane applied for membership to the committee and was refused. If true, it was an effort to infiltrate the vigilantes, just as David Broderick had attempted with Rube Maloney in 1851. See Bancroft, *Popular Tribunals,* 2: 85; *San Francisco Bulletin,* June 2, 1856; *Sacramento Union,* October 31, 1863. According to Hittell, it was another Dutch Charley, Charles Waldeer, who was denied membership. *History of California,* 3: 559.

65. *San Francisco Herald,* June 2, 1856; *San Francisco Bulletin,* June 2, 1856.

66. Bancroft, *Popular Tribunals,* 2: 348–49.

67. Ibid., 2: 278–80; *San Francisco Bulletin,* July 1, 1856.

68. Hittell, *History of California,* 3: 565. John Duane was born in Ireland in 1832. A brick mason, he died in San Francisco on August 9, 1911.

69. Philip J. Ethington, *The Public City: The Political Construction of Urban Life in San Francisco, 1850–1900* (1994), 161–69; Robert J. Chandler, "Vigilante Rebirth: The Civil War Union League," *The Argonaut* (Journal of the San Francisco Historical Society) 3, no. 1, (Winter 1992): 10–18.

70. See Paul Parker, "The Roach- Belcher Feud," *California Historical Society Quarterly* 29 (March 1950): 19–28. On Henry Plummer and vigilantism in Montana, see Art Pauley, *Henry Plummer: Lawman and Outlaw* (1980), and Thomas J. Dimsdale, *The Vigilantes of Montana* (1866, 1953). The literature on the Lincoln County War is extensive; see in particular Robert M. Utley, *High Noon in Lincoln* (1987), Frederick Nolan, *The Lincoln County War: A Documentary History* (1992), and Joel Jacobsen, *Such Men as Billy the Kid* (1994). On the Earp-Clanton feud and the cowboy troubles in southern Arizona, see Casey Tefertiller, *Wyatt Earp: The Life behind the Legend* (1997) and Paula Mitchell Marks, *And Die in the West* (1989).

71. An exhaustive essay on sources up to 1971 appears in Doyce B. Nunis, Jr., ed., *The San Francisco Vigilance Committee of 1856: Three Views* (1971), 9–24. A fine discussion on the historiography of the committee, inclusive to 1985, is in Senkewicz, *Vigilantes in Gold Rush San Francisco,* 203–31.

72. Ethington, *Public City*, 90.

73. Roger W. Lotchin, *San Francisco, 1846–1856: From Hamlet to City* (1974); Richard Maxwell Brown, *Strain of Violence: Historical Studies of American Violence and Vigilantism* (1975); Peter R. Decker, *Fortunes and Failures: White Collar Mobility in Nineteenth Century San Francisco* (1978); Senkewicz, *Vigilantes in Gold Rush San Francisco*. These four, plus Ethington's study, are the major modern scholarly treatments of San Francisco vigilantism. Also important are David A. Johnson, "Vigilance and the Law: The Moral Authority of Popular Justice in the West," *American Quarterly* 33 (Winter 1981): 558–86, and Christian G. Fritz, "Popular Sovereignty, Vigilantism, and the Constitutional Right of Revolution," *Pacific Historical Review* 62 (February 1994): 39–66.

74. Ethington, *Public City*, 92–105, 112–27, 130–34.

75. Martin J. Burke, *Dictation*, 1887, Bancroft Library; *San Francisco Examiner*, March 6, 1881.

76. Bancroft, *Popular Tribunals*, 2: 272.

77. The biographical sketches are located as follows: John W. Bagley, chap. 4, n. 25; Billy Carr, chap. 7, n. 3; James P. Casey, chap. 4, ns. 24, 27, 29; Charles Cora, chap. 6, n. 1; Robert Cushing, chap. 4, n. 26; Martin Gallagher, chap. 7, n. 2; Woolly Kearney, chap. 7, n. 21; Chris Lilly, chap. 8, n. 11; Rube Maloney, chap. 8, n. 10; Edward McGowan, chap. 3, n. 10; Billy Mulligan, chap. 7, n. 1; Yankee Sullivan, chap. 2, n. 12, chap. 7, ns. 6 and 7.

78. *Alta California*, November 17, 1856; James A. B. Scherer, *The Lion of the Vigilantes: William T. Coleman and the Life of Old San Francisco* (1939), 224.

79. *San Francisco Call*, May 15, 1887. In the trial of Duane's lawsuit against Captain Robert H. Pearson, it was alleged by the defense that Dutch Charley's disability was "caused by his own vices." *San Francisco Bulletin*, December 2, 1863.

80. *Sacramento Union*, March 17, 1860; *Alta California*, July 22, 1860.

81. *Alta California*, July 22, 1860.

82. Christian G. Fritz, *Federal Justice in California* (1991), 81–83; *Pearson v. Duane* 71 U.S. 447 (1867); *Sacramento Union*, October 31, 1863, August 23, 1864; *San Francisco Bulletin*, August 13, 1860 and December 2, 1863; *Alta California*, August 15, 1862.

83. James Duane was born in 1829. He settled in New Orleans in 1859, became active in politics, and served as a police officer from 1860 to 64. He was chief of police in 1864, then served one term in the legislature,

1864–65. He died in poverty in Fort Worth, Texas, on November 12, 1876.

84. *San Francisco Bulletin*, October 17, 18, 19, 1864; *Alta California*, October 19, 21, 1864.

85. *San Francisco Examiner*, May 26, 1866.

86. *San Francisco Bulletin*, May 23, 1866; Gary Scharnhorst, ed., *Bret Harte's California* (1990), 53–54.

87. On the killing of Ross, see *San Francisco Bulletin*, May 23, 24, 25, 1866; *San Francisco Examiner*, May 26, 1866; *San Francisco Call*, May 27, 1866. For anti-Duane editorials, see the *Bulletin*, May 24, 1866; *Examiner*, May 24, 1866; *Alta California*, May 24, 1866. For Duane's trial, see the *Alta California*, October 18, 23, 24, 25, 26, 27, 28, 31, November 1, 1866; *Bulletin*, October 22, 23, 24, 25, 26, 27, 28, 30, 31, November 1, 1866; *San Francisco Call*, October 28, 1866.

88. Scharnhorst, *Bret Harte's California*, 53–54.

89. *San Francisco Call*, November 18, 1868; *San Francisco Bulletin*, July 18, 1871.

90. *San Francisco Bulletin*, July 16, 1872; *San Francisco Call*, July 17, 18, 1872.

91. *San Francisco Bulletin*, December 4, 1873, December 12, 1874; *San Francisco Call*, December 5, 1873.

92. *San Francisco Call*, May 21, 23, 1876.

93. *San Francisco Chronicle*, October 22, 1876; Edward Byram, Police Record Book No. 1, 63–64.

94. Hubert Howe Bancroft, *History of California* (1888), 7: 348–62; Bancroft, *Popular Tribunals*, 2: 696–748.

95. *Alta California*, December 10, 1877; *San Francisco Bulletin*, December 17, 1877; *San Francisco Call*, March 22, 1878.

96. *San Francisco Bulletin*, July 20, 1877; *Alta California*, March 5, June 1, 1878; *San Francisco Chronicle*, November 19, 1880; *San Francisco Call*, June 23, 1882; *San Francisco Examiner*, March 6, 1885.

97. *San Francisco Examiner*, January 9, 1881. Duane's memoirs appeared in the following issues of the *Examiner*: January 9, 16, 23, February 6, 13, 20, 27, March 6, 13, 20, 27, April 3, 17, 1881.

98. Ibid.

99. *San Francisco Examiner*, Jan. 16, 1881.

100. *San Francisco Call*, May 15, 1887; *Alta California*, May 15, 1887; *San Francisco Examiner*, May 14, 1887; *San Francisco Post*, May 14, 1887.

CHAPTER 1. GOLD RUSH SAN FRANCISCO

1. Like many Argonauts who craved the prestige of being among the earliest Gold Rush pioneers, Duane wanted to be known as a Forty-niner. But according to his own statement published in his 1856 lawsuit against William Tell Coleman, he did not arrive in San Francisco until April 14, 1850. *Alta California*, November 17, 1856.

2. This fire originated in the U.S. Exchange Saloon and destroyed $4,000,000 worth of property. The cause was widely believed to have been arson. Mullen, *Let Justice Be Done*, 106.

3. Duane's praise of Palmer, Cook & Co. is understandable. This bank, the financial power behind David Broderick's political machine, bore an unsavory reputation. In 1854 charges of bribery were brought in the state senate against its principal, Joseph C. Palmer, who was accused of attempting to bribe a legislator. After a trial, the senate disagreed on his guilt. The bank secured political power through its support for Broderick and also by underwriting the bonds for state officers, who in return allowed the firm to handle state funds that belonged in the state treasury and should not have been deposited in a private bank. Palmer, Cook & Co. failed in 1856, shaking the credit of the state. Bancroft, *History of California*, 6: 616–18, 682–83; 6: 177–80. James King of William in his *San Francisco Bulletin* repeatedly accused the firm of corruption. See Williams, *David C. Broderick*, 115–16, 124–25.

4. This number is plainly wrong. In 1847, there were sixty-six "white women" in San Francisco alone. The 1850 census found a state population of 92,597, of whom 8 percent were women. There were far more than twenty-eight women of European extraction in California in 1850. Joann Levy, *They Saw the Elephant: Women in the California Gold Rush* (1990), xix, 176–77.

5. David C. Broderick (1820–1859) was born in Washington, D.C. and raised in New York City. A natural politician, he operated a popular saloon, made an unsuccessful bid for Congress in 1846, and joined the Gold Rush three years later. His ownership of a private mint and speculation in San Francisco real estate made him wealthy and politically prominent. Broderick built a powerful machine patterned after Tammany Hall, attracting many political operatives, thugs, and prizefighters whom he had probably known in New York. Among them were Charley Duane, Ira Cole, Billy Mulligan, Woolly Kearney, Yankee Sullivan, Chris Lilly, and Rube Maloney. Elected to the state senate, Broderick became the head of the

Tammany wing of the Democratic Party in California. He was elected U.S. senator in 1857 and engaged in a bitter rivalry with California's other senator, William Gwin, to control federal patronage and Democratic Party politics in California. Unsuccessful, Broderick instead became leader of his party's Free-Soil wing, which was outnumbered by the party's Southern proslavery wing, the "Chivalry," or "Chivs," as they were called. The result was a split in the Democratic Party which was an important part of the factionalism that resulted in the Civil War. In 1859 he quarreled with David S. Terry, chief justice of the California Supreme Court and a leader of the proslavery Democrats. On September 13, Terry killed Broderick in one of America's most famous and most significant duels. See Williams, *David C. Broderick* and Quinn, *The Rivals*.

6. Frederick D. Kohler (1810–1864), a jeweler by trade, had been assistant engineer of the New York City Fire Department and was a close friend of David Broderick in New York. With Broderick and John McGlynn, he had helped establish the Democratic Party machinery in California in 1849–50. On December 2, 1849, Kohler was appointed chief engineer of San Francisco's volunteer fire department and elected to the post on January 28, 1850, making him the city's first fire chief. He resigned on August 25, 1851, to take an appointment as adjutant general of California. See Williams, *David C. Broderick*, 26, 28–29, 53; *San Francisco Call*, December 22, 1890; *San Francisco Chronicle*, May 25, 1939.

7. That is highly unlikely. Private mints, of which there were approximately fifteen in San Francisco during the early 1850s, issued private coins that contained less gold than their face value. Otherwise, the private mints would not make a profit. According to Broderick's biographer, his coins contained "a slightly smaller" amount of gold than the value stamped on them. Bancroft, however, who was no admirer of Broderick, reported that the coins contained only 80 percent gold and proved so profitable that their sale laid the foundation for Broderick's fortune. Williams, *David C. Broderick* 28; Bancroft, *History of California*, 6: 661.

8. Moffat & Co. were U.S. assay contractors authorized by an act of Congress. They were authorized by the government to affix the U.S. stamp to the gold assayed at their office. William Gwin, U.S. senator, was the firm's patron and, at his suggestion, $50, $100, and $200 gold pieces were permitted to be manufactured at its office. Duane's comments about the firm's shortchanging no doubt stemmed from his dislike of Gwin. After the office of Moffat & Co. was established, privately issued coins began to be repudiated by the public in favor of the U.S. approved coin. The U.S. mint finally went into operation in San Francisco in April 1854, with machinery

capable of coining $30 million annually. Bancroft, *History of California*, 6: 629; Williams, *David C. Broderick*, 28–29.

9. Gambling was the grand occupation and amusement of all classes in Gold Rush San Francisco. It has been estimated that at the peak of the Gold Rush some $500,000 was on the tables of the popular Parker House at one time. According to an 1854 article first published in the *California Chronicle*, some houses in 1850 paid more than $500 daily for rent and there was one table at which it was reported that "$2,000,000 of gold coin and dust changed hands monthly." Robert K. DeArment, *Knights of the Green Cloth* (1982), 9–14; *San Diego Union*, September 7, 1854.

10. Thomas Maguire (1820?–1896) was a former hack driver, bartender, and gambler from New York City. He came to San Francisco in 1849, made his fortune at the card tables, and built and rebuilt a number of saloons and theaters as they were burned in San Francisco's many fires of the early 1850s. His Jenny Lind Theater and Maguire's Opera House brought to California the greatest names in American theater. He was a close friend of David Broderick, whom he had known in New York. In 1856 the Committee of Vigilance banished him from the state but never enforced its decree. Maguire became a power in Democratic politics in San Francisco during the 1860s. Chris Buckley, San Francisco's Democratic boss in the 1880s, got his start working for Maguire. After losing his fortune, Maguire returned to New York City, where he died a pauper. DeArment, *Knights of the Green Cloth*, 150–59; Lois Foster Rodecape, "Tom Maguire, Napoleon of the Stage," *California Historical Society Quarterly* 20, no. 4 (December 1941): 289–314; 21, no. 1 (March 1942): 39–74; 21, no. 2 (June 1943): 141–82; 21, no. 3 (September 1943): 239–76. See also William A. Bullough, *The Blind Boss and His City: Christopher Augustine Buckley and Nineteenth Century San Francisco* (1979), 11–13, 18–19.

11. James McCabe had been a Mississippi riverboat gambler before he arrived in California in 1849 with his paramour, Irene McCready. He and Thomas Chambers (probably the "Chamberlain" that Duane mentions) opened the El Dorado, which quickly burned but was rebuilt into the city's finest gambling hall. Irene McCready became one of San Francisco's first grand madams, opening her first bagnio in 1849. She and McCabe quarreled often; after one such spat, she reportedly drugged him and shaved his body from head to toe. McCabe did not appear again in public until his hair had grown out. Curt Gentry, *The Madams of San Francisco* (1964), 34–39; DeArment, *Knights of the Green Cloth*, 12–15.

12. Born in Ireland in 1824, Thomas Hayes was active in politics in New York's Fourth Ward before coming to California in 1849. He was

deputy sheriff under Jack Hays in San Francisco in 1850–51 and served as county clerk from 1853 to 1856. He and his brothers, Michael and John, settled in what became known as Hayes Valley, in what is now the area between Van Ness Avenue and Fulton, Fillmore, and Haight Streets. He owned real estate worth $100,000 and died on a steamer to New York in 1868. *Alta California*, June 30, 1868; *San Francisco Bulletin*, November 16, 1895; R. A. Burchell, *The San Francisco Irish* (1980), 8–9.

13. John Coffee "Jack" Hays (1817–1883) had been a famous Texas Ranger, Indian fighter, and hero of the Mexican War. He served as sheriff of San Francisco from 1850 to 1853. See Walter Prescott Webb, *The Texas Rangers* (1935), pp. 67 ff, and James Kimmins Greer, *Colonel Jack Hays: Texas Frontier Leader and California Builder* (1952).

14. Colonel J. J. Bryant was a wealthy Democrat and a famous gambler. The Bryant House was then perhaps the finest hotel in San Francisco and a popular resort for politicians. A veteran of twenty years as a Mississippi River gambler, Bryant arrived in San Francisco in 1849. He was defeated by Jack Hays in the election for sheriff on April 1, 1850. Bryant left California in 1854 and gambled in Mississippi and New Orleans, where he was shot to death in a quarrel over a gaming debt in 1868. DeArment, *Knights of the Green Cloth*, 16–18.

15. This law was in effect in 1851–1852 and permitted a jury, in its discretion, to return a verdict of death for grand larceny. Under this statute at least six men were hanged, mainly for horse theft. Charles Howard Shinn, *Mining Camps: A Study in American Frontier Government* (1948), 217; Bancroft, *History of California*, 7: 195.

16. Empire Engine Company No. 1 was organized in June 1851 with David Broderick as its foreman. It was modeled after the volunteer companies of New York. Its members not only fought fires but were deeply involved in politics. They attended primaries, mustered voters at elections, and supported the political interests of their foreman. Williams, *David C. Broderick*, 54–55.

17. This was actually the second post office in San Francisco. The first had been located briefly at the corner of Stockton and Washington Streets in 1849. Mildred Hoover, Hero Rensch, and Ethel Rensch, *Historic Spots in California* (1966), 357.

18. The fire at the city hospital owned by Dr. Peter Smith occurred on October 31, 1850. It severely injured several patients, and caused $250,000 in damage. Bancroft, *History of California*, 6: 203.

19. John W. Geary was San Francisco's last alcalde and first mayor. Born in Pennsylvania in 1819, he worked as a schoolteacher and railroad surveyor

until 1846, when he raised a regiment of volunteers for the Mexican War. His gallant war record won him promotion to colonel and led to his 1849 appointment by President James Polk as San Francisco's first postmaster. In August he became alcalde, or mayor, under the Mexican system of government still in effect. In May 1850, Geary was elected mayor and served a one-year term. According to Hubert Howe Bancroft, Geary illicitly accumulated a fortune of $200,000 before he left San Francisco in 1852. President Franklin Pierce appointed him governor of Kansas Territory in 1856. A major general during the Civil War, Geary was elected governor of Pennsylvania in 1866 and died in office in 1873. William F. Heintz, *San Francisco's Mayors, 1850–1880* (1975), 3–9.

20. Cornelius K. Garrison, born in New York in 1809, was an architect and shipbuilder. From 1849 to 1853 he acted as agent for the Nicaragua Steamship Line in Panama, then came to San Francisco and was soon elected mayor, a post he held for one year, 1853–54. As mayor he supported the fire department, instituted civic improvements, and took an active role in the suppression of crime. He returned east in 1859, operated his own steamship company, and died in New York City in 1885. Heintz, *San Francisco's Mayors*, 21–25.

21. The incident that Duane describes took place on May 31, 1854, during efforts to fight a large fire on the block bounded by Broadway, Dupont (Grant), and Vallejo Streets. Frank Whitney, assistant foreman of Howard Company, refused to obey Duane's order regarding where to direct a stream of water on the blaze. Duane had Whitney arrested for riotous conduct and seized the company's engine. He ordered that the engine not be run to any alarm until an investigation was completed, but at the next alarm, later that day, the Howard Company showed up with their engine. When Duane attempted forcibly to retake the engine, the Howard men physically resisted him. Mayor Garrison then interfered in the dispute and ordered that the engine be retained by Howard Company. *Alta California*, June 1, 1854.

22. Frank E. R. Whitney had been a fireman in Boston. He succeeded Fred Kohler on November 3, 1851, but served only two weeks due to ill health. In 1854 Duane had him arrested for disobeying his orders at a fire scene. Whitney was elected chief of the volunteer fire department in 1856 and served until 1860. He was chief of the regular fire department from 1866 to 1870 and again in 1873–74. He died in San Francisco on October 19, 1889. *California Chronicle*, June 2, 1854; *San Francisco Call*, December 22, 1890; *San Francisco Chronicle*, May 25, 1939.

23. George H. Hossefross (1826–1864) had been a fireman in Baltimore and arrived in San Francisco in December 1849. Extremely popular,

he served as chief of the fire department from 1851 to 1853. A builder by profession, he was the first in San Francisco to use hydraulic power to move brick buildings. He was a prominent member of both the 1851 and 1856 Committees of Vigilance. *San Francisco Call*, December 22, 1890; Dolores Waldorf, "Baltimore Fire Laddie, George H. Hossefross," *California Historical Society Quarterly*, 23 (March 1944): 69–77.

24. Catherine Hayes was a beautiful Irish singer, known as the "Swan of Erin." She made her debut in November 1852 and "threw the musical world of San Francisco into a fever of excitement." She was a great favorite of the city's firemen; the Empire Engine Company paid $1,150 for a single seat at her opening concert. Edmund M. Gagey, *The San Francisco Stage: A History* (1950), 32–33; George R. MacMinn, *The Theater of the Golden Era in California* (1941), 388–93.

25. Elisa Biscaccianti, a popular singer, was known as the "American Thrush." Born Elisa Ostinelli in Boston, she made her debut in 1848. The first eminent singer of the Gold Rush, she gave ten concerts in San Francisco in March 1852, which were received with tremendous enthusiasm. In 1853 she left for South America, and did not return to San Francisco for six years. By the early 1860s she took to drink and was reduced to singing at the Bella Union gambling hall, leaning unsteadily against a table or a wall. She left California for Italy in the mid-1860s, and died in poverty in Paris in 1896. Gagey, *San Francisco Stage*, 32; MacMinn, *Theater of the Golden Era in California*, 383–88.

26. Lola Montez (1818–1861) was already famed for her shocking love affairs in Europe and her scandalous dancing when she arrived in San Francisco, where she made her debut on May 26, 1853. Although her dancing skill never impressed the critics, the miners loved her. Her "spider dance," in which she simulated searching for a spider in her petticoats, was very popular with her largely male audiences. She lived for several years in Grass Valley and left for the East Coast in 1856. She died in New York City on January 17, 1861; her true name was Maria Dolores Eliza Rosanna Gilbert. See Doris Foley, *The Divine Eccentric: Lola Montez and the Newspapers* (1969), and Horace Wyndham, *The Magnificent Montez* (1935).

27. Matilda Heron, a native of Ireland, came to San Francisco from Philadelphia in 1854 with her agent, who died en route. She was then in her early twenties. She arrived alone and unheralded, and had her debut on December 26, 1853. Her subdued, lifelike acting style proved very popular, but her personality was far from subdued. One San Francisco critic called her a "wild, impulsive, eccentric being" and an "exponent of elemental

passions." Impulsively, while on her San Francisco tour, she married District Attorney Henry H. Byrne. Three months later they were permanently separated. She later achieved a national reputation for her performance as Camille. Gagey, *San Francisco Stage*, 50–56; MacMinn, *Theater of the Golden Era in California*, 97–101, 156–61, 296–99.

28. Catherine Sinclair had been the wife of Edwin Forrest, America's first great tragedian. Her divorce from the actor in 1852 brought her nationwide notoriety. After a brief study of acting, she debuted in New York City in 1852. She came to San Francisco, where she first performed on May 9, 1853. By year's end she was the manager of the Metropolitan Theater, and in 1855 toured with Edwin Booth. She became one of the most dynamic figures of American theater. Gagey, *San Francisco Stage*, 38, 49, 53; MacMinn, *Theater of the Golden Era in California*, 138–46. See also Richard Moody, *Edwin Forrest: First Star of the American Stage* (1960).

29. Henry Haight was born in Rochester, New York, in 1821. Trained as a banker, he was living in St. Louis, Missouri, when gold was discovered and he emigrated overland to California. Haight was cashier of the banking house of Page, Bacon & Co. until it failed in 1855. He died in San Francisco on March 24, 1869. He was the uncle of Henry H. Haight, governor of California from 1867 to 1871. *Alta California*, March 25, 1869.

30. According to Herbert Asbury, Ah Toy came to San Francisco in the summer of 1850 and became a celebrated courtesan, the first in Chinatown. She became wealthy, bought her freedom, and established herself as a principal importer of prostitutes from China. She also operated "a chain of dives in San Francisco, Sacramento, and other cities," and eventually returned to China to live in comfort. According to Curt Gentry, she was the leading Chinese courtesan in Gold Rush San Francisco and differed greatly from most Chinese prostitutes, who were little more than slaves to their pimps. She disappeared from San Francisco in 1859. The Ah Toy who died in San Jose on February 1, 1928, at almost one hundred years of age, may or may not have been the same woman. Asbury, *The Barbary Coast* (1933), p. 172; Gentry, *Madams of San Francisco*, 50–59.

31. Abla A. Selover, born in 1824, arrived in San Francisco in 1850. That year he served as a city alderman and in 1853 formed a real estate and auction firm with Richard H. Sinton. A bitter enemy of James King of William, he was the object of some of King's harshest journalistic attacks. He died in New York on February 23, 1898. Nunis, *San Francisco Vigilance Committee of 1856*, 106n, 110n; Charles P. Kimball, *The San Francisco City Directory* (1850), 99, 122.

CHAPTER 2. FLUSH TIMES

1. Peter H. Burnett was born in Tennessee in 1807 and emigrated in 1843 to Oregon, where he served as a legislator and judge before coming to California in 1848. Inaugurated as governor on December 20, 1849, he served one year and resigned on January 9, 1851. He was a justice of the California Supreme Court in 1857–58, and later engaged in banking in San Francisco. Bancroft, *History of California*, 6: 644.

2. John McDougal was perhaps the most colorful of California's early governors. Born in Ohio in 1818, he served as a captain of a volunteer company in the Black Hawk War and was superintendent of the Indiana state prison in 1846. McDougal distinguished himself as a captain in the Mexican War. He came to California in 1849 with his brother George. Governor for one year, until January 1852, John McDougal was the quintessential Gold Rush politician. Gentlemanly and fine-looking, he favored a ruffled shirt, buff vest and pantaloons, and blue coat with brass buttons. Affable, generous, and socially adept, he was a heavy drinker and enjoyed gambling and carousing with his cronies. One of his gambler friends and target-shooting partners turned out to be the noted outlaw Henry J. "Cherokee Bob" Talbot, although that fact was unknown to McDougal when he associated with Talbot following the latter's escape from San Quentin 1855. He claimed that he feared but two things: "God almighty and Mrs. McDougal." When offended by an article in the *San Francisco Picayune*, he challenged its editor, A. C. Russell, to a duel. They met in Santa Clara County on December 11, 1852, and Russell was wounded in the breast at first fire. On September 22, 1854, he acted as a second for H. P. Dorsey in his duel with Rasey Biven near Oakland. He was known as "I, John McDougal" because that was how he began many of his long-winded proclamations. In preparation of one such speech, Bancroft claimed that he was "three weeks sobering off." McDougal came to Duane's aid twice: first, when he pardoned him in 1851, and later, on shipboard, when Dutch Charley was exiled by the vigilantes in 1856. His health ruined by drink, McDougal died in San Francisco on March 30, 1866. Bancroft, *History of California*, 6: 645.

3. Jonathan Drake Stevenson (1800–1894) was a prominent Tammany Hall politician in New York in 1847 when he raised the New York Volunteers and brought them to California for service in the Mexican War. From its ranks came many of the most famous and infamous men of early California. Stevenson was a friend and associate of David Broderick in New York and California and reportedly financed Broderick's trip to San

Francisco in 1849. In San Francisco he achieved prominence as a real estate developer. Hubert Howe Bancroft, *Pioneer Register* (1964), 734; Williams, *David Broderick*, 26.

4. The Industrial School was located near what is now the site of the City College of San Francisco.

5. Hall McAllister became a very prominent attorney and leader of the California bar. The son of Judge Mathew Hall McAllister, he was born in Georgia in 1826. Father and son arrived in San Francisco in June 1849, and young McAllister quickly established himself as one of the new state's finest legal talents. He died in San Francisco on December 1, 1888. *San Francisco Examiner*, December 2, 1888.

6. This is a somewhat garbled version of the lynching of Irish Dick Cronin in Placerville in October 1850. Cronin (some accounts spell it Crone) was dealing monte in the El Dorado Saloon. Two miners quarreled, which drew gamblers away from Irish Dick's table. Enraged, Cronin pushed through the crowd and stabbed one of them to death. He fled but was soon captured. A mob estimated at one to three thousand took him from the sheriff, gave him a trial, and hanged him. Although Duane saw the original quarrel between the two miners, he may not have seen Irish Dick kill one of them. This may have led him to believe that the man who was hanged was innocent. Either way, Duane surely knew that Irish Dick was hanged for murder and that there was no question that he was the guilty party. His statement that it was later learned that the lynched man was innocent is false. Duane's own prejudices against popular justice clearly colored his recollection of this incident. See *Sacramento Union*, March 27, 1875, April 21, May 1, 1880; Bancroft, *Popular Tribunals*, 1: 155–56.

7. James W. Marshall (1810–1885), an employee of John Augustus Sutter, discovered gold at Sutter's mill in January 1848, setting off the California Gold Rush. He was "old" in 1881 when Duane gave his recollections but was only forty years of age when Duane met him in 1850. Like Sutter, he lost his land to squatters and never profited from his discovery. He received a small state pension from 1872 to 1878 and died a pauper in Coloma, where he had first found gold.

8. A Danish sailor, John W. Kisling arrived in San Francisco in 1846 and was granted a city lot in 1847. In 1859 he moved to San Mateo County, where he died in 1861. Bancroft, *Pioneer Register*, 701.

9. This was evidently Hugo Wilhelm Arthur Nahl (1833–1889), half-brother of Charles Christian Nahl (1818–1878). The Nahl brothers, descendants of a long line of German artists, came to San Francisco in 1851 and soon established themselves as the city's leading painters. Charles

designed the bear on the state flag; Arthur, the state seal. Today their paintings are exceedingly rare and highly prized by collectors of fine art. The fire department certificate was first put on display in San Francisco on November 15, 1855; a copy was issued to all who had been firemen for three years or more. Peggy and Harold Samuels, *Encyclopedia of Artists of the American West* (1985), 341–42; Moreland L. Stevens, *Charles Christian Nahl, Artist of the Gold Rush, 1818–1878* (1976); *San Francisco Herald,* November 16, 1855.

10. The "Van Ness Ordinance" of 1855, named after Mayor James Van Ness (1808–1872), relinquished the city's interest in lands within the city limits, with certain exceptions, to the persons in actual possession on or before January 1, 1855, and to persons holding certain earlier land grants. The result was that millions of dollars of land belonging to the city were rescued from speculators. The ordinance protected those who held title in the downtown area but allowed squatting in the Western Addition, where Duane claimed squatter's rights to a large tract of land in 1854. Thus Duane stood to profit personally from the passing of the Van Ness Ordinance. James Van Ness was mayor of San Francisco in 1855–56. Bancroft, *History of California,* 6: 229–30; Fritz, *Federal Justice in California,* 190; Heintz, *San Francisco's Mayors,* 31–35.

11. Duane refers to the British fighter George Thompson. His true name may have been Bob McClaren.

12. James "Yankee" Sullivan was America's first great bare-knuckle champion. He was born James Ambrose in County Cork, Ireland, on April 12, 1813. A prizefighter in Britain, he was convicted of either murder or burglary about 1838 and sent to the Australian penal colony. He escaped to New York and returned to England under the alias of Yankee Sullivan. After defeating the British boxer Jack "Hammer" Lane, he went back to New York and opened a popular Bowery saloon. He continued prizefighting, sparring, and promoting. As a promoter of the fatal Chris Lilly–Tom McCoy bout in 1842, Sullivan was convicted of manslaughter as an accessory in McCoy's death. Although a jury had found him at fault, Sullivan obtained a pardon through his political connections. On February 7, 1849, he was defeated in his celebrated match with Tom Hyer. He joined the Gold Rush, promoted fights in the mining region, and returned to New York where, in 1853, he fought perhaps his greatest fight against the champion, John Morrissey. Although three inches shorter, thirty pounds lighter, and eighteen years older than Morrissey, Sullivan outfought his opponent for thirty-seven rounds. But when a riot broke out in the ring, the referee awarded the decision and purse to Morrissey. Sullivan returned to San Francisco,

where he and Billy Mulligan ran the Gibraltar Saloon on Merchant Street. His prominence as a ballot-box stuffer led to his arrest by the vigilantes. Yankee Sullivan committed suicide in their custody on May 31, 1856. Gorn, *The Manly Art*, 69–97, 110–12; Bancroft, *Popular Tribunals*, 2: 272–75; *Alta California*, October 19, 1884; *San Francisco Herald*, June 2, 1856.

13. The fight between George Thompson and Jack Willis, of Vermont, took place on June 20, 1852, at the Brighton race course, six miles from Sacramento. A crowd of twenty-five hundred, including not a few women, witnessed the encounter. Thompson was the superior fighter in every respect and the judges awarded the decision to him after nine rounds. According to a newspaper correspondent, "Neither of the parties were much pummeled; and, altogether, it was a very lame affair—hardly worthy the name of a fight." *Alta California*, June 22, 1852.

14. John Morrissey was born in Ireland on February 12, 1831, and grew up in Troy, New York. Compiling a criminal record for burglary and assault, he made his reputation as a brawler on the New York docks and as a political shoulder-striker. In one saloon brawl a stove was knocked over and his opponent pinned him on the coals. His clothes and flesh scorched and smoking, Morrissey kept up the fight until he bested his man. The incident made him famous and earned him his nickname "Old Smoke." He came to California in 1851 at age twenty and fought twenty-seven-year-old George Thompson on August 20, 1852. Morrissey drew first blood in the second round and challenged Thompson strongly until the eleventh round, when the two clinched. With the cry of "Foul!" the crowd broke into the ring and the fight was stopped. According to another account, Thompson outboxed the novice fighter until Morrissey's partisans menaced Thompson with weapons, causing him deliberately to foul Morrissey. Gorn, *The Manly Art*, 109–10; *Alta California*, August 21, 1852.

15. Joe Winrow, a prizefighter from Liverpool, England, fought a spectacular, 119-round battle against an Irishman, Tom O'Donnell, in Natchez, Mississippi, in 1847. He and George Thompson trained Tom Hyer for his great bout with Yankee Sullivan in 1849. Like many of the prize-fighting fraternity, Winrow joined the Gold Rush. He was a San Francisco police officer in 1851. On June 11, 1851, Winrow and several policemen under Police Captains Benjamin Ray and S. C. Harding tried unsuccessfully to rescue John Jenkins from the mob in Portsmouth Square. Gorn, *The Manly Art*, 81,89; Williams, *Papers of the San Francisco Committee of Vigilance of 1851*, 20.

16. Morrissey returned to New York and in 1853 fought a celebrated match with Yankee Sullivan and was awarded the decision by the referee.

He prospered as a saloonkeeper, gambler, and cockfight promoter. His political connections kept him out of prison after an 1856 shooting scrape and several brawls the following year. On October 20, 1858, Morrissey fought his last bout. He defeated John C. Heenan, "The Benecia Boy," in one of the biggest prizefights of that era. Retiring from the ring, he soon became wealthy as the owner of a prestigious gambling house and racetrack in Saratoga, New York. He served two terms in the U.S. Congress and two in the New York State Senate and died in 1878. Gorn, *The Manly Art*, 108–28; Asbury, *Gangs of New York*, 90–100.

CHAPTER 3. HARD CITIZENS

1. Horace W. Carpentier was a notorious attorney and "land shark." Born in New York in 1825, he attended Columbia University and arrived in California in 1849. With his unscrupulous partners, Edson Adams and Andrew Moon, he squatted on the present site of the city of Oakland and swindled the rightful owners, the sons of ranchero Luis Peralta, out of their title. In 1851, when the Peraltas tried to enforce their rights, Carpentier again relied on David Broderick's thugs to aid him. Billy Mulligan and a band of ruffians from San Francisco were called in to protect Carpentier's claim. Carpentier became immensely wealthy and in the 1880s returned to New York City, where he died on January 31, 1918. Perhaps to make amends for his thieving ways, in later life he became a great philanthropist and left more than $2.5 million from his estate to various universities, including scholarships for Chinese and black students. William Halley, *Centennial Year Book of Alameda County*, (1876), 447–51; Bancroft, *History of California*, 6: 475–76; J. P. Munro-Fraser, *History of Alameda County, California* (1883, 1969), 1000; David Weber, *Oakland: Hub of the West* (1981), 42–44.

2. Hyer celebrated his arrival in San Francisco by riding a horse into a saloon. Arrested for drunkenness and disorderly conduct, Hyer was fined fifty dollars after his lawyer argued that Hyer merely wanted to "see the elephant" and to "hunt him out." *Alta California*, August 6, 1850.

3. The Sacramento Squatter Riot took place on August 14 and 15, 1850. Its root cause was the uncertainty of land titles in Sacramento. Located at the upper navigable reaches of the Sacramento River and connected by riverboat service to San Francisco, the city was the center of commerce for the Northern Mines. The bustling settlement grew rapidly after 1848. John Augustus Sutter, who had settled there in 1839, claimed

title to the land based on a vast Mexican land grant and offered lots for sale at steep prices. Sutter's grant had not been confirmed by Congress and many settlers believed that Congress would never allow such huge tracts of land to pass to a single individual. Claiming that Sutter's land was public, they organized a Settlers' Association and squatted on lots both in and outside the town. Their leader was Charles Robinson, a physician, and later governor of Kansas. Litigation ensued between those who had purchased land from Sutter and those who squatted upon it. On August 14, 1850, Sheriff Joseph McKinney evicted squatters from a house on Second Street. A party of armed squatters led by James Maloney retook the house. They were confronted at Fourth and J Streets by a large posse of citizens led by Sheriff McKinney and Mayor Harding Bigelow. Ordered to lay down their arms, the squatters opened fire instead. In the pitched battle that followed, four men were killed and five wounded. The casualties included Mayor Bigelow, who received four wounds; Maloney, who was slain; and Robinson, severely wounded.

The following day Sheriff McKinney led a twenty-man posse to evict a party of squatters near Sutter's Fort. In another desperate shootout, Sheriff McKinney and two squatters were killed and three men were wounded. Duane's visit to Sutter's Fort the following day was an effort to arrest Sheriff McKinney's killers. The courts eventually ruled against the squatters and in favor of those who held John Sutter's title. The irony of Dutch Charley taking sides against squatters could not have been lost on him when he dictated this account. On the Squatter Riot, see Bancroft, *History of California*, 6: 329–34; Josiah Royce, "The Squatter Riot of '50 in Sacramento," *Overland Monthly*, 2d. ser., 6 (September 1885): 225–46.

4. Harding Bigelow, a veteran of the Black Hawk War, was Sacramento's first mayor and an early booster of the city. His death from cholera in San Francisco occurred on November 27, 1850.

5. Andrew Jackson Butler, younger brother of Benjamin F. Butler, Union general of the Civil War, was a political aide to David Broderick when the latter was U.S. senator. In 1859 Andrew Butler encouraged Broderick to fight his duel with David S. Terry and thwarted efforts to avert the clash. He is reported to have told Broderick, "These Chivs have got to learn that there is one man they can't back down. The fight has got to come and this is the best time for it." Williams, *David Broderick*, 175, 235.

6. Benjamin F. Washington was Sacramento city recorder at the time of the squatter riot. It was he who shot and killed James Maloney in the first gunfight of the riot. He became a leader of the Chivalry branch of the Democratic party in California and was a close friend and ally of U.S.

Senator William Gwin. In 1854 Washington fought a duel with Charles A. Washburn, an editor of the *Alta California*. He was appointed U.S. collector of customs in San Francisco in 1857. Hittell, *History of California*, 4: 212, 221.

7. Wakeman Bryarly, editor of the *Sacramento Times and Transcript*, played a prominent role in the second gunfight of the riot. He shot and wounded a squatter named Allen, who had killed Sheriff McKinney. His overland journal, *Trail to California*, was published in 1945 by Yale University Press.

8. Tom Hyer's remaining years were anticlimactic. He ran a saloon in New York City and maintained close ties to the city's gangs, such as the Bowery Boys, and Tammany politics. His efforts at saloonkeeping and gambling were a failure and by the early 1860s he was impoverished. A lifetime of brawling and prizefighting left him with an enlarged spleen; his once magnificent frame was wracked with degenerative arthritis and his liver was diseased from excessive drink. In 1863 a benefit was held to raise funds for Hyer. He was described as "leaning on crutches, almost doubled up, as helpless as a child, ragged, ill-clad, and never free from pain." When Hyer died on June 26, 1864, only a handful of friends came to the funeral. He lived only forty-five years, the typical abbreviated life span of the bare-knuckle fighter of that era. Gorn, *The Manly Art*, 123–24, 277n; Gammie, "Pugilists and Politicians in New York": 293–94.

9. Alexander Campbell (1809–1888), an attorney from New Brunswick, was presiding judge of the Court of Sessions in 1850. A man of integrity, he strongly opposed both the 1851 and 1856 vigilance committees. He issued the warrant for Duane's arrest for the beating of Frank Ball in 1851, and sentenced him to a year in prison. A prominent and very able criminal lawyer, he assisted in the prosecution of Charles Cora for the murder of William Richardson in 1855 and served as District Court judge in San Francisco from 1860 to 1862. Nunis, *San Francisco Vigilance Committee of 1856*, 84–85; Oscar T. Shuck, *Bench and Bar in California* (1889), 123–29.

10. Edward "Ned" McGowan was a noted Gold Rush character. Born in Philadelphia, Pennsylvania, on March 12, 1813, he started in politics in 1838 and served as a superintendent of police from 1845 to 1848. In the latter year he was convicted of complicity in the theft of $51,000 from the Chester County Bank. Released on bail, McGowan soon departed for California. He was county judge in San Francisco in 1850 and a strong supporter of David Broderick. He served as chairman of the state Democratic convention in 1854. A thorough scoundrel, McGowan was suspected of

election rigging and in 1855 was observed fleeing the scene of a bomb explosion at the house of his former lover, a French courtesan. He was accused of conspiring with and aiding James P. Casey in the murder of James King of William. He fled San Francisco to escape vigilante posses but later returned and in 1857 was tried and acquitted of the charges. McGowan then published two newspapers in Sacramento with the avowed purpose of publicly humiliating the vigilantes, or "stranglers," as he dubbed them. Much of what he published against the vigilantes was of dubious accuracy and was libelous in the extreme. In the 1870s and '80s he wrote and published various memoirs of those days and died in San Francisco on December 8, 1893, a well-known and by then—having ceased libeling his enemies—a well-regarded figure. His biography by John Myers Myers, inaptly titled *San Francisco's Reign of Terror* (1966), is heavily biased in McGowan's favor and should be used with caution. A more balanced account is Carl I. Wheat, "Ned, the Ubiquitous," *California Historical Society Quarterly* 6 (March 1927): 3–26.

11. This incident actually took place on February 22, 1851. Several days earlier, on February 19, a storekeeper named Charles Jansen was beaten up and robbed of $2,000 by two thugs. The police arrested two suspects, William Wildred or Windred, and Thomas Berdue, who was mistakenly identified as English Jim Stuart, a notorious criminal and Sydney Duck. On the 22nd, the pair were taken for identification to a house where Jansen was recovering from his wounds. On the return trip to the courthouse the two suspects and their police guard were attacked by a mob in Portsmouth Square. According to most accounts, it was the police who fought off the would-be lynchers. It turned out that Wildred and Berdue were innocent. Wildred soon escaped from jail; Berdue was released. In 1853 a bill was submitted to the legislature asking for $4,000 in reparations for Berdue; it failed. Mullen, *Let Justice Be Done*, 123–24; Stewart, *Committee of Vigilance*, 18; Bancroft, *Popular Tribunals*, 1: 199–200. At the time, Duane himself was being prosecuted for shooting Amedee Fayolle.

12. Berdue, mistaken for James Stuart, was sent to Marysville where he was tried for the murder of Charles Moore, convicted, and sentenced to death. Before he could be hanged, the San Francisco vigilantes notified the Marysville authorities that they had taken the real James Stuart. Williams, *Papers of the San Francisco Committee of Vigilance*, 137–38.

13. John B. Brady lived on the California Street hill, near Powell. On July 2, 1851, he observed James Stuart near his home, and an hour later learned that the house of his neighbor, James Adair, had been burglarized. Brady, Adair, and several other men arrested Stuart and delivered him to the

vigilance committee. Williams, *Papers of the San Francisco Committee of Vigilance*, 140–43.

14. Ira Cole, a close friend of Duane, was one of David Broderick's most loyal shoulder-strikers. He was exiled by the vigilance committee in 1856 but by 1859 he had returned to San Francisco. *Alta California*, August 20, 1859.

15. John Jenkins was the first man executed by the vigilance committee. He was hanged on June 10, 1851. He had been a convict in Australia. Immigrants from Australia were justifiably looked on with suspicion in California. According to a survey of convicts sent from England to the Australian penal colony, some 80 percent were thieves; very few could be classified as political offenders. One-half to two-thirds were habitual criminals, with one and two prior convictions. And according to a study of Australian immigrants to California, 13 percent of immigrants from Sydney in 1848 were ex-convicts. In 1852 there were 2,228 Australians living in San Francisco. Of these, approximately 66 percent were male. It can be extrapolated from these figures that there was a large number of male Australian ex-convicts, many of them habitual thieves, residing in a city with a population in 1852 of only 36,000. It seems clear that convicts were greatly overrepresented in the population of Australian immigrants and that there was a grossly disproportionate number of convicted Australian thieves in San Francisco during the Gold Rush. These figures support the common belief of the Forty-niner that many Australians in the Gold Rush were criminals. The figures are from Robert Hughes, *The Fatal Shore: The Epic of Australia's Founding* (1986), 158–62, and Senkewicz, *Vigilantes in Gold Rush San Francisco*, 78–80.

16. The capture of the Malakoff Tower in Sebastopol took place on September 8, 1855, during the Crimean War. The famous Malakoff Mine (now part of Malakoff Diggings State Park in Nevada County) was named after this battle of the Crimea. News of the Allied victory at Sebastopol arrived in San Francisco in November 1855. On November 26 the French and British hosted San Francisco's largest celebration of the 1850s. The drunken riot is described in detail in the *Alta California*, November 27, 1855. The *Alta* does not mention Duane but provides a similar account and credits City Marshal Hampton North with attempting to restore order. Horace Bell told the story differently: "Charley Duane organized a big crowd of hard hitters, took position, and when the signal was given flung to the midnight air a Russian flag, carried the Malikoff [*sic*] by storm, and planting the banner of the Czar thereon, held the fort." Horace Bell, *Reminiscences of a Ranger* (1927), p. 426.

CHAPTER 4. DUELING IN THE GOLD RUSH

1. This was Caleb C. Smith, son of William Smith of Virginia. The former governor and Broderick engaged in a war of words in Sacramento that was amicably settled. But Caleb Smith was not satisfied, and in a card in the *Democratic State Journal*, published Broderick as a "liar, scoundrel, and blackguard." Mutual friends attempted to negotiate a resolution of the dispute, but Smith withdrew the card and challenged Broderick. The resulting duel, which Duane describes, took place on March 17, 1852. Hubert Howe Bancroft, *California Inter Pocula* (1888), 752–53; Williams, *David C. Broderick*, 68–69.

2. Austin E. Smith was an associate of Broderick and in 1859 was navy agent for California. He was a delegate to the Breckenridge Democratic National Convention in 1860, and was arrested as a Southern sympathizer in New York in 1861. He later joined the Confederate forces and was killed in action in the battle of Fair Oaks, Virginia, on June 1, 1863. Williams, *David C. Broderick*, 227; Nunis, *San Francisco Vigilance Committee of 1856*, 91.

3. John A. McGlynn was a close associate of David Broderick who, with Fred Kohler, was instrumental in setting up the Democratic Party machinery in San Francisco in 1850. Born in Ireland in 1824, he came to New York with his family while an infant. He arrived in San Francisco in 1849 and was the city's first recorder. In 1851 he was president of the Roman Catholic Orphan Asylum and for years was connected with charitable work. During the Civil War he became a Republican and later was that party's unsuccessful nominee for sheriff and for harbor commissioner. He died in San Francisco on August 17, 1874. *San Francisco Examiner*, August 18, 1874.

4. This presentation must have occurred after 1851, as the Colt Navy Model revolver was not manufactured until that year.

5. "Natchez" was Andrew J. Taylor, the leading gunsmith of San Francisco in the 1850s. He operated a pistol gallery on Clay Street, opposite the plaza, and kept a large stock of firearms and knives. He supplied the weapons used in some of California's most noted duels. Bancroft wrote that he "was the general armorer of belligerent San Franciscans" and claimed that Taylor loaded the pistol which Charles Cora used to kill U.S. Marshal William Richardson, as well as the pistol with which James Casey killed James King of William. Taylor died on September 24, 1858, when a customer examining a Colt revolver in his shop accidentally shot him in the face. *Alta California*, September 25, 1858; Bancroft, *Popular Tribunals*, 2: 608–9.

6. Vicesimus Turner was another of Broderick's shoulder-strikers. Like Rube Maloney, he joined the 1851 vigilantes, apparently so that he could keep Broderick posted on their movements. Judge Stephen J. Field called Turner "a well known desperado" and described how he drew a pistol on him in a hotel bar in San Francisco in 1851. David Broderick interfered and saved Field's life. Stewart, *Committee of Vigilance*, 262, 276; Stephen J. Field, *Personal Reminiscences of Early Days in California* (1893), 77–83.

7. The Rancho San Leandro was owned by Jose Joaquin Estudillo, born in Monterey, California, on May 5, 1800. He became a prominent and wealthy ranchero of the East Bay and died in San Francisco on June 7, 1852. One of his daughters, Magdalena, married John Nugent, the dueling editor of the *San Francisco Herald* and opponent of the 1856 Committee of Vigilance. Bancroft, *Pioneer Register*, 794; Mildred Brooke Hoover, Hero Eugene Rensch, and Ethel Grace Rensch, *Historic Spots in California*, 3rd. ed. (1966), 15–16.

8. Henry B. Truett and his brother, Miers F. Truett, were prominent San Francisco merchants. In 1856, Henry Truett opposed the Committee of Vigilance, while his brother was a member of its executive committee. Miers Truett was honest and impartial and, despite his vigilante connections, acted as defense counsel for both Charles Cora and Judge David S. Terry before the vigilance committee. These acts endeared him to Charley Duane and resulted in Duane's protecting Truett in New York, as described in Chapter 8.

9. Hampton North hailed from Philadelphia. In 1850 he was a police sergeant in San Francisco; by 1853 he was captain of police. North served as city marshal of San Francisco from July 1, 1855, to June 12, 1856. When the vigilance committee demanded that all city officials resign, North complied. He did not even bother to serve out the remaining weeks of his term, which expired on July 1. North soon returned to Philadelphia, having somehow managed to accumulate $50,000 on his police officer's pay. He died there in 1860. Martin J. Burke, San Francisco's highly reputable chief of police from 1858 to 1866, considered North highly disreputable and called him "a creature of the worst elements of the city." Kimball, *The San Francisco City Directory, 1850*, 123; Gladys Hansen, *Behind the Silver Star* (1981), p. i; *California Police Gazette*, July 7, 1860; Martin J. Burke, *Dictation*, 1887, Bancroft Library.

10. This duel took place in October 1855. Truett and Smith fought with Colt revolvers at ten paces.

11. Former governor John McDougal did not fight an *Alta California* editor, but he did fight A. C. Russell, one of the editors of the *San Francisco*

Picayune, in Santa Clara County on December 11, 1852. Bancroft, *California Inter Pocula* (1888), 756.

12. San Francisquito Creek.

13. Edward Gilbert was born in 1819 in Otsego County, New York, worked as a printer and newspaperman in Albany, and came to California with the New York Volunteers in 1847. He founded the *Alta California* in 1849, became prominent in public affairs, and the same year was elected as the first congressman from California. He died in the duel with Denver, August 2, 1852. John F. Wilhelm, "Shootout at Oak Grove," *Golden Notes* (Bulletin of the Sacramento County Historical Society), vol. 29, no. 3 (Fall 1983): 4; Bancroft, *Pioneer Register*, 756.

14. James W. Denver, born in 1817, was a native of Winchester, Virginia. Educated at Cincinnati Law School, he practiced law and ran a Democratic newspaper in Xenia, Ohio. In 1842 he relocated in Platte City, Missouri, and in the Mexican War served as a captain in the Twelfth U.S. Volunteer Infantry. Returning to Missouri at war's end, he journeyed overland to California in 1850. He was elected state senator in 1851, was secretary of state in 1853–1854, and served in Congress from 1855 to 1857. He was governor of Kansas Territory when the city of Denver was named in his honor. During the Civil War he was a general in the U.S. Army, and twice was an unsuccessful candidate for Congress from Ohio. In 1876, 1880, and 1884 his name was offered as Democratic candidate for president, but negative publicity from the Gilbert duel helped quash his presidential ambitions. Denver died in Washington, D.C., on August 9, 1892. See George C. Barns, *Denver the Man* (1949).

15. Henry Frederick Teschemaker, born in England in 1823, arrived in California in 1842 as a shipping clerk. He invested in San Francisco real estate, joined the 1851 Committee of Vigilance, and served as the city's mayor from 1859 to 1863. With the wealth from his investments he returned to Europe and died in Switzerland in 1904. Heintz, *San Francisco's Mayors*, 48–53.

16. Henry B. Livingston was a pioneer California journalist. Born in Litchfield, New York, August 19, 1825, he graduated from Williams College in 1847. He read law, joined the Gold Rush, and arrived in California in June 1849. He worked as a newspaperman in Sacramento in the early 1850s, then moved to San Francisco, where he was on the staff of the *Alta California* and later the *Herald*. Livingston was an active member of the Southern wing of the Democratic Party. For ten years he was historian of the Society of California Pioneers. He died in San Francisco on April 1, 1897. *San Francisco Call*, April 2, 1897.

17. The Denver-Gilbert duel was one of California's most noted affairs of honor. See Benjamin C. Truman, *The Field of Honor* (1884), 308–13; Wilhelm, "Shootout at Oak Grove," 1–16.

18. Duane, in his original account, confused Edward C. Kemble with A. C. Russell. I have corrected his error. This duel occurred in September 1851, when George McDougal twice met Kemble, editor of the *Alta California*. According to Bancroft, each time the proposed duel was stopped by law officers. Bancroft, *California Inter Pocula*, 751.

19. George W. McDougal was the younger brother of Governor John McDougal. Born in Clermont County, Ohio, he served with his brother in the Black Hawk War in 1832 and journeyed overland to California with the Swasey-Todd party in 1845. He was in San Francisco when gold was discovered in 1848, invested in town lots, and was the first storekeeper in Sacramento. A popular man of herculean proportions and great eccentricity, he suddenly disappeared from California in 1853. Erroneously reported as killed by Indians, he wandered through the western territories and lived with Indian tribes in Arizona and Mexico. In 1867 he was found by a naval commander living in South America as chief of a Patagonia Indian tribe. He returned to the U.S. and committed suicide in Washington, D.C., in 1872. Bancroft, *Pioneer Register*, 723; William L. Willis, *History of Sacramento County* (1913), 835–36; *Sacramento Union*, May 20, 1872.

20. The Red House was located near the present intersection of 23rd and Mission Streets.

21. John Cotter of New York served one term as alderman in San Francisco, 1852–53. His sons were Edward Cotter and John C. Cotter. *San Francisco Call*, March 23, 1889.

22. John Nugent was born in Galway, Ireland, in 1829, and emigrated to America as a boy. College educated, he worked for the *New York Herald* as a correspondent. In 1849 he was in San Antonio, Texas, and joined Jack Hays's overland party to California. In 1850 he started the *San Francisco Herald*, which quickly became one of the most prominent of the city's twenty-six newspapers. A fiery partisan, he supported the 1851 Committee of Vigilance but was one of the most vocal opponents of the 1856 committee. His acid pen resulted in his fighting several duels. The first, against Cotter, took place on July 15, 1852, not in 1854, as Duane erroneously states. The same year he met Edward Gilbert, an editor of the *Alta California*. Gilbert lost his nerve on the dueling ground and avoided a fight by retracting his offensive language against Nugent. In 1853 he fought his last, against Thomas Hayes. Nugent later became an attorney and in 1860, still an enemy of the vigilantes, he represented Duane in his lawsuits against Captains

Watson, Pearson, and Goodall. Nugent died at San Leandro, California, on March 29, 1880. Dan L. Thrapp, *Encyclopedia of Frontier Biography*, vol. 2 (1988), 1065–66; Bancroft, *Popular Tribunals*, 2: 618–19. His memoirs were published in six installments of the *Argonaut*, as follows: February 23, 1878, p. 7; March 9, 1878, p. 3; March 16, 1878, p. 6; March 23, 1878, p. 11; March 30, 1878, p. 6; and April 13, 1878, p. 3. These reminiscences deal mainly with his adventures in the Southwest and, unfortunately, contain nothing about his important role in San Francisco journalism and public affairs or his opposition to the 1856 Committee of Vigilance.

23. The Nugent-Hayes duel occurred on June 9, 1853.

24. James P. Casey was born in New York City about 1817. A political thug, he lived with a prostitute and served two years in Sing Sing (1849–51) for grand larceny before coming to San Francisco in 1853. He took part in various brawls and shooting scrapes, all arising out of politics. In 1855 he was chosen a member of the board of supervisors in a rigged election. Yankee Sullivan boasted to Martin J. Burke that he had used a trick ballot box to elect Casey. James Casey ran a newspaper, the *Sunday Times*, in 1856, which William Tecumseh Sherman, then a prominent San Francisco banker, charged was a blackmail sheet. On May 14, 1856, Casey shot and mortally wounded newspaper editor James King of William, for which he was executed by the vigilantes on May 22. Secrest, *Lawmen and Desperadoes*, pp. 76–82; Burke, *Dictation*.

25. John W. Bagley was a Democratic politician; he served one term as a member of the state assembly in 1854–55. The incident that Duane describes took place near the Mission Dolores in August 1854. On May 25, 1856, Bagley was banished by the vigilance committee. Evidently he did not leave but fled to the interior of the state, for on September 19 the committee ordered "that if J.W. Bagley is found in San Francisco after the 20th inst., he will be immediately executed without trial." *California Chronicle*, August 26, 1854; Secrest, *Lawmen and Desperadoes*, 77; Bancroft *Popular Tribunals*, 2: 348, 528.

26. Robert Cushing was born in Ireland in 1829 and came to California in 1849. Active both in politics and in the volunteer fire department, he was foreman of Columbia Engine Co. No. 11. On June 2, 1856, he was placed on the vigilantes' blacklist and ordered to leave the state on pain of death. Cushing later returned to San Francisco where he was long active in Republican politics and died there on May 18, 1881. *San Francisco Post*, May 19, 1881.

27. The Bagley-Casey feud continued in 1855. In June, Casey fought with Bagley and Cushing when they attempted to remove him from his

position as sixth ward inspector of elections. The cutting and shooting scrape which Duane describes took place on August 21, 1855, and demonstrated amply the stern stuff that Casey was made of. When Casey came into his precinct to learn the election results, he was attacked by Cushing, Bagley, and three other men, armed with knives and pistols. Casey was unarmed and, although he was grazed by several pistol balls, he grabbed a knife from one of his assailants and cut Cushing severely. Casey then seized a pistol and exchanged gunfire with his attackers, wounding Bagley and putting the rest to flight. *Alta California*, August 25, 1855; O'Meara, *The Vigilance Committee*, 25–26. For a sketch of Casey's life see Secrest, *Lawmen and Desperadoes*, 76–82. Both Bagley and Cushing were placed on the vigilance committee's blacklist in 1856. Although not actually deported like Charley Duane, they were ordered to leave the state or be executed without trial. Bancroft, *Popular Tribunals*, 2: 348.

28. Dupont Street is now Grant Avenue.

29. Casey's election as supervisor in 1855 was the most celebrated example of voting fraud in Gold Rush San Francisco. Although Casey had never even been a candidate for supervisor, Yankee Sullivan and two cronies, while running an isolated polling place, stuffed the ballot box with 150 votes for Casey. A Democratic judge on the court of sessions refused to set aside the ballots and Casey was declared legally elected. Senkewicz, *Vigilantes in Gold Rush San Francisco*, 116–17.

CHAPTER 5. A BULLET FOR JAMES KING OF WILLIAM

1. He was born James King in Georgetown, District of Columbia, on January 28, 1822. He added the surname "of William" after his father to avoid confusion with other James Kings in the area. After working as a journalist and a banker, he journeyed to California in 1848 to improve his health. En route, he learned of the discovery of gold. He made a brief tour of the mines and in 1849 opened a banking house in San Francisco. By 1853 he was reportedly worth $250,000, but his bank failed the following year. He went to work for the Adams & Co. bank and persuaded that institution to take over his assets and debts, which may have weakened it financially and helped lead to its failure. Senkewicz, *Vigilantes in Gold Rush San Francisco*, 156–58; Nunis, *San Francisco Vigilance Committee of 1856*, 105–6.

2. James King of William was cashier of the Adams & Co. bank, owned by the Adams Express Co. of Boston. It went out of business on February 23, 1855. Alfred A. Cohen, who was appointed by the court as

receiver of the failed bank's assets, publicly accused King of fraud and of mishandling the firm's funds. O'Meara, *The Vigilance Committee*, 62–63; Nunis, *San Francisco Vigilance Committee of 1856*, 105–106n; Senkewicz, *Vigilantes in Gold Rush San Francisco*, 54–57.

3. James King of William began publishing the *San Francisco Bulletin* on October 8, 1855. In a colorful and reckless style he attacked corruption, particularly the political machine of David Broderick, and made personal journalistic attacks on his political enemies and those who had accused him of dishonesty in his failed banking ventures. The *Bulletin* quickly became a prominent and profitable newspaper. Senkewicz, *Vigilantes in Gold Rush San Francisco*, 158–67.

4. John C. Cremony was a journalist, frontiersman, and soldier. Born in Portland, Maine, about 1817, he went to sea, later serving as second lieutenant of the First Massachusetts Infantry in the Mexican War. A member of the U.S. Boundary Survey Commission from 1850 to 1852, he served as Spanish interpreter and helped survey the southeastern boundary of the U.S. In 1852 he led a mining exploration party into what is now Arizona, and later came to San Francisco, where he worked as a newspaperman. Cremony joined the Union Army in the Civil War, and as a captain in the California Column took part in the Battle of Apache Pass against Apaches led by Mangas Coloradas and Cochise on July 15, 1862. An authority on the Apaches, he compiled a vocabulary of their language. In 1868 he published *Life among the Apaches*. His writings were often exaggerated and unreliable. Cremony died in San Francisco on August 24, 1879. Thomas Edwin Farish, *History of Arizona* (1915), 1: 184, 271, and 2: 127ff; Jay J. Wagoner, *Arizona Territory 1863–1912: A Political History* (1970), 19; Franklin Walker, *San Francisco's Literary Frontier* (1939), 114, 352; Thrapp, *Encyclopedia of Frontier Biography*, 1: 342–43; *Alta Californian*, August 25, 1879.

5. James Hennessey was banished by the Committee of Vigilance, but he fled to the interior of the state. Bancroft, *Popular Tribunals*, 2: 528.

6. Here Duane's memory failed him. The fact that Casey had served a prison term in New York came out in his testimony during his trial for assault following his gunfight with Bagley and Cushing on August 21, 1855. This fact was published in the contemporary newspaper accounts of his trial; Casey was bitterly criticized in the *California Chronicle* of November 2, 1855, more than six months before he shot James King of William. Nunis, *San Francisco Vigilance Committee of 1856*, 96–97n.

7. Franklin Soule, born in Maine in 1810, was an 1838 graduate of Wesleyan College. First a teacher, then a journalist, he joined the Gold Rush in 1849, mined for a year, and then became editor of the *Alta*

California. With a partner, William L. Newell, he published the *California Chronicle* in San Francisco from 1853 to 1858. Soule opposed the vigilance committee. In 1864 he became editor of the *San Francisco Call,* later rejoined the *Alta,* and died in San Francisco on July 3, 1872. Nunis, *San Francisco Vigilance Committee of 1856,* 107–108n.

8. Duane refers to James Nisbet, who was associate editor of the *California Chronicle* and later, at the time of the murder of James King of William, associate editor of the *San Francisco Bulletin.* Nisbet was born in Glasgow, Scotland, in 1816. He worked as a San Francisco journalist until his death on July 30, 1865, as a passenger on the ill-fated *Brother Jonathan,* which sank off the California coast near Crescent City. Some ninety passengers and crewmen perished. Nunis, *San Francisco Vigilance Committee of 1856,* 109n.

9. James King of William was shot on May 14, 1856, and died on May 20, 1856. On his deathbed he denied that Casey ever said, "Draw and defend yourself." Contrary to Duane's assertion, there is no reliable evidence that King was carrying a pistol when he was shot.

10. The passage that Duane refers to is probably the following, which King published in the *San Francisco Bulletin* on December 6, 1855, after he had been threatened by Abla A. Selover. It is quoted in Bancroft, *Popular Tribunals,* 2: 28.

> Mr. Selover, it is said, carries a knife. We carry a pistol. We hope neither will be required, but if this recontre cannot be avoided why will Mr. Selover persist in periling the lives of others? We pass every afternoon, at half past four to five o'clock, along Market Street from Fourth to Fifth Street. The road is wide and not so much frequented as those streets farther in town. If we are to be shot or cut to pieces, for heaven's sake let it be done there. Others will not be injured, and in case we fall our house is but a few hundred yards beyond, and the cemetery not much farther.

11. The leading members of the Law and Order Party were David Broderick; David S. Terry, justice of the California Supreme Court; John Nugent, editor of the *San Francisco Herald*; and Edward D. Baker, a prominent attorney. Greatly outnumbered by the vigilantes, they had no success in opposing the committee.

12. Lafayette Byrne was a deputy sheriff at the time that Casey killed James King of William. He took Casey to the police station house following the shooting.

13. Henry H. Byrne was a lawyer from New York. He was San Francisco's district attorney from 1851 to 1855 and from 1868 to 1871. He prosecuted Charles Cora for the killing of Marshal Richardson. Byrne died in San Francisco on March 2, 1872. Nunis, *San Francisco Vigilance Committee of 1856*, 86n.

14. Duane fails to mention that several ruffian friends of Casey, including Billy Mulligan, were also present on the hack, as were Police Captain Isaiah W. Lees and Officer John L. Durkee. According to Lees, Casey was still armed and tried to draw his revolver to defend himself from the mob but Lees disarmed him. Hittell minimized Duane's role, writing that he "tried to get into the carriage; but, failing in that, he clung to the back of it, as it was driven furiously along." Bancroft, *Popular Tribunals*, 2: 58–59; Hittell, *History of California*, 3: 483.

15. David Scannell was born in New York City on January 31, 1820. As a young man he gained experience in New York's volunteer fire department and served as a captain of volunteers in the Mexican War. He arrived in San Francisco in 1851, served as undersheriff for William R. Graham, and was elected sheriff in 1855. He opposed the Committee of Vigilance, and was accused by William T. Sherman of being a New York shoulder-striker. Scannell joined San Francisco's volunteer fire department in 1851. Exceedingly popular, he was foreman of Broderick Engine Company No. 1 and was chief of the volunteer fire department from 1860 to 1866, and chief of the regular paid fire department (organized in 1866) from 1871 to 1873 and from 1874 until his death in San Francisco on March 30, 1893. Nunis, *San Francisco Vigilance Committee of 1856*, 79–80n; *San Francisco Daily Report*, January 31, 1881; *San Francisco Call*, December 22, 1890, March 31, 1893.

16. The "prominent men" whom Duane fails to mention include the disreputable judge, Edward McGowan, and gambler Dan Aldrich, who was soon afterward deported by the vigilance committee. Hittell, *History of California*, 483.

17. Here Duane is uncharacteristically modest. What he fails to mention, of course, is that every man in the mob knew him, either personally or by reputation. They were not afraid of "a single weapon" but rather of the man who wielded it.

18. The vigilantes moved into their headquarters, which became known as Fort Gunnybags, on May 17, 1856. A large, two-story building, it was divided into a courtroom, committee rooms, guardrooms, dormitories, and prison cells. On the roof was mounted a large signal bell, and the street level was fortified by a breastworks of sandbags, hence its nickname.

CHAPTER 6. "CORA AND CASEY ARE HANGED!"

1. Charles Cora was born in Genoa, Italy, about 1816, and came to the U.S. as a boy. By 1835 he was a gambler in the notorious sporting town of Natchez, Mississippi. He came to California in 1849 with his mistress, Belle Cora, and several gambler comrades. They reportedly brought $40,000 with them to open a gambling house. After a tour of the mining country, he settled about 1852 in San Francisco, where he soon became one of the city's best-known professional gamblers. Curt Gentry, *The Madams of San Francisco* (1964), chap. 6; DeArment, *Knights of the Green Cloth*, 9–10, 17–21, 25–40.

2. Belle Cora was born Arabella Ryan in Baltimore, Maryland, about 1826. The daughter of a clergyman, she reportedly met Charles Cora in New Orleans in 1848. They came by ship to California via Panama, arriving on December 28, 1849. According to Ben Bohen, a San Francisco police detective of the 1860s and '70s, "She was a voluptuous creature." She toured the mines with Charles Cora and by November 1852 she owned a bagnio on Dupont Street, now Grant Avenue. Later she ran a brothel on Waverly Place, and in 1855 Charles Cora built her an ornate house on Pike Street. She died in San Francisco on February 18, 1862, and is buried next to Charles Cora in Mission Dolores Cemetery. Gentry, *The Madams of San Francisco*, chaps. 6–8; Nunis, *San Francisco Vigilance Committee of 1856*, 80; DeArment, *Knights of the Green Cloth*, 26–27, 30–33.

3. William H. Richardson was born in Baltimore, Maryland, in 1819. He came to California in 1850 as sutler for the surveying party of the U.S. Boundary Commission and became quartermaster of the California state militia in 1851, acquiring the rank of general. In March 1852, he was appointed U.S. marshal of California. He was shot and killed by Charles Cora on November 17, 1855. Nunis, *San Francisco Vigilance Committee of 1856*, 76.

4. The difficulty between them began on November 15, 1855, when U.S. Marshal Richardson brought his new bride and a lady friend to the New American Theater. The two women made negative comments about Belle Cora, who was seated nearby, and sought unsuccessfully to have the theater management remove her. Later that evening Richardson had a chance meeting with Charles Cora at the Blue Wing Saloon. The gambler jocularly mentioned the theater encounter and Richardson took offense, but a friend of the marshal talked him into going home instead of quarreling with Cora. The marshal brooded over the incident and two days later was shot in what may well have been self-defense by Cora. Senkewicz, *Vigilantes in Gold Rush San Francisco*, 5–6.

5. Edward D. Baker was born in London, England, on February 24, 1811. Brought to the U.S. by his parents at the age of four, he was raised in Pennsylvania and Illinois. A lawyer by 1830, he was elected to Congress in 1844 and resigned to fight in the Mexican War as a colonel of the Illinois Volunteer Infantry. Baker was a close friend of Abraham Lincoln. After serving another term in Congress from 1849 to 1851, he came to San Francisco, where he was one of the city's most prominent attorneys. In 1860 he moved to Oregon and was elected U.S. senator. In the Civil War he commanded the Fourth Regiment of California Volunteers. Baker was killed in action at the battle of Ball's Bluff, Virginia, on October 21, 1861. Nunis, *San Francisco Vigilance Committee of 1856*, 81–82.

6. Several recent commentators have written that there is scant evidence of election fraud in San Francisco during this period. Yet this admission by Duane, who was arguably the most prominent shoulder-striker in the city's early history, gives substantial weight to the traditional view of political and electoral corruption in Gold Rush San Francisco. See also Ethington, *The Public City*, pp. 117–24. For evidence against voter fraud, see, in particular, Senkewicz, *Vigilantes in Gold Rush San Francisco*, 116–19.

7. Christopher Dowdigan was a typical New York shoulder striker and friend of Billy Mulligan and Woolly Kearney. On May 10, 1854, he fought a duel at the San Francisco presidio with James Hawkins. They used rifles at forty paces and Dowdigan was wounded in the left arm. In an 1855 trial he testified that he had known Woolly Kearney for twenty years in both New York and California. Dowdigan was blacklisted by the vigilantes in 1856. Hubert Howe Bancroft, *California Inter Pocula* (1888), 758–59; *Alta California*, January 28, 1855.

8. According to Bancroft, the funeral procession included eighty-four carriages, eighty horsemen, and four hundred on foot. Just six hacks accompanied Charles Cora's remains. *Popular Tribunals*, 2: 242. The pro-vigilance *Bulletin* reported that "hundreds" of Irish laborers had attended Casey's funeral and that "there were not over a dozen American born citizens" in the procession. Senkewicz, *Vigilantes in Gold Rush San Francisco*, 173. Casey's impressive burial marker can be viewed today in the small cemetery at the Mission Dolores in San Francisco.

CHAPTER 7. CAPTURED BY THE VIGILANTES

1. Few fighting men of the Gold Rush ran up a worse record than Billy Mulligan. Born in Ireland in 1825, Mulligan emigrated to New York

when still a youth and was apprenticed to a cooper. Despite his small
stature, he became well known as a prizefighter and shoulder-striker for
Tammany Hall. His companions in New York included Charley Duane,
William "Woolly" Kearney, Chris Lilly, and Yankee Sullivan. He was jailed
on a burglary charge in 1847 but escaped and fled to New Orleans. There
he enlisted in the Louisiana Mounted Volunteers and saw action during the
Mexican War. He then joined the Gold Rush, arriving in San Francisco in
1849. By 1850 Mulligan was active as a gambler, prizefight promoter, claim
jumper, and general ruffian in the mining region. On February 9, 1851,
Billy shot and mortally wounded a young gambler, William Anderson, in a
saloon brawl in Sonora. In the fall of 1851 he fought a celebrated duel near
Mokelumne Hill with another ruffian, Jimmy Douglass. On November 18,
1851, Mulligan was wounded in a shootout with another gambler in the
Bella Union in San Francisco. Six days later he was again wounded as a
bystander in yet another gunfight. In San Francisco Mulligan was a
shoulder-striker for David Broderick and served as tax collector and later as
deputy sheriff under David Scannell. Mulligan, his brother Bernard, or
Barney, and Chris Lilly played prominent roles in the San Mateo County
election frauds of 1856. After being deported by the vigilance committee,
he lived in New York for a number of years and delighted in thrashing San
Francisco vigilantes who happened to visit the city. In 1860 Mulligan
received a prison term for shooting at a New York policeman. By 1863 he
was back in San Francisco, and the following year fought a duel in Austin,
Nevada. In San Francisco on July 7, 1865, suffering from delirium tremens
and believing that the vigilantes were again after him, he killed two men in a
violent gun battle before he was slain by a police sharpshooter. Secrest,
"There Once was a Badman"; Secrest, *Lawmen and Desperadoes*, 241–45.

2. Martin Gallagher was a notorious political hack, ruffian, and bare-
knuckle fighter. Born in New York City about 1830, he came to San
Francisco, worked as a boatman, and was a prominent First Ward shoulder-
striker and election rigger. In 1856 he was a night watchman at the
customshouse. On June 5, Gallagher was exiled to Hawaii, but returned to
San Francisco on October 5 under an assumed name. A manhunt for him
was unsuccessful; it developed that he had returned to get his new wife.
Gallagher left for South America with her and came back to San Francisco
on January 14, 1858. The vigilante excitement had blown over in March,
when he brought a lawsuit in federal court against James Smith, master of
the bark *Yankee*, asking for $25,000 in damages. Judge Ogden Hoffman,
ruling in Gallagher's favor, held that "the deportation of a citizen to a
foreign country in an American ship, commanded by an American master,

in pursuance or execution of a sentence of an illegal and self-constituted body of men, must remain a marine tort of a most flagrant character," and awarded $3,000 in punitive damages. Martin Gallagher did not live long to enjoy the money. On June 14, 1859, he was stabbed and mortally wounded in a drunken Barbary Coast brawl. Bancroft, *Popular Tribunals*, 2: 595–96; Fritz, *Federal Justice in California*, 81–83; *Alta California*, June 17, 18, 1859.

3. Billy Carr, formerly a printer in New York City, was a boatman, shoulder-striker, and political operative for David Broderick in San Francisco's First Ward. He was arrested several times for assault and battery and once for murder. On June 5, 1856, Carr was deported with Martin Gallagher and Edward Bulger on the bark *Yankee* to Hawaii. He returned to California in 1858. Still a troublemaker, in 1861 he was arrested for forcing his way into the National Theater in San Francisco. Bancroft, *Popular Tribunals*, 2: 597, 601; Nunis, *San Francisco Vigilance Committee of 1856*, 117, 119; *Alta California*, March 1, 1861.

4. Edward Bulger returned to San Francisco on the same ship, arriving July 24, 1856. He was promptly rearrested by the vigilantes. Bulger was the only one of the deportees to be rearrested and retried while the vigilance committee was still in power. On August 5, 1856, he was again deported, with three others, on the steamer *Sonora*. He returned to California in 1857. Bancroft, *Popular Tribunals*, 2: 593–97.

5. During the trial of Duane's lawsuit against Captain Robert Pearson in 1863, Isaac Bluxome, secretary of the 1851 and 1856 committees, testified that Dutch Charley had been deported because "he said the Vigilance Committee had murdered Yankee Sullivan, and felt disposed to express himself very plainly on the subject." *Sacramento Union*, October 31, 1863. Duane had no regard for Yankee Sullivan because of the animosity between Sullivan and Tom Hyer.

6. The report of the postmortem examination of Yankee Sullivan by Drs. A. J. Bowie and A. F. Sawyer was made on May 31, 1856, and published in the *San Francisco Herald* on June 2, 1856. It read as follows:

At a post mortem examination held at half-past five o'clock this evening on the body of James Sullivan, there was found to be a well marked muscular rigidity, the jaws being firmly locked, the lips and gums as well as the surface of the body presenting a pale and bloodless appearance. A little above the left elbow there was a large, ragged incised wound, extending transversely from near the outer condyle of the humerus to the inner, superficial through the skin in its outer form, but seriously involving the deeper textures towards its inner termination. On a further inspection of the wound it was found that the brachial artery, with its accompanying veins, had been divided. The cut extremities were somewhat retracted, and were not closed by a coagulum. The artery was severed in its connection with the tendon of the biceps muscle about an inch and a quarter from its division into the radial and ulnar arteries.

The viscera of the chest, abdomen, and head were carefully examined, and with the exception of these being drained of blood, presented a perfectly healthy and natural appearance. No further traces of injury or violence was found on the body. The wound was unmistakably made during life, and probably with a dull cutting instrument. The brachial artery having been severed, the hemorrhage from it must necessarily have proved fatal within a very short period of time.

These findings tended to confirm the verdict of the coroner's jury. The wound, on the inside of the left arm above the elbow, was more consistent with self-infliction by a powerful right hand than by a thrust from a vigilante's sword. The wound had been caused by a dull cutting instrument, such as Sullivan's own case knife. Lastly, there was no evidence of any other trauma to the body such as would have been found if Sullivan had been cut to death during a physical altercation with his guard.

Yankee Sullivan was a heavy drinker. According to Bancroft, who probably exaggerated, he customarily took fifty to eighty drinks a day and when he was denied alcohol in vigilante custody he suffered an attack of delirium tremens. That morning Sullivan told one of his guards that he had dreamed the night before that he had been hanged. The vigilance committee supporters claimed that Sullivan was an escaped convict from the Australian penal colony and that he killed himself rather than be returned to prison. It is more probable that delirium tremens prompted his suicide. He left a widow, Emily Mary Sullivan, and an adopted son. See Bancroft, *Popular Tribunals*, 2: 272–75; *San Francisco Herald*, June 2, 1856.

7. Yankee Sullivan was buried in Mission Dolores cemetery, where his grave can be viewed today. The marker, erected by a friend, states bluntly that he "died at the hands of the V.C."

8. Joseph Capprise was born in Baltimore, Maryland, in 1825, where he was a volunteer fireman. He came to San Francisco in the Gold Rush and with George Hossefross and other Baltimore firemen was one of the founding members of the Monumental No. 6 Fire Company in 1850.

Capprise was a member of Sterling Hopkins's vigilante posse that attempted to arrest Judge David S. Terry when the latter stabbed Hopkins. In 1860 Capprise joined the Exempt Fire Company. He later moved to San Rafael, where he was head carpenter of the public schools when he died on December 27, 1872. *Marin Journal*, December 28, 1872; *San Francisco Bulletin*, December 30, 1872, January 30, 1897.

9. Duane's version of his arrest by the vigilantes agrees in its main particulars with the accounts published in the *San Francisco Herald*, June 2, 1856, and *Bulletin*, June 2, 1856.

10. Bancroft claimed that Duane "always carried a dose of poison on his person to cheat the hangman with." This claim was evidently based on the following report from the *San Francisco Bulletin* of June 2, 1856: "Yesterday, before his arrest, Duane was boasting that he had a dose of poison always secreted about his person, which in the event of the Committee arresting him, he said he would use and so cheat the fellows." Bancroft also claimed that Dutch Charley later tried to kill himself with laudanum in New York. These accounts appear unlikely. The *Bulletin* was strongly biased in favor of the vigilantes and against Duane, who never exhibited suicidal behavior. Further, he had never committed any offense in California that law or vigilance punished by death. Thus there was no hangman for him to cheat and no reason for him to carry poison. After Duane's lead poisoning in 1857, he was hospitalized in New York City; this may have been the basis for the laudanum story. Bancroft, *Popular Tribunals*, 2: 598–600; *San Francisco Bulletin*, June 2, 1856; *Alta California*, August 15, 1862.

11. Richard M. Jessup was a member of the executive committee of both the 1851 and 1856 Committees of Vigilance. A native of New York, he arrived in California in September 1849. A successful merchant, Jessup was one of the principal stockholders of the California Steam Navigation Company. He died at sea on February 3, 1865. *Alta California*, February 20, 1865.

12. Aaron M. Burns was a member of the vigilantes' executive committee.

13. Richard Porter Ashe was born in North Carolina about 1823. After service as a Texas Ranger, he came to California and was sheriff at Stockton in 1850. He was appointed naval agent for San Francisco's port in 1853 by President Franklin Pierce. Later he was a prominent farmer in San Joaquin County. He died in 1871. *San Francisco Examiner*, September 7, 1871.

14. Thomas J. L. Smiley was born in Philadelphia in 1821 and was employed as schoolteacher. He arrived in San Francisco in 1849 and

engaged in the auction business. Active in the volunteer fire department, he was a member of Howard No. 3 and president of Brannan Engine Company. As vice president of the Committee of Vigilance, he was second in command under William T. Coleman. Later Smiley was a stockbroker. In 1890 he served as the city's registrar of voters. He died in San Francisco on April 23, 1897. *San Francisco Call*, April 24, 1897.

15. Charles H. Gough was born in Maryland in 1828. A pioneer resident of San Francisco, he helped frame the first city charter and was elected to the state legislature. Gough helped map the city's boundaries; Gough Street was named in his honor and Octavia Street was named after his sister. In 1856 he was captain of Company 27, Fourth Regiment of the Committee of Vigilance; his company consisted of 110 men. Like many early Californians, he made a small fortune in land but lost most of it in litigation. He died in San Francisco on July 25, 1895. *San Francisco Call*, July 27, 1895.

16. The principal reason behind the French community's antipathy toward Duane was, of course, his shooting of Amadee Fayolle in 1851 and his successful machinations to avoid punishment.

17. On the ethnic makeup of the 1856 vigilantes, see Ethington, *Public City*, 96–97. He found that somewhat less than 2 percent of its six to eight thousand members were Irish, far more than Duane's figure of fifteen. But since Irish-born males composed 19 percent of the city's population, they were greatly underrepresented in the vigilance committee.

18. John S. Ellis was a member of the executive committee of the 1851 Committee of Vigilance. In 1856 he was lieutenant colonel of the First Regiment of the Committee of Vigilance. He played a prominent role in the capture of the jail on May 18, 1856, when Charles Cora and James P. Casey were seized by the vigilantes. Ellis personally manned the cannon that was trained on the jail. He later served as brigadier general of the California National Guard.

19. Charles Goodall was captain of the steam tug *Hercules*, owned by the Sausalito Water and Steam Tug Company. Later he was the partner of George Perkins; their firm was one of the principal California shipping firms of the 1870s. Perkins was governor of California from 1880 to 1883. In 1862 Duane sued Goodall for $2,000 in federal court for his role in exiling him from California. Hittell, *History of California*, 4: 647; *Alta California*, August 15, 1862.

20. The "soldiers" Duane mentions were the rank and file of the vigilance committee, many of whom wore local militia uniforms and carried rifles seized from various militia armories.

21. William "Woolly" Kearney was a notorious prizefighter and ballot-box stuffer for David Broderick. James O'Meara called him, "The homeliest, ugliest looking mortal I ever saw. . . . His battered, flattened, twisted, gnarled nose was at every point of the compass, and more hideous at every turn." Kearney came to California from New York City. On February 16, 1850, on Yerba Buena Island, he fought and won a twenty-five-round bareknuckle battle against an Australian fighter thirty pounds his superior. When Irish Dick Cronin was lynched in Placerville in October 1850, Kearney unsuccessfully tried to rescue him from the mob. In 1851 Kearney fought a second prizefight on Yerba Buena Island, this time with a fellow ruffian, William Harding; they fought for money and to settle a personal dispute. In San Francisco he ran a tavern, the Ripton House, on the Mission Road. On February 17, 1854, Kearney, with James P. Casey, Martin Gallagher, Bill Lewis, and other ruffians engaged in a violent brawl at a political meeting in the Mercantile Hotel in San Francisco. Arrested after a vicious battle with the police, they were promptly released by Supreme Court Justice Alexander Wells, a corrupt Broderick associate. Wells was later seen drinking with the rioters in a saloon. Two days later Woolly Kearney and two other ruffians attacked Police Officer Isaiah W. Lees in retaliation for their arrest. Lees fought them off and arrested Kearney, but he was released again. In January 1855 he was arrested for stabbing a man to death in San Francisco but was released due to lack of evidence. Deported by the vigilantes in 1856, he returned to California in 1859. That May he was twice arrested in San Francisco for disturbing the peace. Always a heavy drinker, Kearney made two attempts to hang himself in his San Francisco home in 1861. He was badly beaten in a saloon brawl on Kearny Street in 1864. His fate is unknown. O'Meara, *Vigilance Committee of 1856*, pp.49–50; Bancroft, *Popular Tribunals*, 2: 333–34; Secrest, *Lawmen and Desperadoes*, 76–77, 197–98; Williams, *Papers of the San Francisco Committee of Vigilance of 1851*, 556–57, 578–79; *San Francisco City Directory for the Year 1854*, 78; *Alta California*, February 18, 1850, January 28, 1855, May 24, 1859, June 26, 1861, October 20, 1864.

22. This scenario seems unlikely, for Bulger was not the only captive on board who was seasick. In his 1856 vigilante lawsuit Duane alleged that while he was on the steam tug he was "very sick and without any means of relieving his [Duane's] illness." *Alta California*, November 17, 1856.

23. R. M. Hooley was the instrumentalist for Tom Maguire's theater in 1855. Later he became a famous manager and operated Hooley's Theater in Chicago in the 1870s. Gagey, *San Francisco Stage*, 64–65.

24. Eph Horn was a well-known white minstrel who performed in blackface. In January 1855, he was one of the principal performers of Christy's Minstrels at Tom Maguire's theater, and continued his popular burlesques up to the vigilante period. Some writers have incorrectly identified him as African-American. Gagey, *San Francisco Stage*, 64–65; MacMinn, *Theater of the Golden Era in California*, 426–27.

CHAPTER 8. EXILED TO PANAMA AND NEW YORK

1. This was Robert H. Pearson of the Pacific Mail and Steamship Company. Born in Massachussetts in 1817, he went to sea at an early age on packets running from New York to London and Liverpool. During the 1850s he was master on Pacific Mail ships between Panama and San Francisco. Duane recovered $4,000 from Pearson in his 1863 lawsuit. Pearson died a wealthy man in San Francisco on July 10, 1868. *Alta California*, July 11, 1868.

2. Mathew Hall McAllister, distinguished attorney and father of Hall McAllister, was born in Savannah, Georgia, in 1800. He served as mayor of Savannah, U.S. attorney, and Georgia state senator before coming to California in 1849. He was appointed judge of the U.S. Circuit Court in 1855 and served until poor health caused him to retire in 1862. McAllister died in San Francisco on December 19, 1865. Nunis, *San Francisco Vigilance Committee of 1856*, 100n; Fritz, *Federal Justice in California*, 33–34, 161–62.

3. Dr. J. D. B. Stillman, one of the passengers on the *Stephens*, gave a different view of Dutch Charley's voyage:

He was a bully and a high-cockalorum on board the ship. If he wanted wine or anything else he got it; they gave him whatever he asked for because they did not dare to refuse him. A high official, one of the passengers on board our steamer, advised Duane not to leave the ship unless they used force to put him off, and if they did then to go. The official was in high dudgeon [and considered] that an outrage had been committed on the high seas, for which the officers of the ship and the company ought to be made responsible and punished. That was all that saved Duane's life. If he had come back at that time, at the height of the excitement about Terry, he would have swung before sundown. Bancroft, *Popular Tribunals*, 2: 599–600.

The "high official" was Judge McAllister.

4. Duane viewed his eagerness to return to San Francisco and face the vigilance committee as a courageous action in response to a great affront to his personal honor. Years later the U.S. Supreme Court expressed a decidedly different view. In an 1867 ruling on Duane's lawsuit against Captain Pearson for ejecting him from the ship, the court expressed sympathy for "the outrages which he suffered at the hands of the Vigilance Committee [and] his forcible abduction from California" but added, "It was sheer madness for Duane to seek to go back there. Common prudence required that he should wait until the violence of the storm blew over, and law and order were restored." *Pearson v. Duane* 71 U.S. 447 (1867).

5. Duane refers to a riot in Panama in April 1856 between American travelers and Panamanians in which some fifteen Americans were reported killed.

6. William Walker was famous as a filibuster in the age of Manifest Destiny. Born in Nashville, Tennessee, May 8, 1824, he studied medicine at the University of Pennsylvania, toured Europe, then studied and practiced law briefly in New Orleans. Next he became a journalist and arrived in California in 1850, where he worked for the *San Francisco Herald*. Walker fought several duels: against one Kennedy, an editor in New Orleans, against W. H. Carter in 1850, and against Will Hicks Graham in 1851. In 1853 he led a failed filibustering expedition to La Paz, Baja California. Returning to San Francisco, he again worked as a newspaper editor and in 1855 led a second invasion, this time to Nicaragua. His forces captured Granada and Walker became president of Nicaragua but in 1857 he was forced to surrender to the U.S. Navy. In 1860 he invaded Honduras. Captured, Walker was executed by firing squad on September 12, 1860. See Laurence Greene, *The Filibuster: The Career of William Walker* (1937) and Albert Z. Carr, *The World and William Walker* (1963).

7. Charles Wheatleigh was a favorite on the San Francisco stage for many years. He left San Francisco for a tour in Australia in 1856 but returned to perform in California many times over the years. Gagey, *San Francisco Stage*, 40, 51.

8. Edward T. Batturs was born in Baltimore, Maryland, in 1823. He arrived in San Francisco on February 28, 1849, on the steamer *California*. Active in San Francisco politics, he was tax collector in 1856 and served for years as deputy assessor. In Duane's lawsuit against Captain Goodall of the *Golden Age*, Batturs testified that he met Duane in Panama and helped pay his passage to New York. Batturs died in Oroville, California, on September 13, 1897. *Alta California*, August 15, 1862; *San Francisco Call*, September 14, 1897.

9. William Tell Coleman, famous as "the Lion of the Vigilantes," was born in Kentucky in 1824. He arrived in California in 1849, settled in Sacramento and a year later founded a mercantile firm in San Francisco. Tall, handsome, and a natural leader of men, he was second in command, behind Sam Brannan, of the 1851 Committee of Vigilance. In 1856 he was the leader of the reorganized Committee of Vigilance. During the anti-Chinese riots in San Francisco in 1877, Coleman once again came to the forefront as head of the Committee of Public Safety. His "Pick Handle Brigade" of more than five thousand men assisted the police in suppressing rioting. When Coleman died in San Francisco in 1893 newspapers lauded him as "the most heroic figure in California history." A laudatory biography is James A. B. Scherer, *The Lion of the Vigilantes* (1939).

10. James Reuben Maloney was born in Illinois in 1824 and moved to New York City at age twenty. Two of his brothers served in Congress, one from Illinois and one from Maine. After coming to California in 1849, he was a political ruffian on behalf of David Broderick. Maloney joined the 1851 Committee of Vigilance, reportedly as Broderick's spy, but he was not considered trustworthy; the secret password was changed and was not revealed to Maloney. He was deported by the vigilantes on July 5, 1856. In New York City he brought lawsuits against several vigilantes who returned home: William T. Coleman in 1856, Miers F. Truett in 1857, and James Dows in 1859. Maloney lost these cases on the ground that New York courts had no jurisdiction over events that took place in California. In these lawsuits Maloney alleged that he had suffered large financial losses due to his being deported. But the *Alta California* published San Francisco court records showing that he was insolvent in December 1855, with some $28,000 in debts and no assets. Maloney died in New York City on August 19, 1861. James O'Meara said of him, "His bravery was in his mouth; his mouth beyond his own control." Nunis, *San Francisco Vigilance Committee of 1856*, 98–99n, 107; Bancroft, *Popular Tribunals*, 2: 509, 612–15; *Alta California*, November 20, 1856.

11. Chris Lilly was one of the most prominent bare-knuckle prize-fighters and was the first professional American pugilist to kill a man in the ring. In a bloody mill at Hastings, New York, on September 13, 1842, Lilly defeated Thomas McCoy before a crowd of 2,000. After 119 rounds, the badly battered McCoy drowned in his own blood. Lilly fled to England to avoid prosecution. He returned to the U.S., lived in New Orleans, and served with distinction as a lieutenant of Louisiana mounted volunteers in the Mexican War. He came to California in 1850, a fellow passenger of Duane's on the *Tennessee*, and toured the mines with Billy Mulligan and

Yankee Sullivan, promoting prizefights. In 1855 he ran a popular cock-fighting pit in San Francisco, and the following year owned the Abbey House, a tavern located at the intersection of Mission Street and San Jose Avenue in what is now Daly City. With Billy Mulligan, he played a prominent role in the San Mateo County election frauds in May 1856, which led to his arrest by the vigilantes on July 8. Lilly was deported to Central America on August 15. He gambled and traded in Nicaragua until 1857 when he was accused of aiding the filibuster William Walker and executed on February 16. Gorn, *The Manly Art*, 73–78; Edna Bryan Buckbee, *The Saga of Old Tuolumne* (1935), 111, 192; *History of San Mateo County* (1883), 158–63; Bancroft, *Popular Tribunals*, 2: 280–82, 601–2; *Sacramento Union*, May 17, 1856; *San Francisco Bulletin*, November 6, 1857.

12. On one occasion in New York, Billy Mulligan assaulted Coleman "but inflicted only slight damage." Scherer, *Lion of the Vigilantes*, 224.

13. Miers F. Truett was a prominent San Francisco merchant and member of the executive committee of the vigilantes in 1856. Born in 1822, he settled in Galena, Illinois, where he served one term as mayor. A man of great strength and unquestioned courage, he once battled the leaders of a Galena lynch mob to rescue a prisoner from death. In 1856 he used his influence with the vigilantes on behalf of Judge Terry. On August 12, 1871, he was aboard a stagecoach in Sonoma County, California, when it was attacked by the John Houx gang; Truett and a Wells Fargo agent killed one bandit and wounded another. He died in San Francisco on September 27, 1885. *San Francisco Call*, September 29, 1885; John Boessenecker, *Badge and Buckshot: Lawlessness in Old California* (1988), 47–48.

14. Trenor W. Park was born in Woodford, Vermont, December 8, 1823. He practiced law on the East Coast and came to California in 1852, where he resided for ten years. He invested in land, mines, and railways, becoming president of the Panama Railway. A wealthy philanthropist, he died at sea on December 13, 1882. Zoeth Skinner Eldredge, *History of California* (1915), 4: 218.

CHAPTER 9. JUDGE TERRY AND THE VIGILANTES

1. William Tecumseh Sherman (1820–1891) graduated from West Point in 1840, served in the Second Seminole War (1840–1842), and was stationed in California from 1847 to 1850. In 1853 he resigned from the army and returned to San Francisco as a banker. Recommissioned in the Civil War, he soon became one of the nation's most prominent military

figures. On Sherman's western career, see Robert G. Athearn, *William Tecumseh Sherman and the Settlement of the West* (1956), and Dwight L. Clarke, *William Tecumseh Sherman: Gold Rush Banker* (1969).

2. It was not Sherman, but General Volney E. Howard, who had succeeded him as commander of the state militia, who sent the schooner *Julia* after the weapons.

3. John L. Durkee achieved prominence as a member of the 1856 vigilance committee. Born in Baltimore, Maryland, on June 29, 1829, he arrived in San Francisco on November 23, 1849, as second officer of the ship *Balance*. After a brief tour of the mines, he returned to San Francisco where he became a police officer in 1851. Later he was a deputy sheriff under Jack Hays, and in 1855 he captured the notorious outlaw "Tipperary Bill" Morris. In 1856 he joined the vigilance committee as deputy chief of police. He rejoined the regular police department under Chief Martin J. Burke in 1858 and became deputy superintendent of streets in 1862. Long active in the volunteer fire department, Durkee was appointed San Francisco's first fire marshal in 1864, a post he held until 1886, when he retired. He arrested Charley Duane after the Ross shooting in 1866. Durkee died in San Francisco on January 29, 1897. *San Francisco Call*, January 30, 1897; *San Francisco Bulletin*, January 30, 1897.

4. Sherman actually resigned before this. His successor, Volney E. Howard, was a prominent lawyer. Born in Maine in 1809, Howard at age twenty-one went to Mississippi, where he took an active part in politics. He later moved to Texas, where he served several terms in Congress. In 1853 Howard arrived in California as U.S. attorney for the Land Commission and became an important member of the San Francisco bar. The part he played as general of the state militia in opposing the vigilance committee made him many enemies. He lost numerous clients and as a consequence moved to Los Angeles in 1861. There he practiced law and served as district attorney and Superior Court judge. Howard died in Santa Monica on May 14, 1889. Bancroft, *History of California*, 7: 374–75; *San Francisco Examiner*, May 15, 1889.

5. Sterling A. Hopkins was born in Ellsworth, Maine, in 1823, and later lived in Boston. An artesian well-borer, he came to California in 1849 and was active in the Know-Nothing Party in San Francisco. One of the most energetic of the vigilante policemen, he acted as James Casey's hangman. He recovered from his knife wound and in the Civil War was a sergeant in the Fifty-Seventh Massachusetts Regiment. Hopkins was killed in action during the Battle of the Wilderness in May 1864. *Alta California*, June 22, 1856; June 19, 1864.

6. David S. Terry was born in Kentucky, March 8, 1823. His family moved to the Texas frontier when he was a boy. He studied law in the office of an uncle and served in the Texas Mounted Volunteers during the Mexican War. Terry rode overland to California in 1849. He became a prominent attorney in Stockton and a leader of the state's southern, or Chivalry, wing of the Democratic Party. In 1855 he was elected a justice of the California Supreme Court, and as such was an important opponent of the 1856 vigilance committee. Terry's quick, ungovernable temper obscured his many fine qualities of courage, intelligence, and leadership. See A. Russell Buchanan, *David S. Terry of California: Dueling Judge* (1956).

7. Joseph Rodman West, born September 19, 1822, in New Orleans, studied at the University of Pennsylvania. He served in the Mexican War as a captain of mounted volunteers. West came to California in 1849 and worked as a newspaperman in San Francisco. In 1861 he enlisted as a lieutenant colonel of the First California Infantry. Soon promoted to brigadier general, West served in Arizona and New Mexico and carried on a ruthless campaign against the Apaches. It was reportedly on his orders that the noted Apache chief Mangas Coloradas was shot while under arrest. After the war he returned to New Orleans, served as U.S. senator from 1871 to 1877, and died in Washington, D.C., on October 31, 1898. Thrapp, *Encyclopedia of Frontier Biography*, 3: 1534–35; Alvin M. Josephy, *The Civil War in the American West* (1991), 275–80; *San Francisco Call*, November 1, 1898.

8. David Glasgow Farragut (1801–1870), one of America's great naval heroes, served in the U.S. Navy from the War of 1812 through the Civil War. His biographers have ignored his involvement with the San Francisco vigilantes. Nunis, *San Francisco Vigilance Committee of 1856*, 16.

9. George S. Evans hailed from Texas, where his brother had been killed in the siege of the Alamo. He served in the Mexican War, joined the Gold Rush, and settled in Tuolumne County. As undersheriff of Tuolumne County in 1851, he shot and killed Augustus Kauffman, who resisted arrest. Several years later Evans was elected county clerk. Although aligned with pro-Southern Democrats, he remained loyal to the Union during the Civil War and served as the state's adjutant general and colonel of the Second Cavalry of the California Volunteers. In 1862 he led an expedition against the Paiute Indians in the Owens Valley and established the post of Camp Independence. Evans was later elected state senator several times. He died in San Francisco on September 17, 1883, while serving as harbor commissioner of the port. Carlo M. DeFerrari, ed., *Annals of Tuolumne County* (1963), 141; Roger D. McGrath, *Gunfighters, Highwaymen and Vigilantes* (1984), 26–32.

10. Theophilus W. Taliaferro was well known in legal and political circles in San Francisco. Born in Demopolis, Alabama, in 1820, he was trained as a lawyer and served with distinction in the Mexican War. In the spring of 1850, he came to California, where he engaged in the practice of law. In 1853 he was alcalde, or justice of the peace, in Calaveras County, and later was justice of the peace in San Francisco. He held various offices in the city government and died in San Francisco on December 6, 1889. *San Francisco Call*, December 8, 1889.

11. The Bowie knife that Duane described was probably a dress knife made by Michael Price of San Francisco, one of America's premier knife makers of the nineteenth century. Michael Price knives are even more prized by collectors today than they were in the 1850s. As Major Horace Bell, commentator on men and events in pioneer California, observed, "None of the California chivalry of that day was of the elite unless possessed of one of Price's knives." Terry carried a Michael Price knife the rest of his life; in a celebrated courtroom brawl in 1888 (see note 13 below), he was disarmed after flourishing a Michael Price Bowie knife. The knife he carried in 1888 is illustrated in *The Terry Contempt* (1888), following p. 50.

12. Broderick's friends charged that Terry had inside knowledge of the dueling pistols, and that the weapon given to Broderick had a hair-trigger, and this caused his gun to discharge prematurely. Broderick's own seconds denied this charge, and stated that the trigger pull was identical in both weapons. Buchanan, *David S. Terry*, 108–9; Williams, *David C. Broderick*, 243–44.

13. Duane's account was written several years before the final tragic events in David Terry's life. He served as a colonel in the Confederate Army during the Civil War and returned to Stockton in 1869. His stabbing of Hopkins, his killing of Broderick, and his Confederate service seriously damaged his reputation with many in California. Nonetheless, he was an extremely able lawyer and prospered. In 1884 he was retained by the beautiful but unstable Sarah Althea Hill in her sensational divorce suit against U.S. Senator William Sharon. Although she was thirty years his junior, Terry fell in love with her and they were married in 1886. During an acrimonious 1888 hearing in federal court in San Francisco, Judge Terry pulled his knife and was sentenced to six months in jail. He blamed Justice Stephen J. Field of the U.S. Supreme Court for unfavorable rulings and threatened Field. On August 14, 1889, Terry accidentally encountered Justice Field in the train depot restaurant in Lathrop, near Stockton. Once again Terry's hot temper brought him trouble. He struck Justice Field twice in the face. Field's bodyguard, the noted gunfighter David Neagle, promptly

shot Terry dead. Buchanan, *David S. Terry*, 191–231; Robert H. Kroninger, *Sarah and the Senator* (1964), 189–232. A friend of Wyatt Earp and his brothers, Dave Neagle had been chief of police of Tombstone, Arizona Territory. See Secrest, *Lawmen and Desperadoes*, 252–56.

Bibliography

THE memoirs of Charles P. Duane were published in thirteen installments in the *San Francisco Examiner* in 1881, during the twenty-fifth anniversary of the 1856 Committee of Vigilance. They appeared in the following issues: January 9, 16, 23; February 6, 13, 20, 27; March 6, 13, 20, 27; April 3, 17, 1881. The other sources cited in the introduction and notes are listed below.

BOOKS

Asbury, Herbert. *The Barbary Coast*. New York: Alfred A. Knopf, 1933.

————. *The Gangs of New York*. New York: Alfred A. Knopf, 1928.

Athearn, Robert G. *William Tecumseh Sherman and the Settlement of the West*. Norman: University of Oklahoma Press, 1956.

Ayers, Edward L. *Vengeance and Justice: Crime and Punishment in the Nineteenth Century American South*. New York: Oxford University Press, 1984.

Bancroft, Hubert Howe. *California Inter Pocula*. San Francisco: The History Company, Publishers, 1888.

————. *History of California*. Vols. 6–7. San Francisco: The History Company, 1888.

————. *Pioneer Register*. Los Angeles: Dawson's Book Shop, 1964.

————. *Popular Tribunals*. Vols. 1–2. San Francisco: The History Company, 1887.

Barns, George C. *Denver, the Man*. Wilmington, Ohio: Pub. by author, 1949.

Bell, Horace. *Reminiscences of a Ranger*. Santa Barbara, Calif.: Wallace Hebberd, 1927.

Boessenecker, John. *Badge and Buckshot: Lawlessness in Old California*. Norman: University of Oklahoma Press, 1988.

Brown, Bertram Wyatt. *Southern Honor: Ethics and Behavior in the Old South*. New York: Oxford University Press, 1982.

Brown, Richard Maxwell. *No Duty to Retreat: Violence and Values in American History and Society.* New York: Oxford University Press, 1991.

——. *Strain of Violence: Historical Studies of American Violence and Vigilantism.* New York: Oxford University Press, 1975.

Buchanan, A. Russell. *David S. Terry of California: Dueling Judge.* San Marino, Calif.: The Huntington Library, 1956.

Buckbee, Edna Bryan. *The Saga of Old Tuolumne.* New York: Press of the Pioneers, 1935.

Bullough, William A. *The Blind Boss and His City: Christopher Augustine Buckley and Nineteenth Century San Francisco.* Berkeley: University of California Press, 1979.

Burchell, R. A. *The San Francisco Irish.* Berkeley: University of California Press, 1980.

Carr, Albert Z. *The World and William Walker.* New York: Harper and Row, 1963.

Clarke, Dwight L. *William Tecumseh Sherman: Gold Rush Banker.* San Francisco: California Historical Society, 1969.

DeArment, Robert K. *Knights of the Green Cloth.* Norman: University of Oklahoma Press, 1982.

Decker, Peter R. *Fortunes and Failures: White Collar Mobility in Nineteenth Century San Francisco.* Cambridge: Harvard University Press, 1978.

DeFerrari, Carlo M., ed. *Annals of Tuolumne County.* Sonora, Calif.: Tuolumne County Historical Society, 1963.

Dimsdale, Thomas J. *The Vigilantes of Montana.* Norman: University of Oklahoma Press, 1953.

Eldredge, Zoeth Skinner. *History of California.* New York: Century History Co., 1915.

Ethington, Philip J. *The Public City: The Political Construction of Urban Life in San Francisco, 1850–1900.* New York: Cambridge University Press, 1994.

Farish, Thomas Edwin. *History of Arizona.* Phoenix: Filmer Brothers Electrotype Co., 1915.

Field, Stephen J. *Personal Reminiscences of Early Days in California.* Privately printed, 1893.

Foley, Doris. *The Divine Eccentric: Lola Montez and the Newspapers.* Los Angeles: Westernlore Press, 1969.

Fritz, Christian G. *Federal Justice in California.* Lincoln: University of Nebraska Press, 1991.

Gagey, Edmund M. *The San Francisco Stage: A History.* New York: Columbia University Press, 1950.

Gentry, Curt. *The Madams of San Francisco*. Garden City, N.Y.: Doubleday, Inc., 1964.

Gorn, Elliot J. *The Manly Art: Bare-Knuckle Prize Fighting in America*. Ithaca, N.Y.: Cornell University Press, 1986.

Greene, Laurence. *The Filibuster: The Career of William Walker*. New York: Bobbs-Merrill, 1937.

Greer, James Kimmins. *Colonel Jack Hays: Texas Frontier Leader and California Builder*. New York: E. P. Dutton, 1952.

Halley, William. *Centennial Year Book of Alameda County*, Oakland, Calif.: pub. by author, 1876.

Hammond, George P., ed. *The Larkin Papers*. Berkeley: University of California Press, 1953.

Hansen, Gladys. *Behind the Silver Star: An Account of the San Francisco Police Department*. San Francisco: San Francisco Archives, 1981.

Heintz, William F. *San Francisco's Mayors, 1850–1880*. Woodside, Calif.: Gilbert Richards Publications, 1975.

History of San Mateo County. San Francisco: B. F. Alley Co., 1883.

Hittell, Theodore H. *History of California*. San Francisco: N.J. Stone and Co., 1897.

Hoover, Mildred, Hero Rensch, and Ethel Rensch. *Historic Spots in California (3rd ed.)*. Stanford, Calif.: Stanford University Press, 1966.

Hughes, Robert. *The Fatal Shore: The Epic of Australia's Founding*. New York: Random House, 1986.

Isenberg, Michael T. *John L. Sullivan and His America*. Chicago: University of Illinois Press, 1988.

Jacobsen, Joel. *Such Men as Billy the Kid*. Lincoln: University of Nebraska Press, 1994.

Johnson, David R. *Policing the Urban Underworld*. Philadelphia: Temple University Press, 1979.

Josephy, Alvin M. *The Civil War in the American West*. New York: Alfred A. Knopf, 1991.

Kimball, Charles P. *The San Francisco City Directory*. San Francisco: Journal of Commerce Press, 1850.

Kroninger, Robert H. *Sarah and the Senator*. Berkeley, Calif.: Howell-North, 1964.

Joann Levy. *They Saw the Elephant: Women in the California Gold Rush*. Hamden, Conn.: Archon Books, 1990.

Lotchin, Roger W. *San Francisco, 1846–1856: From Hamlet to City*. New York: Oxford University Press, 1974.

Marks, Paula Mitchell. *And Die in the West: The Story of the O.K. Corral Gunfight.* New York: Touchstone, 1989.

MacMinn, George R. *The Theater of the Golden Age in California.* Caldwell, Idaho: The Caxton Printers, 1941.

McGowan, Edward. *Narrative of Edward McGowan, Including a Full Account of the Author's Adventures and Perils While Persecuted by the San Francisco Vigilance Committee of 1856.* San Francisco: Pub. by author, 1857.

McGrath, Roger D. *Gunfighters, Highwaymen and Vigilantes.* Berkeley: University of California Press, 1984.

Monaghan, Jay. *The Great Rascal.* Boston: Little, Brown and Co., 1951.

Moody, Richard., *The Astor Place Riot.* Bloomington: Indiana University Press, 1958.

————. *Edwin Forrest: First Star of the American Stage.* New York: Alfred A. Knopf, 1960.

Mullen, Kevin J. *Let Justice Be Done: Crime and Politics in Early San Francisco.* Reno: University of Nevada Press, 1989.

Munro-Fraser, J. P. *History of Alameda County, California.* Oakland, Calif.: M. W. Wood, 1883.

Myers, John Myers. *San Francisco's Reign of Terror.* Garden City, N.Y.: Doubleday, 1966.

Nolan, Frederick. *The Lincoln County War: A Documentary History.* Norman: University of Oklahoma Press, 1992.

Nunis, Doyce B., Jr., ed. *The San Francisco Vigilance Committee of 1856: Three Views.* Los Angeles: Los Angeles Westerners, 1971.

O'Meara, James. *The Vigilance Committee of 1856.* San Francisco: James H. Barry, 1887.

Pauley, Art. *Henry Plummer: Lawman and Outlaw.* White Sulpher Springs, Mont.: The Meagher County News, 1980.

Quinn, Arthur. *The Rivals: William Gwin, David Broderick, and the Birth of California.* New York: Crown Publishers, 1994.

Ranney, R. H. *Account of the Terrific and Fatal Riot at the Astor Place Opera House.* New York: n.p., 1849.

Roberts, Gary L. *Death Comes for the Chief Justice.* Niwot, Colo.: University of Colorado Press, 1990.

Samuels, Peggy and Harold. *Encyclopedia of Artists of the American West.* Secaucus, N.J.: Castle, 1985.

San Francisco City Directory for the Year 1854. San Francisco Herald, 1854.

Scharnhorst, Gary, ed. *Bret Harte's California.* Albuquerque: University of New Mexico Press, 1990.

Scherer, James A. B. *The Lion of the Vigilantes.* New York: Bobbs-Merrill, 1939.

Secrest, William B. *Lawmen and Desperadoes.* Spokane, Wash.: Arthur H. Clark Co., 1994.

Senkewicz, Robert M. *Vigilantes in Gold Rush San Francisco.* Stanford, Calif.: Stanford University Press, 1985.

Shinn, Charles Howard. *Mining Camps: A Study in American Frontier Government.* New York: Alfred A. Knopf, 1948.

Shuck, Oscar T. *Bench and Bar in California.* San Francisco: Occidental Printing, 1889.

Soule, Frank, John H. Gihon, and James Nisbet. *The Annals of San Francisco.* New York: D. Appleton, 1855.

Stevens, Moreland L. *Charles Christian Nahl: Artist of the Gold Rush, 1818–1878.* Sacramento, Calif.: E. B. Crocker Art Gallery, 1976.

Stewart, George R. *Committee of Vigilance: Revolution in San Francisco, 1851.* Boston: Houghton Mifflin, 1964.

Sullivan, Joseph A., ed. *McGowan v. California Vigilantes.* Oakland: Biobooks, 1946.

Tefertiller, Casey. *Wyatt Earp: The Life Behind the Legend.* New York: John Wiley & Sons, 1997.

The Terry Contempt. San Francisco, 1888.

Thrapp, Dan L. *Encyclopedia of Frontier Biography.* 3 vols. Glendale, Calif.: Arthur H. Clark Company, 1988.

Truman, Benjamin C. *The Field of Honor.* New York: Fords, Howard & Hulbert, 1884.

Utley, Robert M. *High Noon in Lincoln.* Albuquerque: University of New Mexico Press, 1987.

Wagoner, Jay J. *Arizona Territory 1863–1912: A Political History.* Tucson: University of Arizona Press, 1970.

Walker, Franklin. *San Francisco's Literary Frontier.* New York: Alfred A. Knopf, 1939.

Webb, Walter Prescott. *The Texas Rangers: A Century of Frontier Defense.* New York: Houghton Mifflin, 1935.

Weber, David. *Oakland: Hub of the West.* Tulsa, Okla.: Continental Heritage Press, 1981.

Williams, David A. *David Broderick: A Political Portrait.* San Marino, Calif.: The Huntington Library, 1969.

Williams, Mary Floyd. *Papers of the San Francisco Committee of Vigilance of 1851.* Berkeley: University of California Press, 1919.

Willis, William L. *History of Sacramento County.* Los Angeles: Historic Record Co., 1913.

Wyndham, Horace. *The Magnificent Montez.* London: Hutchinson, 1935.

ARTICLES

Chandler, Robert J. "Vigilante Rebirth: The Civil War Union League," *The Argonaut* (Journal of the San Francisco Historical Society) 3, no. 1 (Winter 1992).

de Massey, Ernest. "A Frenchman in the Gold Rush," *California Historical Society Quarterly* 6, no. 1 (March 1927).

Fritz, Christian G. "Popular Sovereignty, Vigilantism, and the Constitutional Right of Revolution," *Pacific Historical Review* 62 (February 1994).

Gammie, Peter. "Pugilists and Politicians in Antebellum New York: The Life and Times of Tom Hyer," *New York History* 75, no. 3 (July 1994).

Johnson, David A. "Vigilance and the Law: The Moral Authority of Popular Justice in the West," *American Quarterly* 33 (Winter 1981).

Mullen, Kevin J. "Dutch Charley Duane," *Old West* 33, no. 1 (Fall 1996).

———. "Torching Old-Time San Francisco," *The Californians* 8, no. 5 (January-February 1991).

Parker, Paul. "The Roach-Belcher Feud," *California Historical Society Quarterly* 24 (March 1950).

Rodecape, Lois Foster. "Tom Maguire, Napoleon of the Stage," *California Historical Society Quarterly* 20, no. 4 (December 1941); 21, no. 1 (March 1942); 21, no. 2 (June 1943); 21, no. 3 (September 1943).

Royce, Josiah. "The Squatter Riot of '50 in Sacramento," *Overland Monthly*, 2d ser, 7 (September 1885).

Secrest, William B. "There Once Was a Badman Named Mulligan," *Real West*, 27 (August 1984).

Waldorf, Dolores. "Baltimore Fire Laddie, George H. Hossefross," *California Historical Society Quarterly* 23 (March 1944).

Wheat, Carl I. "Ned, the Ubiquitous," *California Historical Society Quarterly*, 6 (March 1927).

Wilhelm, John F. "Shootout at Oak Grove," *Golden Notes* (Bulletin of the Sacramento County Historical Society) 29, no. 3 (Fall 1983).

COURT RECORDS

John H. Baird, et al. v. Charles P. Duane, et al. District Court, Fourth Judicial District, San Francisco, February 13, 1864. California Historical Society Library, San Francisco.

Pearson v. Duane 71 U.S. 447 (1867). U.S. Supreme Court case decisions.

UNPUBLISHED MATERIALS

Blunt, Phineas. *Journal*. Bancroft Library, Berkeley, California.
Burke, Martin J. *Dictation*, 1887. Bancroft Library, Berkeley, California.
Byram, Edward. Police Record Book No. 1. John Boessenecker Collection.

NEWSPAPERS

Alta California (San Francisco)
California Chronicle (San Francisco)
California Police Gazette (San Francisco)
Democratic State Journal (Sacramento)
Fireman's Journal (San Francisco)
Marin Journal (San Rafael)
Sacramento Daily Union
San Diego Union
San Francisco Bulletin
San Francisco Call
San Francisco Chronicle
San Francisco Daily Report
San Francisco Examiner
San Francisco Post
San Joaquin Republican (Stockton)

Index

Acapulco, Mexico, 31, 39, 137, 141–42
Adair, James, 181n.13
Adams, Edson, 178n.1
Adams & Co., 105–107, 188nn.1,2
Ah Toy, 62–63, 173n.30
Aitken, George, 82
Aldrich, Dan, 34, 191n.16
Alexander, William, 43
Allen (squatter), 180n.7
Anderson, William, 194n.1
Arrington, Nick, 155–56
Ashe, Richard Porter, 132, 152–54, 157, 197n.13
Aspinwall, Panama, 144–45
Astor Place Riot, 8–10
Australian convicts. See "Sydney Ducks"

Bagley, John W., 35, 102, 104, 107, 187nn.25,27, 189n.6
Baker, Edward D., 121, 190n.11, 193n.5
Baker, George, 11, 51, 63
Ball, Frank, 18–19, 180n.9
Barbary Coast, 12, 195n.2
Barmore, John, 21
Barter, Richard A. ("Rattlesnake Dick"), 36
Batturs, Edward T., 147, 201n.8
Baxter (squatter), 42

Bell, Horace, 182n.16, 206n.11
Benecia, Calif., 151
Berdue, Thomas, 17, 77–79, 181nn.11,12
Bideman, Joseph, 56
Bigelow, Harding, 76, 179nn.3,4
Biscaccianti, Elisa, 62, 172n.25
Biven, Rasey, 174n.2
Blunt, Phineas, 21
Bluxome, Isaac, 30, 195n.5
Bohen, Ben, 192n.2
Booth, Edwin, 173n.28
Bowery Boys, 7, 180n.8
Bowie, A. J., 127–28, 195n.6
Boxing. See Prizefighting
Brace, Philander, 31, 34
Brady, James, 66
Brady, John B., 77–78, 181n.13
Brady (combatant), 37
Brannan, Sam, 29, 202n.9
Broderick, David C., 3, 11–12, 16, 18–20, 25–26, 33–34, 36–37, 53, 55, 57, 65–66, 70, 74, 77, 87–91, 93–95, 98, 100, 110, 150, 157–58, 167nn.3,5, 168nn.6,7, 169n.10, 170n.16, 174n.3, 178n.1, 178n.5, 180n.10, 182n.14, 183nn.1,2,3, 184n.6, 189n.3, 190n.11, 194n.1, 195n.3, 199n.21, 202n.10, 206nn.12,13
Brown, Harvey S., 19, 77

217